AVIATION'S WATERGATE

On March 3, 1974, a Turkish Airlines DC-10 crashed nine minutes after takeoff from Paris. The cause: *a faulty cargo door*. 346 died in the shocking carnage. What is more shocking is that the crash needn't have happened at all. . . . This is the story of that electrifying catastrophe, of the subsequent monumental litigation involving the cold dollar calculus of human lives, and of the people—the passengers, the crew, their families—unwilling participants in a consuming human drama.

"AN ABSOLUTELY GRIPPING, INTENSELY WELL-WRITTEN weighing of human values against technological achievement."
The Kirkus Reviews

"Combining the realism of Ernest Gann with the poetic genius of Antoine de Saint-Exupery, THE LAST NINE MINUTES will arouse profound feelings in even the most veteran pilots and provide unbelievable fascination to the most seasoned air traveller."

Captain Charles Simpson, *Vice President, International Federation of Airline Pilots' Association*

"FASCINATING. . . . A MAGNIFICENT PIECE OF INVESTIGATIVE JOURNALISM."
Best Sellers

(Turn page . . .)

"AWESOMELY DETAILED . . .

a dreadfully engrossing account of the worst airplane crash in history."
The Washington Post

"Exploding into prominence in *The New York Times Book Review*, THE LAST NINE MINUTES unravels the Byzantine mysteries of the crash, and reads like a novel."
New West Magazine

"TOTALLY ABSORBING, COMPLETELY AUTHENTIC . . . should be read by every airplane manufacturer. . . . It will certainly be read with fascination by every pilot and air traveler."
Pilot Magazine

"A RIVETING READ. . . . Moira Johnston has done a brilliant job of research. . . . Here is the story behind the headlines, and everyone who's ever buckled a seatbelt will want to read it."
Elizabeth Janeway

"A STUNNING ACCOUNT . . . written with compassion and empathy."
The Seattle Times

"A MINOR MASTERPIECE . . . Moira Johnston has taken the worst crash in history and written an engrossing account of its genesis and aftermath, breaking fresh soil on every page."
The Houston Post

THE STORY OF FLIGHT 981

BY MOIRA JOHNSTON

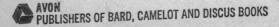

AVON
PUBLISHERS OF BARD, CAMELOT AND DISCUS BOOKS

"There was no agony of death. Only agony for those left behind."

from *The Last Nine Minutes*

This book is dedicated
to those thousands who have endured
the agony of Ermenonville.

Grateful acknowledgment is made by the author for the use of the following:

Lines from "The Most Beautiful Girl." Words and music by N. Wilson, B. Sherrill and R. Bourke. Copyright © 1973 Al Gallico Music Corporation and Algee Music Corporation. Used by permission.

Lines from the quote on death on page 25 from *The Lives of a Cell* by Lewis Thomas, reprinted by permission of The Viking Press.

AVON BOOKS
A division of
The Hearst Corporation
959 Eighth Avenue
New York, New York 10019

First Avon Printing, January, 1978

AVON TRADEMARK REG. U.S. PAT. OFF. AND IN
OTHER COUNTRIES, MARCA REGISTRADA,
HECHO EN U.S.A.

Printed in the U.S.A.

On March 3, 1974, Flight 981, a DC-10 aircraft owned and flown by Turkish Airlines and carrying 334 passengers and a crew of 12, took off from Orly Airport in Paris. Nine minutes later, it crashed into the Ermenonville Forest, killing all 346 aboard. It was the first crash of a fully loaded "wide-body" jet and the largest air disaster in aviation history.

AUTHOR'S NOTE

In reconstructing events or behavior I have used verifiable details whenever possible. Where no details have been available I have projected behavior with the aid of aviation physiologists and psychologists from the Human Factors Department of the University of Southern California's Safety Center.

Where italics have been used within quotes, emphasis is the author's.

PART I

The Human Experience

Chapter One

The 77 Seconds

WITH ITS REAR ENGINE speared on the tail like a silver cigar and poised over 30 feet above the ground, the big plane was the most commanding sight at Orly airport.

But Prudence Pratt had no time for tail watching. She was rushing to get home to Stephen after a week-long modeling job in Spain. These trips were always tiring—on location at dawn, trying to dress in a cramped trailer with all the models grabbing for mirrors and accessories, trying to stay fresh and glamorous in wilting heat. But to be delayed a whole day by French incompetence! Air France had overbooked her Malaga–Paris–London flight and bumped her. She had made her way to Paris and called Stephen the night before to tell him what had happened. He'd be at Heathrow to meet her. If she could make her way to the plane through this madhouse.

Swinging the big, soft bags that were a model's trademark, she and the others pressed into the crush of people who were all trying to get back to London. It was like the last train from Berlin—this anxious army of people dashing from ticket counter to ticket counter, trying to get confirmation, change flights, get aboard with friends. What a shambles strikes created. The ground engineers' strike at Heathrow that had caused this chaos was apparently already over. But it had put them so far behind in servicing planes that all BEA and

Air France flights to London that day had been canceled. And now thousands of people were being shuffled, with the urgency of Dunkirk, aboard every available craft.

But even in the confusion, Prudence and her friends were a commanding sight. Simply coming home from work, they were playing their looks very low key. Prudence was wearing the flared jeans overalls she'd picked up in New Mexico under her blue military greatcoat and her black boots. But when seven models and their coterie move through an airport on their way to or from a modeling assignment, an aura of glamour and excitement spins up around them. Prudence had matured well beyond thinking that life was all about turning heads in a restaurant. But it was impossible not to feel heads turn and be pleased by it. And when you had Prudence's theatrical flair, and a shiny mane of red hair flying behind you, every airport scene was like the disembarking of a movie star from the old *Queen Elizabeth*.

She and her friends had got tickets on Turkish Airlines' Flight 981 that would be leaving at noon—the four girls and three male models, the stylist, fashion buyer, and editor of the mail-order catalog they had been shooting in Spain.

A pretty, brisk American-looking mother held tightly to her little girl's hand, steering her through the crowd. Her two other children stayed close, as the husband led them through the maze of check-in, security, and boarding passes.

Fay Wright was eager to get home, too. There was school tomorrow, and it was her turn for car pool. The family had had a week's vacation in Spain. Tom had just been made managing director of Merrill Lynch-Brown Shipley Bank's corporate finance activities in London, and Fay had finally been able to break him free of his obligations at work. American corporate families living abroad, as they were, were always under strains of ambition, absence, alien customs. They had needed this week to be together and get in touch.

4

Stranded in Marbella by the strike, they'd had the option of flying to Manchester and taking the train down to London, or flying home via Paris. They'd discussed the alternatives with friends they'd run into at the airport in Spain. The friends had gone to Manchester. They had decided on Paris.

Several other families from the American School in London were coming home from Turkey and the Alps. It was a difficult place for children that day. The crowds of men flying home from the England v. France international rugby match the day before gave Orly-Sud terminal the atmosphere of a pub at closing time. Men had come from rugby clubs all over England. Among the dozens of young men trading jokes and tickets were the team and officers of the Bury St. Edmunds rugby club—eighteen men. At that moment, they should have been pulling on their rugby shirts, getting ready to run on the field for an exhibition game against a French team—the windup to their big weekend in Paris. But the strike had made an evening flight home so uncertain that they had canceled the game and grabbed seats on the Turkish plane.

The quiet orderliness of a large group of young Japanese men was like a collective frown at the boisterous rugby boys. All in their early twenties, their purposes were far loftier than a rugby game. For the thirty-eight men, this was a brief educational hiatus between graduation from university and the beginning of work for the companies that would employ them for the rest of their lives—a chance to travel and see at first hand the sights and the corporate and industrial techniques of Europe. An academic elite chosen from thousands of applicants for the jobs they were about to begin, all had prospects of senior management opportunities before them. And each was the focus of family pride and obligations that surpass anything known in the Western world.

There were other Japanese faces in the crowd. Atsuko and Takehiro Higuchi had been married less than a month, and were honeymooning in Europe before

5

Takehiro returned to his architectural practice and, as eldest son, to heavy family obligations.

Prudence rushed aboard with the rest, 216 of them —196 at first, and then a last-minute flurry of twenty people who were hurriedly found seats, delaying the flight half an hour. Changes kept being made until the moment the doors were locked—changes that would mean life and death. Several people got on, and then got off and gave their tickets to others. One man got word after he had boarded that his wife had surprised him by flying to Paris, and he dashed from the plane to meet her. Ticket switching was easy to do, as immigration does not check the name on the passport against the name on the ticket. Friends flipped coins to see who'd get aboard. Two men with hangovers missed the plane. In the rush, few knew or cared what kind of plane they were boarding. But on the phone the night before, when Prudence had told Stephen that she was coming on Turkish Airlines, he had made some comment about flying on "that" airline, implying that Turks might be better at flying carpets. But she knew it was just that he hated flying. He loathed and feared it as much as she loved it. And yet he traveled all the time.

He was a partner in a successful law practice that negotiated claims for Lloyd's of London underwriters, and he often flew to Hong Kong, the Bahamas, New York, or Beirut on business. He frequently packed off on the trail of lost emeralds, silver coins . . . deteriorating frog's legs, of damaged, delayed, or stolen shipments of all kinds, protecting Lloyd's interests. It was delicate work, carrying Lloyd's rigorous ethics and reputation for fair and fast payment of claims through a maze of conflicting stories, international smuggling, networks of thieves, and sophisticated attempts at fraud. Lloyd's was a legend. But it was also a business. Its cases called for discretion, shrewd judgment, and able help.

Whether in a suit or with his dark hair curling over the collar of an open-necked print shirt, he displayed an enigmatic air he carefully nurtured. His good looks and lazy charm made him compellingly attractive. And with his head lowered over a glass of wine and a cigarette, he could make even the description of a boxing match sound sensuous and conspiratorial. But as he talked of his days in Muscat, of drinking with mercenary soldiers on their way to Biafra, dressing for dinner in borrowed "Gulf rig," probing the pink desert city for ways to liberate a trapped shipment of Kuwaiti dinars insured at Lloyd's, he could laugh at his own role in a bad movie.

He did not want his relationship with Prudence to end up as a bad movie. They had been together for two years now, two cautious and independent personalities, and it had worked. They both resisted a relationship based on need. Need made you vulnerable, something neither of them wanted to be. If they did marry, it would never be to hold each other up. He felt the trips were good. He had had a previous relationship where there had been no chance to escape, and he sometimes wondered if trips didn't operate as a pressure valve, preventing tensions or, worse, boredom.

As he hurried into Heathrow airport, he checked with BEA, which acted as handling agents for Turkish Airlines. The flight was late, and Stephen waited. He had spent much of his life waiting for planes. He settled in with the Sunday papers, a London ritual. He lit a cigarette and flicked ashes from his suit. He wondered why he'd worn a suit. He'd even shaved. He supposed it was a spontaneous gesture of pleasure at her coming home. He flipped through the color supplement and spotted a picture of Prudence as a housewife. Or was it Prudence? He was embarrassed to admit that he wasn't always sure. Several times he'd congratulated her on some pictures in such and such a magazine only to be told that they were of somebody else. Prudence played her roles so well—the seductress, the chic matron, the bride. He only knew her natural style, which was one of "cultivated casualness," of blue jeans and battered mini cars. His favorite picture of her was one he had taken the day they'd gone to Brighton—a color snap of her in blue jeans and macintosh, standing on Brighton Pier

7

with her red hair blowing free, the strong jaw giving her face character, the blue-green eyes laughing. Brighton had been one of their very best days together—a silly, spontaneous day when they'd done all the things they *never* did—take a day off, ride the train to Brighton like daytrippers, hike the honky-tonk Pier in pouring rain, eat slimy fish and chips doused in ketchup, and buy mildly pornographic mementos. The picture would shatter the illusions of the hundreds of thousands of housewives who would revel vicariously in sundrenched glamour when they read the catalog she'd shot in Spain. He wanted her home. He wanted to see the ivory heart and silver letter *P* he'd given her around her neck. Their symbol of commitment. He checked with BEA again, and they told him the plane was still over forty-five minutes away. It was only a fifty-minute flight, and it sounded to him as if she hadn't even taken off yet. He decided to drop in on friends who lived nearby and have a drink.

The DC-10 was still a novelty in Europe in the spring of 1974. Many eyes at Orly followed it, fascinated, as the tail with the red streaks and symbol of Turkish Airlines wove its way through the Caravelles, 707s, and Tridents in the stately gavotte of the modern jet.

They read the strip of words that ran the length of the fuselage—*THY TURK HAVA YOLLARI—TURKISH AIRLINES TC-JAV*. En route to London from Istanbul that first Sunday in March, the Turkish DC-10 did have a commanding presence. With its huge rear engine apparently pierced by the fin—a phallic symbol—it was the most virile aircraft around. Clean and workmanlike, it had its vital power source right up where you could see it. Functional, direct, the DC-10 moved the air in a straight line from intake to exhaust. No sacrifice of efficiency for visual elegance.

It was the youngest in the distinguished family of Douglas aircraft, successor to the legendary DC-3, the -4, the -6 and the -7, and the pure jets, the DC-8 and

-9. It had been tested more than any of Douglas's previous planes, all to achieve the mission of "building an airplane that's not going to cause the guy any trouble," as a Douglas executive had described it. Douglas, like the rest of the aviation industry, was driven by the concept of *mission*—the striving for goals as if for the Holy Grail. Douglas was proud of the DC-10. It was their baby.

It had had some problems, but all new planes had a debugging period. Debugging was built into cost estimates. Certain cautious passengers stayed away from any new plane for the first two years on general principle, for everybody in aviation knew that an airplane got better as it got older. The DC-10's cargo door had been causing some operational delays—something airlines didn't like. And a door had blown out over Windsor, fifteen months ago. . . .

But pilots loved the plane. The two Turkish pilots had landed Turk Hava Yollari's Flight 981 at 11:02 that morning, completing the first and longest leg of the journey to London. As TC-JAV nosed into the arrival gate, a telescoping ramp moved out to meet it. Fifty of the passengers disembarked. Men from the service company, Samor, attacked the cargo holds. They left the front compartment untouched, unloaded the center one of empty pallets and mail bags, and began to load on the baggage of passengers who were boarding at Paris. With passengers still buying tickets, last-minute luggage would have to go later, on another plane. Four Samor men unloaded baggage and mail from the rear cargo compartment, and when it was empty, one of them, a big young Algerian named Mohamed Mahmoudi, called out from the hold to his supervisor to ask if there was any more baggage to load. The supervisor hollered back "No." Mahmoudi climbed out of the hold onto a conveyor belt that had been driven over for him and proceeded to close the door as he had forty or fifty times before. He pressed the toggle switch that electrically closes the door and, he later claimed, kept his finger on it until he heard the characteristic "click"

9

and saw the usual light go out. He reached up and pulled down the handle that locks the door. The handle stowed easily, confirming closure. The small truck carrying the conveyor belt moved Mahmoudi swiftly away from the plane. It must not obstruct the plane at departure.

He had closed the rear cargo door at 11:35, just 33 minutes after landing and 5 minutes after completion of the refueling. The door had delayed them before when they couldn't get it closed, and sometimes the baggage handlers had had to close it manually. There had been nearly a dozen recorded cargo door delays in the past year. But this morning, it would not be the door causing delays. From the chaos at the ticketing counters, it was clear that it would be the passengers.

Captain Nejat Berkoz would undoubtedly have welcomed the delay and a chance to stretch. It had been a long flight from Istanbul. The rest of his cockpit crew got up and moved around the airplane. They were virtually pioneers on the airline's DC-10s. All three—Berkoz, his cocaptain, Oral Ulusman (in Turkey, all pilots are captains), and his flight engineer, Erhan Ozer, had been sent to the manufacturer's plant at Long Beach, California, for simulator training on the same day, January 24, 1973, just over a year before, and just six weeks after Turk Hava Yollari had taken delivery of the first of its three DC-10s.

Now flights were routine. Berkoz had 438 hours on the DC-10, Ulusman had 628, and Ozer had 775 hours, a respectable body of experience. The plane itself had 2,955 hours and 52 minutes, still just the beginning of the 60,000 flight hours she'd been built for.

Berkoz would have checked his watch. The stop in Paris was running over schedule. Loading of passengers would delay them half an hour. Departure was now set for 12:30. The crew settled back into the cockpit to prepare for the 50-minute flight that would complete their long mission. At 12:11 and 30 seconds, they made their first contact with Orly Control and began the preflight procedures and checklists, getting routing, altitudes, checking fuel, weather, systems. Everything was going smoothly. There was no hint of trouble. Pilots are acutely aware of air safety, always—as they like to joke—the first one at the scene of an accident. They have a fierce will to live and a positive attitude toward flight. Though Ozer had talked of death to his wife through his poetry, he worked to deny it by these methodical preparations for flight.

On the ground, the service men had loaded all the baggage they were going to load and closed the doors of the center hold at 12:10, but the loading of passengers was continuing. By 12:18, they had their clearance from Orly Control, the first of four control agencies that would monitor TC-JAV, handing it from one to the other as it moved out to the runway and through the first stages of flight. At 6,000 feet, Orly Control would hand the big plane off to Paris Control.

Departure from the gate had been delayed at the last minute, as the twenty extra passengers rushed aboard and hunted for the few remaining seats. With no seat assignments, it had been everyone for himself, and the 8 cabin attendants were smilingly plying the aisles trying to get everyone seated in the three big compartments, settling and soothing the people who had boarded at Paris, stowing parkas and coats, checking that children were strapped in. Semra Hidir, who had been with the airline for a year, was anticipating London as much as the passengers. She had already made out her shopping list for the gifts she wanted to buy for her family.

Most of the passengers pressing aboard that morning had never flown in a DC-10, but there was casual assumption of a safe flight. In the sixty-five years since Louis Blériot had made the first precarious crossing of the English Channel by air, the awe had gone out of it. Psychologically, Paris to London was now a shuttle run. The passengers, nearly two hundred of them British, began to lean back and settle in. The final weight and balance forms were handed into the cockpit. Even with all the extra passengers, they were still well within their maximum weight allowance of 430,000 pounds.

At 12:19 the cabin door was locked, closing out the confusion of the airport and severing almost the last of the physical support links with the ground. The most symbolic act of any flight, the closing of the door shifts almost baronial powers and obligations to the captain's shoulders, and gives each flight its own unique dynamic. To an engineer, the closing of the doors gives the aircraft back the integrity it was designed to have, making it once more a sealed pressure vessel ready to test itself in the thin, alien air of cruising altitudes. And to him, the humbler act of closing the rear cargo door is as important as the more symbolic closing up front.

Mahmoudi, the baggage handler, had completed that 45 minutes ago at the rear of the DC-10. The amber light in the cockpit that warns of an improperly locked door was out. The wheel chocks were removed, and at 12:20, a tractor pushed TC-JAV back from the gate. The aircraft taxied out to Runway 08, escorted to the threshold by two mobile gendarmes. Berkoz would take off to the east. He was cleared to climb initially to 4,000 feet, and then to 6,000 feet. Weather conditions were good. Temperature was 43 degrees Fahrenheit, chilly but well above freezing. Light cumulus clouds between 1,500 and 3,000 feet. Visibility more than 9 miles.

He taxied onto the runway and held, waiting for takeoff clearance. Momentarily still, he kept his right hand firmly on the throttles, adjusting his grip and flexing his fingers, waiting. The cocaptain's hands performed a deft cockpit ballet, moving with graceful precision over the final buttons and switches, double checking. 334 passengers and the crew of 12 were strapped in for takeoff.

The takeoff roll started at 12:31. As the captain pushed the throttles decisively forward, three mighty turbo-fan engines, each with 40,000 pounds of thrust, accelerated the DC-10 down the runway. The plane reached V1—the go/no go speed—the speed at which they could still have chopped the throttles and aborted.

Everything checked out. Past V1, the captain moved his right hand swiftly from the throttles to the wheel, irreversibly committed to flight. They raced on, gaining a speed of 143 knots and rotated, lifting the nose into the air at a speed 4 knots below the precalculated takeoff—or V2-speed—when the airplane could safely take off even with the loss of an engine. The great bird lifted easily. Flight 981 was committed to the last leg of its long mission. It was almost 12:32.

Still under Orly Control, the plane climbed through lofty cumulus and light winds to 6,000 feet. Berkoz would follow Departure Number 18, which would vector him to three checkpoints—Tournan, Coulommiers, and Montdidier. At 12:34, Flight 981 contacted Orly Departure Control to report reaching 6,000 feet and was handed off to Paris Control. Flight 981 contacted Paris Control at 12:36—4 minutes into the flight—and was cleared to Flight Level 230—an altitude of 23,000 feet. They were then instructed to turn left, toward the Montdidier checkpoint. Flight 981 turned to the northwest on a heading of 345 degrees. At 12:37, the flight called in to report reaching 7,000 feet, it last coherent transmission.

They climbed swiftly through 7,000 feet . . . 9,000 feet, at an air speed of 300 knots—345 miles per hour.

In the cabin, everyone was relaxing after takeoff, lighting cigarettes, and chatting. The young rugby fans would have carried their high spirits with them into the air, with laughing and joking up and down the aisle. Steve Backhouse, traveling with friends from the Davenport Rugby Club, had headed to the airport in a very happy mood, according to a friend who had seen him off in a taxi. Two of the rugby boys from Bury St. Edmunds hadn't got out of bed and had missed the flight.

With so many men aboard, it was impossible for the four models not to be actively looked at. Prudence had never liked being "chatted up." She was intent on London and knew Stephen would be on his way to Heathrow.

There were six people at the rear of the plane whose

13

random choice of seats beside each other would cast them in a special destiny, one that was to become symbolic of the special fears that haunt a plane crash. Omer Faruk Afir had been on the plane since Turkey. One of a number of young Turkish students aboard, he was on his way to London to attend medical school and looked forward to becoming a doctor like his father. In Paris, others had taken the seats around him. Three women and two young Japanese men. Daniele Cam-ha Nguyen Thi was a twenty-three-year-old Vietnamese girl studying in France; and Georgiana Byatt, a forty-six-year-old primary schoolteacher from Middlesex returning from a holiday in Spain, traveling with a friend, Bessie Brown, a crossing guard at the same school. The two Japanese men were new friends on the trip—Tsukuro Yoshitake, who would be joining the Tomen trading company, and Tadaharu Sakata, who would join a bank. Sakata would have to make his own way in the business world, unaided by money or position. His only brother had died five years earlier in a gas leak accident, and now it would be his duty to support his father, already sick wth diabetes. But he had finished fifth out of eight hundred in his graduating class. And like the rest of the thirty-eight young men, he had been tapped to become part of the managerial elite of Japan.

The six sitting at the left rear of the fuselage in two banks of triple seats were a random sampling of any international flight in Europe. Their choice of seats bound them to a macabre destiny.

The plane climbed through 9,000 . . . 10,000 feet into the thinner air that makes climbers and skiers gasp, their hearts palpitate. But passengers sat back breathing normally, taking for granted the sophisticated environmental control system that maintained the air in the plane at comfortable pressures. Now it meant simply comfort. But at 40,000 feet, this cocoon of thick, compressed air meant survival for the human organism.

But who notices air? Innocent. Invisible. Apparently the same on both sides of the window.

14

There was no way to see or to feel that, with every foot of altitude, the air trapped in the fuselage was growing more frustrated by containment. It was roiling with eagerness to expand, to escape. And as it responded to the suck of the partial vacuum outside, it pressed out, putting stress on every rivet, latch, and window, every square inch of the thin, silvery skin. Pushing against the shell with several times the force of a hurricane, it searched for a way out.

The plane climbed through 11,500 feet, sprinting up at 2,200 feet a minute toward its assigned flight level, with the pressure differential between the cabin and the air outside building rapidly.

At 12:39 and 56 seconds*—a moment frozen in time by the plane's cockpit voice recorder—the air found its escape route. In one explosive microsecond, the caged hurricane burst through the rear cargo door, shearing off the bolts that held it to the fuselage, and flinging it—with six passengers still in their seats—down to the quiet French countryside.

On radar, stunned controllers watched, helpless. A battery of radar screens had been monitoring the moving blip that was Flight 981. At the instant the door came off, the image on the screens changed. On secondary radar, the blip simply vanished, leaving for several seconds the imprint of its altitude—13,000 feet. On the primary radar screen, the controller watched in horror as the image of Flight 981 split in two and became a double image. He had "seen" the door come off. As he watched, the two blips separated from each other on the screen. One stayed fixed at 24 miles northeast of Orly, frozen on the screen for two or three minutes. It was the door and the bodies free falling to the freshly plowed fields of St. Pathus. The second image followed a trajectory to the left, reached a heading of 280 degrees, to the northwest, and vanished.

* There is a 30-second discrepancy between this time taken from the cockpit voice recorder and times taken from the flight data recorder. Both, however, are in agreement on duration of flight and crisis.

It disappeared from his screen 77 seconds after the image had split.

Shortly after the image split, there were alerts by radio, too, that something had gone wrong with Flight 981. At 12:40 and thirteen seconds, Paris Control heard a garbled transmission of Turkish voices above the blaring of the depressurization alarm and, then, the overspeed klaxon. All transmissions ceased as the blip disappeared from the screen.

The controller tried to reach Flight 981. "981, come in . . . 981 do you read me? . . . Come in, 981 . . . 981 . . . " Eight times he tried to reach them. There was no response. After 9 minutes of flight, she had vanished.

In the cockpit, the crisis had hit the crew like a lightning strike. There was the sudden, thunderous noise of decompression as the air evacuated and violent jolts kicked the plane sideways. An explosive burst of dust and debris flew up into the cockpit, temporarily blinding them. From a climb of 3 or 4 degrees, the nose pitched down violently into a dive. The plane yawed hard left because of a 10 degree rudder deflection, forcing the left wing down. The autopilot disengaged instantly and the crew grabbed for control. Scanning instruments with ferocious speed and intensity, they had no idea what had happened, though Ulusman snapped out, "The fuselage has burst!" They did not know that the cabin floor had collapsed, severing and jamming the control cables that ran through the floor from cockpit to tail—their lifeline. They knew they were yawing hard left. And that elevators were forcing the nose down, jammed, inoperative—their prime means of pitch control. Within 22 seconds, the nose was down 20 degrees. They had to get the nose up. Berkoz yelled, "*Bring it up . . . pull her nose up!*" Ulusman pulled back with all his strength on the controls. But he could not overpower the dive. "*I can't bring it up. She doesn't respond!*"

Speed, increasing with pitch, had risen viciously from 300 to 362 knots. Number 2—the mighty engine on the tail—was already out. Dead. Windmilling uselessly. Now they cut the power on the underwing engines 1 and 3 in a desperate effort to stop the buildup of speed. But speed kept rising. They were diving at over 10,000 feet a minute. They would crash in seconds unless they could get the nose up. They were fighting for their lives, and for the lives of 334 passengers. But the rudder was jammed left. Elevators had locked the nose down. Number 2 engine was out. The exchanges were terse, as they searched frantically for an answer. *"Nothing is left."* Thirty-four seconds into the crisis. Speed was still rising . . . 400 . . . 410 knots. The aerodynamic scream was jerking up heads of Sunday strollers in the woods below. *"7,000 feet!"* Forty seconds to impact at the speed of their dive. *"Hydraulics?"* Hydraulics powered all their controls. Were they all gone?

But maybe something was left. For gradually the nose was coming up. It was coming up! Was it the one-in-a-thousand chance that they were flying the plane through the autopilot, using its limited authority to save them from crashing? Or was it simply the effect of the increasing speeds, for speed itself will pull the nose up. It came up from 20 degrees to 10, 9 . . . to 6, 5. They were leveling out. And speed had stabilized at 430 knots. But it was too late. They were too low. Flight 981 was a doomed and helpless bird. There were the desperate words, *"We've lost it."* The straight pines of Ermenonville Forest were rushing toward them like spears as they came in, left wing 17 degrees low, pitch nearly level, 4 degrees down, and speed at 423 knots. The final voiceless emission from Flight 981 ended at 12:41 and 13 seconds. At impact.

Impact is an experience that is beyond integration. An event so violent that the mind refuses it.

Disintegration of the fuselage began instantly. Number 1 engine, hung from the low left wing, impacted first, and began to break up immediately. As it impacted with a large tree, the stage 1 fan disk acted as a punch die, cutting a core right through the tree and driving it, like a wooden plug, into the bore of the

17

engine where it was later found. The rear engine told a story of even more appalling violence. As the momentum that had built up at a speed of almost 500 miles an hour was suddenly slowed by the convulsive impact of the hull, the massive rear engine, poised on the tail like a stone in a slingshot, was catapulted in an arcing trajectory at two thirds the speed of sound for half a mile beyond the main impact area. The same forces ripped off the rear of the hull and sent it, with ninety-five passengers, hurtling along the same path.

Within ten seconds, the hull—stripped of wings and engines—thundered through half a mile of forest, disintegrating progressively as it decelerated, literally raked to bits by the stiff pines. Before the bodies had even completed initial reaction to impact—feet shooting up and hips jamming down into the seat—the violent destruction of their protective envelope, the turmoil of flailing, crushing, and wrenching, of impaling by flying beams, metal, and sharp trees, would have killed all but the ninety-five catapulted to the far end of the crash site when the rear of the fuselage snapped off. For them, annihilation of sensation would be doubly guaranteed by lethal whiplash.

Within ten or fifteen seconds, the last piece of metal would have tumbled to rest, and there would have been no more sound. A small hand lay on the snow, still clutched by a larger female hand. For that child, for her mother—for all the humans who perished with them—there had been no "agony of death." Only agony for those left behind.

In those last few seconds of silence and certainty of death, the poem Flight Engineer Ozer had written just weeks before to his wife took on an unbearable poignancy:

> I want to call you,
> I want you to hear me.
> I wonder if you can feel
> One day my last breath.

Chapter Two

Did They Feel Anything?

BEFORE THE INITIATION of the 77 second nightmare, all had been perfectly normal in the cabin. Babies frightened by the noise and unfamiliarity of takeoff were probably fussing. Mothers would be trying to comfort them. Flight attendants would be moving up the aisles within six or seven minutes of takeoff, pitched forward as if walking against a wind. But passengers would still be in their seats. The NO SMOKING sign would have gone off shortly after the gear was raised, and many would already have lit up a cigarette. Between eight and nine minutes into the flight, a contagious click of seat-belts would riffle through the cabin, as a sense of confidence began to spread. The FASTEN SEAT BELT sign would probably still be on, though, and most passengers would be loosening, rather than unbuckling, their belts. People who had been apprehensive at take-off would be relaxing tensed muscles, still going through a period of adjustment. They would be settling back, interested primarily in comfort, unprepared for emergency as they might be at landing, the most dangerous phase of flight.

When the decompression hit, it would not be the sound of a bomb or gun blast, but a more thunderous rush, as if a car window had been suddenly opened at 350 miles an hour. The explosive blast of escaping air would sweep loose objects with it, pull down ceiling panels and pop panels up from the floor. As the pressure and temperature dropped, fog would fill the cabin, making many think, "SMOKE . . . FIRE!" The initial response would be the startle reflex, with arms and legs snapping out, spread eagled, muscles tensing. Fingers would go straight, though anyone already gripping the armrest would probably dig his fingers in harder, instinctively trying to hold the plane up. In the shock, air would escape from the lungs, making people say a dead "Oh." If some panicked at decompression, they would probably not try to undo their seat belts and run from the threat; they would sit silent, paralyzed from action. Simultaneous with the first reflex bodies would be jerked up hard against their seat belts, as the nose suddenly dropped. For an instant, they would experience negative G, the sensation of cresting a hill on a roller coaster, or of going over a big rise in the road—the sensation that hits you in the pit of the stomach and makes children scream "Wheeee!" It may have lifted them out of their seats. Then, torsos would lean, perhaps flail, to the right as the airplane yawed and the left wing dropped. But the yaw would not be precipitous; it would not be a convulsive, heart-stopping movement. But the two events combined—the wing down, and a dive angle that was many times steeper than anything most would ever have experienced, and getting steeper—would be alarmingly abnormal.

Though most would not panic, a general feeling of anxiety would sweep the pressure vessel. Bodies would become hyperactive, muscles tense, senses supersharp. Awareness and memory would become acute. Stress would shrink the range of vision to a narrow focus in which each detail would be seen and remembered. Time would snap into a new dimension, with seconds lengthening to vivid detail-filled lifetimes in the remarkable phenomenon that lets a fighter pilot take an hour to describe a three-minute aerial battle. Life's vignettes would be relived as if time had stopped. Physical movements would be discoordinated as people tried to handle their newly hypertense bodies. Stress would strip them of the ability to judge their own forces, and movements would be overdone, like bad acting.

All would be alert, intent on "What's happening? What hit us?" trying to figure it out, waiting for the next event. In an instant, the initial violence would pass, and they would fall back into their seats as almost normal G forces returned. There might be a certain sense of relief. And *hope* would be heard in a flurry of comments that put danger in the past tense, behind the—"What do you think it was?" "I wonder what hit us?" But there would be no end to the anxiety, for wasn't the plane going faster? The dive getting steeper? —a sensation exaggerated by the banking of the plane. Everyone would be vibrantly alert now to ANY abnormality, retrieving more rapidly than a computer any information that could help them figure out what was happening. What had they seen, read, heard, been taught? They would search for clues. But there were few physical references to help them. The seat in front. The people immediately adjacent. No answers outside the small windows.

Most would think "MIDAIR!" Seeing the fog, some would think "SMOKE!" and search for signs of fire. All would release tension in their own way, grasping desperately for normalcy, exaggerating it. There would be nervous laughter. Mothers would hug and soothe their children, diverting their own fears. The dependent would be more dependent; strong husbands more reassuring. Strong relationships would be reconfirmed by holding hands tightly, quietly. No protestations of love. Mostly silence, as minds raced. Cigarettes would be grabbed. And magazines. The strongly religious might pray, or handle beads or crosses. Cultural differences would become distinct. People from the Middle East, Italy, or any of the Latin countries might cry out and fling their arms; a man from the northern Anglo-Saxon countries might bolster his own self-control by saying with disgust, "What a bloody fuss she's making!" Others would be drawing on every four letter word they knew. People are profane in crisis. Some would run a frantic checklist of all the eventualities, finding comfort in the process of elimination. Others would find security in tightening their seat belts, or in pulling their clothes around them. A bloodied parka proved to Japanese parents that their son had pulled his hood up over his head.

There would be a compulsion to act to overcome the danger, but few actions were possible. As they quickly discovered that there was nothing constructive to be done, they might hurl hostility at the pilot and crew. "Why doesn't he come on and tell us what's happening?" He was their window on the world. What was he doing up there? And yet, things were not getting worse. Some might be conscious of an increase in speed and the rapid loss in altitude, but at least the dive wasn't getting any steeper. In fact, was it only wishful thinking . . . or was it actually decreasing? Gravity forces would be pressing them forward so gently that many would not notice it. Some would think, "He's diving to a lower altitude." For safety.

And then, before impact, the nose was clearly coming up. And up! "We're leveling off, we're pulling out!" "Whew! Thank God!" Mother would squeeze small hands with hope. "It's going to be all right, darling . . . going to be all right." Relief would wash through the pressure shell.

Most of the 328 passengers still aboard Flight 981 were probably looking around, apprehensive but hopeful, as they came into the trees, unaware that these were the last moments of their lives.

The experience of the six who fell from the plane was quite different; images of their ordeal will always haunt the crash. The collapse of the floor was violent enough to tear loose one of the flight attendants' seats and two banks of triple seats, to hurl them and their six passengers into the cargo hold below to be sucked out into the slipstream. The three men and three women at the left rear had no time to think about their fate. As seats and bodies ripped past shattered metal beams, torn cables, sharp floor panels, and out the hole, the six were almost certainly knocked unconscious, or killed. The young Turk was still strapped in and fell attached to his seat. Reportedly, all except him suffered severe and similar head damage that suggests death may have been caused during the terrible exit. Probably all were spared awareness as they were whipped into the slipstream.

If any were swept out cleanly, without damage, there could have been consciousness, but not awareness in the normal sense. For the mind would throw up protective walls around the delicate human mechanism. The initial experience would be so violent that there would be complete disorientation, with a rush of events the mind would not begin to catalog and comprehend in any rational way. Within seconds, this could be replaced by panic, the negative panic that throws people into a catatonic state. Eyes could close. The mind would either blank out or race uncomprehendingly. Thoughts or words, if there were any, would be repeated over and over. In this state, they could have fallen the 2 miles insulated from awareness. For others, the initial disorientation could have passed in four or five seconds, and awareness could have returned. But in crisis, it could have been a detached awareness, allowing a passenger to view the incomprehensible events happening to her as if she were a dispassionate observer: "Mary's falling. She's bleeding. I hope she survives. She wants it to be over." If there was blood—if Mary had been damaged by the tumult of exit—she would not feel it; for there would be too many other more acute sensations fighting for dominance, crowding out the sensation of pain. The fall could even have been euphoric, silent, with no sensation of plummeting to earth. The earth would not rush up until the final seconds, and Mary might have imagined herself suspended, perhaps from the plane.

Yet the six had fallen fast, reaching a maximum speed of 135 mph and impacting at a terminal velocity of about 120 mph in the denser air of lower altitudes. Attached to their seats, or falling free, they would have tumbled uncontrollably, probably never regaining clear

23

orientation to events or their environment, never seeing the ground. In spinning, blood pressures could have dramatically altered consciousness. But if any had been aware and clearly oriented to their situation, they would have fought for life, turning every fiber of mind to finding a way out. For "the habit of living has become an addiction." But attempts to fight back would be thwarted by the complete physical helplessness of their situation. There was nothing to grasp. No way to control the fall. No hope that they could survive it. Not prepared as skydivers would have been, they would not know to flip onto their backs and spread eagle as they fell to distribute the energies at impact, or to use the half-mile circle-of-choice they had to maneuver away from trees and pavement to green or plowed fields. It was chance that brought them down in plowed fields, a factor that could conceivably have worked toward their survival. Though the odds of preparedness making any difference are very slim indeed, people have fallen remarkable distances and lived. A Russian stewardess survived a fall of 3,000 feet; a Russian pilot has survived a fall of 29,000 feet. A navy parachute rigger jumping in a test program free fell 16,000 feet with only his streaming unopened chute slowing his fall, and recovered to become a flight instructor and charter pilot.

Pilots fight all the way down for their own lives, and for the ship's. Unlike passengers, they are actively in command of their fates and keep very busy. When they do realize that, for reasons known or unknown, they have lost control—blown it!—they respond with frustrated resignation. Though the words are always edited out for the sake of the surviving families, it is well known that the pilot's last words on the cockpit voice recorder are often "Oh, shit!" It is said as if he had just hit his thumb with a hammer. Or missed the last train.

With no survival tasks to preoccupy them, there would be loss of hope for those falling. And then, knowledge of death. This is the part that would cause nightmares to the families. But from the little we know, it seems that in that flash of transition from the fight for life to the recognition of imminent death, another threshold is leaped. Fighter pilots coming in for a crash have described it as a state of anticipation, of exhilarated fascination with "What will it be like?" A woman, brought back by doctors from "death," resented the interference with her dying. It has been described as "a remarkable sensation of detachment, of an extraordinary sense of peace, calm, and total painlessness. . . ." "The dying appear to go through a withdrawal, a preparation for death, as though intuitively familiar with the process." The renowned physician William Osler believed that there was "no agony of death."

Impact in the field at St. Pathus would have occurred at almost the same moment as impact in the forest. Death would have been instantaneous. There would be no conscious screams of terror. If there were human sounds, they would be the involuntary expulsions of air. If anything had been heard as they neared the ground, it would more likely have been the vibration of their clothes at high speed, making the tumbling bodies sound like an approaching artillery barrage. Then, a thud, as they impacted deeply into the earth.

Aboard the plane, there would have been a ring of panic around the hole where the seats had vanished. A zone of partially collapsed floor, seats askew, people hanging from their seat belts, trying to resist the suction that would continue through the flight, terrified to breathe or move. There would be a tangle of shiny bent or snapped cables that any mechanically aware passenger would quickly guess were vital to control. Here, there would probably be no noise or movement. Only the blanked minds and physical paralysis of negative panic. People resort to the mobile panic glorified in disaster movies only when there is a clearly marked exit to safety, and it is blocked, as when crowds jam the door from a burning theater. There would be no stampede toward this exit.

In the cockpit, the crew would be obsessed with "What the hell is happening?" and with saving the plane.

After the crash, there were rumors that, in crisis, Turkish pilots would throw up their hands and wait the will of Allah. There were fears that they might have reverted to old culture patterns. Pilots who had trained with them in NATO remembered that "flying wing" on a Turk was a "near-*kamikazi*" experience; that they would shrug off incredible errors with a resigned, "I didn't understand." And maybe they didn't. Turks are not yet fully at home with twentieth century technology, as demonstrated by the training of DC-10 flight engineers who would prepare for takeoff with 40,000 pound errors in takeoff weight, and without fuel logs. But with experience, they can be among the world's best—highly motivated and intelligent. Clearly, they would fight to save a plane. With origins as barbarous steppes horsemen, Turks have historically been the most aggressive of the Islamic groups, long in contact with the West's adversary spirit. The captains of Flight 981 were seasoned military and commercial pilots with well over 12,000 flight hours between them—enough for imprinting sound crisis responses. Turkish pilots are potentially perhaps even better than U.S. pilots because they obey rules and more easily suppress their egos for the good of the mission. If the Turkish crew *did* engage the autopilot to try to use its limited control to recover from the dive—a remote but tantalizing possibility—it was a cool and positive response. Without final proof that they had lost all hydraulics that powered the autopilot, there will always remain the intriguing possibility that they were flying her out on autopilot at the moment of impact.

On March 3, 1974, a cargo door failure had initiated a series of secondary failures that, in 77 seconds, had brought a giant plane screaming down at nearly 500 mph into the pine trees of Ermenonville Forest, 23 miles northeast of Paris. With the sturdy pines acting "like a giant shredding machine," the aircraft and its occupants had been utterly destroyed.

It was the worst, the largest, the most unspeakable

crash in aviation history. It was the crash that had been haunting the aviation insurers since the 747 had started commercial flights in 1970. The crash of a fully loaded wide-body airplane.

Statistically, it was overdue. The loss of one wide-body plane had been predicted for the first year of operation.

But when it came, only a small, highly specialized group of professionals was ready to respond. Of all those who may have speculated, few had really accepted the possibility. Compulsive Peter Pans, Westerners have tried to deny death in any form. But death by air crash has a special terror.

There is still a mystique about moving through the skies. And our ability to get us up there has raced ahead of our ability to handle it emotionally. As Canadian author Hugh McLellan suggested, perhaps our technological society has "outtraveled its own soul." Getting into a plane is an act of faith in high technology. And when a transport falls from the sky, we suffer not only the shock of loss, but also a shaken faith in the mechanistic way. A faith that must be reaffirmed. So a frantic search for cause follows. "Fixes" are made. And we try to believe it will never happen again. We keep trusting that if the wax is going to melt, it won't be on *our* wings.

Committed to the perfectibility of men and machines, we force air safety up to higher and higher levels, until flying becomes safer than taking a bath. Yet we fly suspecting that flight itself is a violation of one of the most tyrannical of all physical forces—gravity—and knowing that implicit in getting off the ground are some basic compromises, one of which is the compromise with perfect safety. One of the most popular pieces of received wisdom in aviation is: "Sure, we could build a perfectly safe plane. But it wouldn't fly."

An air crash is a public, highly visible event. And this was the most visible of all air crashes. The glare of public attention would be on it from minutes after the crash. The grim horror of it would be brought to many families by television hours before they had any idea that they would be involved.

From the stark lights that lit the barren hangar where the wreckage was examined, to the white-hot scrutiny by journalists, investigators, lawyers, and governments, the DC-10 crash would become a prisoner held under harsh lights until he has told everything he knows.

From the moment of impact, the *Paris Air Crash*, as it quickly became known on legal briefs, would become the most publicized, most controversial, and potentially most influential aviation disaster in history. The world's shock at the enormous loss of life would put unprecedented pressure on getting at the truth. And before the last ripples died away, the search for cause and culpability would carry us far beyond the testing of the structural integrity of a cargo door and the pressure vessel it should have sealed, to the testing of the most basic institutions, systems, strengths, and values of all the nations and individuals involved.

Chapter Three

Was It a Door?

HENDRIK WOLLESWINKEL HEARD the news at his home in Amsterdam and said to his wife, "That must be a door."

It had finally happened, just as they had warned it would—he and his two senior colleagues in the Netherlands Department of Civil Aviation, the RLD. For more than three years, the Dutch had railed at Douglas, at Boeing, at the Federal Aviation Administration and the international aviation community to wake up and act upon the decompression dangers in the wide-body jets.

Wolleswinkel had first been alerted to the potential hazard in the wide-body planes during precertification studies of the 747. Toying with numbers in the terse shorthand of the structural engineer, he had become aware of an alarming fact: Engineers seemed to be ignoring the "size-effect," the dynamics of the dramatically larger volumes of pressurized air that would fill the big planes. In sudden decompression—if a hole were knocked in the shell when a plane was pressurized —there would be vastly greater volumes of air rushing to get out of the hole, pressing down on cabin floors. If the pressures were great enough, cabin floors could collapse, bending and tearing the control cables that ran through the flors, with the potential for catastrophe for some of the wide-bodies. Fuselages could be punc-

tured any number of ways—by a bomb, a midair collision . . . a door coming off.

The new planes *must* be built to withstand a large
hole in the shell. They had yelled it to the aviation
world—but no one had listened.

Was it the door? Was it that damn door again? This
was one of the thoughts that raced through Chuck
Miller's mind when he heard that the crash at Paris
was a DC-10. Miller had just buckled his ski boots for
some Sunday skiing, and was heading for the slopes at
Masanatten just outside of Washington, D.C., when his
friends called out to him to say they'd heard a radio
report of a bad crash in France. Miller was the director
of the National Transportation Safety Board's Bureau
of Aviation Safety and one of America's most authoritative and concerned watchdogs of air safety. His
bureau's job was to investigate all significant U.S.
crashes or incidents to determine probable cause and to
try, by recommendations to the Federal Aviation Administration and others, to prevent them. There had
been only one fatal wide-body crash prior to Paris.
When Miller called his deputy, Marion Roscoe, and he
had confirmed that it was a DC-10 that had gone in,
Miller found his mind jumping to the Windsor Incident
more than two years ago . . . when a DC-10 had lost
its aft cargo door in flight. The bureau had investigated
the Windsor Incident, made a report and recommendations. Since then, he'd heard very little about the DC-10
cargo door problem. His bureau was always short-
staffed, and at the time it was just one of five thousand
problems. Now he couldn't get *Windsor* off his mind.
He instructed the GO team to leave for Paris. The GO
team are the crash investigation specialists who are
always standing by, ready to go. They do not sit around
a ready room, like SAC pilots poised for the alarm that
blasts them into the skies. They don't *wait* for accidents.
But when on call, they must be reachable at all times
via the portable "beeper" they carry with them, ready
to depart within two hours, night or day. Many carry

bags in their car, ready to rush to National airport, to the hangar—the closest thing they have to a ready room—that houses the FAA planes they use. Or they go commercial, bumping passengers or sitting in the cockpit, getting to the crash site any way they can, as fast as they can.

This time they'd be on a commercial flight to Paris. Miller knew they would have to have an invitation from the French, "but that doesn't mean you can't buy an airplane ticket, and wait in Paris just as well as here." He ordered the GO team into the air. Senior investigator Doug Dreifus would act as U.S. accredited representative for the American team that would gather in Paris—men from the manufacturers of the plane and engines, the FAA, and the GO team. They were on TWA's Flight 800—the first available flight to Paris—with their kits, flight suits, and high international reputations. They would be on the scene by Monday morning, French willing.

With every international crash, the men who *must* be there had to play the delicate game of protocol, pushing the rights they had under the United Nations' International Civil Aviation Organization (ICAO) to the very limit, hoping they didn't insult someone, hoping they could break through the pall of secrecy that often fell over a foreign inquiry. With so little crash experience on wide-bodies, it was desperately important for them to be there. Armed with ICAO's Annex 13, the official crash investigation procedures booklet that defined their rights, they flew off to Paris.

The French were eager for American help, and Dreifus had no difficulty gaining access to the site.

In Paris Monday morning, he had raced so quickly to the forest that he had not even changed into his old flight suit. In sports coat and slacks, he had hiked "the whole distance the first visit. . . . Walk a bit, then think about what I'd seen. Rugged terrain. Getting ideas all the way." He was looking for rational patterns in the wreckage. With information exchanged with the French and the Turks added to their own visual inspection, he and the team quickly did a tentative analysis of the crash.

The major and initial ground contact was synonymous in a rough area where stone had been quarried. The terrain was subsequently so devastated that precise impact locations were difficult to establish. A tremendous explosion occurred near the initial impact point. Pine trees to the side of the flight path had been uprooted with no mechanical forces evidence. The percussive force of the explosion had blown them out. Tree stubs were discontinuous and irregular, indicating the wreckage had been broken into many pieces during the initial heavy ground impact. The wipeout of trees was essentially complete for an approximate one-half-mile distance.

The pieces were so small that identification of parts was difficult. The tail, usually intact in a crash, had been destroyed almost beyond recognition. The largest chunk of fuselage was only about 10 by 17 feet. Of the thousands of feet of cable that had run the length of the 181-foot-long plane, only one 6-foot length could be found. No instruments were seen. A crumpled *boîte noire* containing the Digital Flight Data Recorder was found the first day, but the precious Cockpit Voice Recorder could not be located at first. They found floor planking structure but its normal location in the plane could not be identified, and "the only seat structure that remained relatively intact were the seats that separated from the aircraft in flight." The seats that fell over St. Pathus. Because of the tremendous momentum this big plane generated at high speed, a logical sequence of wreckage was hard to distinguish.

Yet even in this shambles, investigators were able to pick up the threads of a logical scenario. There had been momentary explosions and flash fires with a few persisting for a few seconds. But unburned fuel had been found smeared on trees at the point of impact with the wing engines, indicating that the bulk of the fuel on the plane had not burned. The seats that had fallen with their passengers at St. Pathus held valuable clues. The seats had torn away with small pieces of the metal track at the base of the seats still attached. Structurally a load-bearing part of the floor, the failed track indicated collapse of the cabin floor. The power plant group of the American team found that the engines had not exploded in flight, for there was none of the metal splatter or hot spots that would have indicated "pre-impact distress" in any of the engines. But from the scattered confusion of fan blades, turbine shafts, and compressor sections they were able to deduce that the condition of the rear engine, which is dependent for control on cables running through the floor to the tail, "is as would be expected following the cabin floor failure and resultant destruction of engine control cables." There was still enough residual heat left in the engine to discolor tree debris, but the temperatures were low, pointing to a shutdown in flight that had left number 2 engine without power, in a "windmilling" condition. It was all consistent with the severing or jamming of engine control cables prior to impact, further supporting the theory of floor collapse.

Enough rotating components were recovered to tell them that the underwing engines, 1 and 3, had been operating at the time of the crash, though perhaps in flight idle. To the relief of General Electric, the engines did not appear to be a causal factor.

The combined investigative groups of all the countries involved started writing up their preliminary evaluations—evaluations that were to be kept confidential until the official French report was issued. "The impact swath was oriented southeast to northwest and was approximately 2,624 feet long and 245 feet wide at its widest part. All personnel were killed." It was the biggest "non survival accident" yet, a significant new point on the curve.

Late Monday night, Doug Dreifus called Miller with a routine confidential report. He confirmed that bodies and some pieces of "structure" had been found 9 miles from the crash, along the airplane's flight path. Was the "structure," Miller asked, a door? They *knew* it was,

Dreifus reported, but it had not yet been confirmed by the French.

Miller had just learned, too, that McDonnell Douglas had already sent wires out to all DC-10 operators urging them to be sure the cargo doors were fully latched and locked before flight. Douglas clearly feared that the cargo doors *might* be involved. Grasping the chilling implications, Miller ordered out all the files on *Windsor* and told Walt Sweet, the investigator who had handled it, to pack his bag.

Chapter Four

The Windsor Incident

On JUNE 12, 1972, Sante Facca, a farmer, was puttering with the flowers around his home near Windsor, Ontario, when he heard a loud *bang*. He looked up, searched the sky, but saw nothing. Seconds later he saw what looked like an airplane door bumping across a field in front of his house. Then he heard a *thump* at the back of his house. And there he found a coffin. Though it was still partially covered by a tarp, the belts securing it were broken. He opened it a little and saw the distorted legs of a woman. A dummy? He touched it with a stick and promptly shut the lid. It was a body. He called the police.

The coffin was the first clue to what was happening two miles above him. The first clue to a stark drama involving a flight crew and fifty-six passengers—a drama that became known as the Windsor Incident.

One of the passengers was Brad Reed, an engineer with General Electric. The kind of man the DC-10 was designed for, he often traveled for his company through the heavily industrialized northeastern United States and, less often, across the continent. When he boarded the American Airlines DC-10 in Detroit that day, he was on his way back to his office in Pittsfield, Massachusetts, from Muskegan, Michigan.

Called back ahead of time, he had phoned United to saddle him up for the journey. They had booked him on a 3:55 flight direct from Muskegan to Hartford,

35

Pittsfield's closest airport. Good. That was efficient. Even the rushed packing, check-out, and race to the airport in a rental car were so well practiced from previous trips that they did not ruffle him.

Then, the first catch. No 3:55 flight. Computers spat out an alternative routing that was Byzantine in its complexity. It required him to drive from Muskegan to Grand Rapids to catch a North Central flight to Detroit, connect there with American Airlines Flight 96 to Buffalo, make a tight connection at Buffalo with an Allegheny flight to Hartford, then drive to the office. But that was life. Brad did not do an on the spot comparative analysis of the safety record and equipment of the three lines he would be flying. His decisions were not based on safety factors. He just booked aboard whatever flights would get him back to the office most directly.

At Detroit, the captain carried his flight bag aboard the DC-10 as if it were a briefcase. Without the hat and captain's stripes, Bryce McCormick could have been the company's controller, as comfortable with the cryptic language of an annual report as with the cockpit instrumentation of a jumbo jet. At fifty-two, he looked . . . reliable. Stuffy, even. Metal-rimmed glasses. Hair clipped short and neatly parted, with a mature sprinkling of gray at the temples. Chin settling firmly into the incipient jowls of the sedentary executive reaching his middle years.

To American's Flight 96, en route from Los Angeles to New York via Detroit and Buffalo on June 12, McCormick was the most visible symbol of the vast complex of service systems with which an airline competes: maintenance, catering, computerized ticketing, in-flight care, convenient schedules, baggage retrieval, and so on. To the experienced corporate traveler, the captain was not so much a symbol of safety—for low risk is assumed—as he was an expression of all those efficiencies that were sold, though not spelled out, in the "contract of carriage" made when you purchased a ticket.

American is a businessman's airline. And through dress and demeanor, its pilots strike an unspoken bargain with the corporate passengers who are the airline's bread and butter. "You fly my airline. I'll give you bland sensation-free flight that will not distract you from *your* mission. Check your digital watches and relax. I will be in charge of your office in the air, assuring you of elbow room for writing up your reports, smiling girls and service that will remind you of your secretary, a cabin kept at the correct temperature for a suit, so that you can go directly from the exit gate to your conference. I'll have to wear a cap—this *is* my ship, and you and my girls both need authority symbols—but apart from that, I'll be in a conservative suit, just like you. Pretend we're in the board room together, and trust me. And if I cause you to expend one scrap of those corporate energies on delays or a hard landing, then I've failed *my* mission."

A smooth landing was part of the bargain. And McCormick was proud of his landings. He'd never blown a tire.

For Brad, United had broken the bargain back there in Muskegan. And American was now pressing its luck. The flight was already behind schedule; the connection in Buffalo would be almost impossible. Quietly organized, he retrieved his bag from the checked luggage and checked it as "escort luggage" that would be handed to him the moment he deplaned. It would buy him a few extra minutes at the other end. Also, he broke a long-standing habit and sat near the front of the tourist section—a window seat on the left—so he could be among the first to get off. For years, he had made it an unvarying practice to sit in the very last row in the plane—a vestige of his single days when he had sat back there to meet the stewardesses. Unconcerned with the equipment, he thought he was on a Boeing 747.

Flight 96 was now posted for a 6:50 P.M. departure, and the passenger load was light. Most of his fifty-five fellow passengers were seated along the windows, with the center sections almost empty. Looking out the window on the right side, a middle-aged black lady seemed nervous, apprehensive; it was her first flight. An Italian couple was having its concern compounded by a language problem. A black girl soothed a baby. A retired woodworker and his wife were chatting with a friend traveling back to Tonawanda, New York, with them; the wife had carefully stowed a cardboard pretzel box containing an antique cut-glass water pitcher under the seat in front of her. With eight stewardesses patrolling the aisles, they would all be well attended.

It was a wet, gray evening for mid-June. And the 46-minute delay in departure from L.A. had put pressure on the ground crew trying for a fast turn-around—an economic imperative. Brad Reed's bag and the rest of the escort luggage had been loaded aboard the rear cargo hold, and they were ready to lock up the door. But the ramp service agent was having trouble with the aft cargo door—the door that had reportedly caused two additional delays on American DC-10s on the L.A.–Detroit run within the last three days. As soon as the baggage was stowed, he had pressed the toggle switch that closed the door electrically and had then held it down, listening for the motor to stop running—the sign that the door was properly closed and latched. Then he tried to close the door handle, an act that would guarantee safe flight by locking the latches, sealing the plane, making it ready for pressurization by closing a little vent door—a door within the cargo door—turning off the cockpit light, assuring the flight crew that the aft cargo door was locked.

But he couldn't get the handle down. And it was eating up seconds. In the cockpit, the initial checklists would have been completed; the crew would be waiting for the cargo door to be closed before firing up the engines. He was holding up the flight—failing in *his* mission. He put his knee against the handle and shoved. The handle closed flush with the door. But the little vent door looked a little cockeyed. He called a mechanic over to take a look and release the aircraft.

Whatever they decided on the ground, the men in the cockpit still had the final responsibility. They were the ones with the stripes of authority, and the warning light on the annunciator panel to tell them whether or not the door *was* properly locked. The mechanic checked the door, approved it, and let her go.

The cargo door warning light had finally gone out in the cockpit, and Flight 96 had started taxiing out to the runway. Bryce McCormick had been taxiing American planes out for takeoff for twenty-eight years. This evening, however, he would monitor while First Officer Paige Whitney made the takeoff. It was common practice to give the first officer the controls for the day when he would be sitting in the left seat, captain of his own ship. Also, co-pilots like to fly too.

No matter how many times you've done it before, there is drama in getting airborne. Even pilots whose home is the cockpit periodically sit back and appreciate the small miracle they routinely work with the maze of instrumentation before them. It is a sensation of being special that may be surpassed only by an astronaut heading for the moon.

For the three on the flight deck, the drama was heightened by the fact that they were all relatively new to the DC-10. McCormick had 56 hours; Whitney had 75; and Flight Engineer Clay Burke had only 45—just a few months on a wide-body, a profoundly different type of plane. Vastly fewer hours on the DC-10 than the Turkish crew. But with McCormick's 24,000 hours, Whitney's 8,000, and Burke's 14,000 hours, they were professionals taking pride in doing their job well.

In one of the most sedentary of all occupations, the tiny cockpit was their world. There are few habitats in which a species is so highly specialized. A flight crew's sole mission is the safe completion of the flight, achieved through skilled reading and manipulation of an electronic smorgasbord of controls, dials, switches, and lights. They work under a self-imposed pressure to perform well and competently. It is a pride that goes beyond the obvious necessity to fly well for your passengers, for a company check pilot looking over your shoulder, or for the voice and flight data recorders that make your mistakes living history. It is the way you "move in the cockpit"; handle your radio transmissions; your calm and decisive responses; the smoothness of your controls handling; the systematic flow of fingers over buttons, knobs and switches, the economy of movement that grows into a style—the things that show you are at home and in command of your habitat, that give you class among your peers.

Part of it is taking down radio information correctly and firing it back in a cool, deep voice. Paige Whitney had listened to the latest recordings giving him the local winds, visibility, runway frequencies, and altimeter setting—Information Delta—and was now ready to get the special information governing their flight to Buffalo— their clearance. It would come from air traffic control, one of a myriad of controlling agencies that make for the safe, orderly conduct of flight: ground control, the tower, departure control, air traffic control centers, approach control. They would oversee Flight 96 in a series of handoffs from one agency to the next all the way to the arrival gate at Buffalo. You had to obey instructions. If you were initially cleared to 4,000 feet, it probably meant that there were aircraft at 5,000 feet, and in cloud you had no way of seeing them. If your initial climb heading was 060, to the northeast, it probably meant there were aircraft in adjacent sectors. To make sure you had the numbers right, it was essential to read them back, verbatim. Paige had his pad out, ready to copy. You talked and wrote in pilot's shorthand. You had to. You had to be fast and accurate to make efficient use of your radio transmission. There were always lots of others out there waiting to make transmissions, too.

He told them he was ready for their clearance: *"Metro Clearance Delivery, American 96. Information Delta and Airways Buffalo."*

The instructions came at normal talking speed. He was given a zero six zero heading—60 degrees. Salty

40

and romantic as "east by nor'east" may be, there's no room for that kind of imprecision in flying, just as the old mariner's "keeping a good look out" is not enough in the three-dimensional environment of the flyer. You can't rely on visual scanning, vital as it is. So control gives you lateral and vertical separation; tells you when other aircraft are on a course that could come near you, and tells you where to look for them.

They got their altitudes and radio frequency. They would fly Airway J-554 to Buffalo, either vectored by ground radars or directed by on-board navigational equipment. They were assigned the transponder code that would identify their aircraft from others on radar.

Whitney read back their clearance:

American 96 cleared to . . . er . . . Buffalo airport. After takeoff turn right, that's as filed. After take-off turn right to . . . er . . . heading . . . er . . . zero six zero for radar vectors J-554. Maintain 5,000 . . . that's maintain 4,000. But expect Flight Level two five zero 10 minutes after departure. One eighteen niner five. And zero 200 transponder.

Not too smooth. He'd messed it up a bit. But he had got it.

On the final pre-takeoff checklists, the amber warning light for the troublesome cargo door was still off. The captain handed over control to his copilot. They rolled and lifted off.

They crossed the Canadian border, swinging over Windsor as they climbed. The climb was so steep that Margaret Innes, whose cut-glass water pitcher clung to its perch under the seat, observed that a stewardess walked up the aisle "as if she was climbing a steep hill." As they broke through the cloud into the shock of brilliant sunlight at about 11,700 feet, her eyes, and the eyes of almost everyone on the plane, were riveted on the spectacle. But as she turned to comment on the "fleecy white clouds" to her husband, Don, and her friend, the calm came apart. With a fury of sound and

41

motion, the protecting womb was punctured. *Explosive decompression.* One of the most terrifying events that can be experienced in flight. It hit like a hurricane.

The hull shuddered with a series of horizontal jolts, as if it had been kicked in the side by a giant boot. In one furious *whoosh,* the air whipped through the fuselage, sucking and tearing loose anything it could as it roared toward its exit. Ceiling panels the size of table tops fell like lethal blades. Some swung from wires that dangled like intestines from the gaping holes in the ceiling. Smoke—or was it vapor?—poured in through the holes, swirling around Margaret Innes like a smokescreen. Floor panels leaped up in the aisles between her husband and her friend. The paneled interior of the plane seemed to be collapsing like a house of cards. Thank Heaven there were storage bins—not panels— above the heads of passengers sitting on the sides!

Don Innes looked back toward the rear and saw that the carpeted floor of the cockpit lounge had collapsed. Through the debris and fog he could see "shiny, new-looking cables and wires" in the hole—the plane's control cables—taut, and exposed like veins.

Something made passenger Cindi Breloff look toward the front of the plane; and as she did, "particles of dust came flying toward me and someone in back of me screamed, 'Oh, my God!' " The dust flying around was "just like in the movie *Airport,*" and she knew there was a hole in the plane, somewhere.

A galley hatch cover blew up and hit a woman in the cheek, cutting her. The elderly Italian couple who spoke no English were in terror. People counted rosary beads. And Victor Perez prayed to God.

Brad Reed heard a loud rushing noise. He had been watching the sky, too, when "a series of severe jolts occurred—it felt like a violent shudder, sideways, not up and down. . . . I thought at first it was turbulence, then the front of the tourist section filled with white foglike vapor—very thick—and a panel on the ceiling about six feet ahead of me in the center section came down. The fog was pouring in through the hole where the panel was missing." This was not part of the bargain.

Margaret Innes's first thoughts had been, "A bomb's gone off . . . and I hope we aren't over Lake Erie!"

For most, a bomb or a midair collision were the first thoughts. The stewardesses knew it was decompression, though none had experienced it in their training, as military pilots do. All but two had completed their emergency procedures training within the previous month, and it had at least been graphically described. Most instinctively thought "Oxygen." But the masks had not come down. One grabbed an oxygen bottle and started up the aisle. Carol McGhee had grabbed for her mask, couldn't find it, and had realized she was breathing normally. They had been 2,000 feet below the danger level of 14,000 feet, where the masks pop out automatically. She saw the cockpit door burst open, hats fly out, and a sandy cloud come gushing out, murky and different from the fog that was filling the cabin. She started calming hysterical passengers and helping the woman hit by the hatch cover.

"First Lady" Cydya Smith saw the captain's hat on the floor near the cockpit and felt an urgent need to get up there. Having made one of her major executive decisions on the flight—the bar would *not* be opened—she had been fixing coffee and had just missed having her face smashed by a service door that flew open. She grabbed a handle to keep from falling. Then, a sensation of weightlessness and, after the wild moments of decompression, an eerie silence—like a vacuum. She raced toward the cockpit.

Scheduled for her regular emergency procedures training the next day, Sandi McConnell had unfastened her shoulder harness and seat belt, but was still in her jump seat at the very rear of the plane, chatting with Bea Copeland, when the jolt hit her. She was thrown from her seat to the divider partition that was behind the circular cocktail bar. What had been the lounge floor was now a gaping hole, and she had the sensation that she was slipping down into it, down into

43

the cargo hold. Bea was hurled to the floor and found herself trapped, with a piece of ceiling on her head, the upended bar lying beside it, and her foot caught. She was staring into the luggage compartment below the cabin floor. She could not pull her foot free; as she struggled, she could feel the floor give way beneath her. The escaping air had almost taken her with it, and could still succeed.

Brad heard one of the girls scream to a man who'd stood up, "Get back in your seat, please!" and another yell, "Get me out of here!" He didn't know yet that the floor at the back of the plane had caved in with the bar and three of the seats, and that two stewardesses were trapped. Instinct was to get away from the threatening hole, and stewardesses started herding people away from it to the forward seats. Though the stewardesses were generally responding well, most of them seemed frantic to Brad. As passengers were shunted around, he saw one group moved into the very seats that another had just vacated. A man clutching a five-gallon can of antisize compound like a security blanket was put beside him.

In the cockpit, the flight had been going well. Captain McCormick was so pleased with his plane that he was giving it testimonials. "Whoever designed that thing, I'll tell ya, he . . . ooooooooh!" They broke out into the sunshine. Flight Engineer Clay Burke thought, "What a beautiful day!" Then there was a loud, thudding *bang*. A jolt. A whirling sandstorm. The rudder pedals under the captain's and first officer's feet slammed to the hard left position, the left pedals going all the way forward, and the right pedals snapping back with such force that it smashed the captain's leg back against the seat. The three throttle levers flew back, with number 2 whacking hard against its stop. This put the engines into flight idle, killing forward thrust with a lurch, turning the vessel into a massive glider.

The blast was like a firecracker going off in the captain's face. His headset blew off, cutting radio contact; and he got a faceful of flying dirt and debris that almost blinded him to the brownish-gray fog that billowed through the cockpit. The cockpit door flew open, and three hats shot into the cabin. "A midair!" the captain and flight engineer thought. A collision. When McCormick could see again, he looked for the windshield. He "just knew it had to be gone." But it was there. In disbelief, he started to reach out and touch it. But the cockpit had come alive with red emergency flags and lights, and they demanded his attention.

Airspeed was falling. They were yawing and rolling to the right, a condition that could lead to a spiraling dive. The initial pitch down of the nose that had caused zero G and the momentary feeling of weightlessness had eased, but the nose was continuing to drop, pulling them back into the clouds. In cloud, they'd have to go back on instruments—instruments they could no longer fully trust—giving them that much more to do during the crisis. Also, altitude means time and options. Precious options.

When Cydya Smith stuck her head in the cockpit and asked, "Is everything alright up here?" McCormick snapped back "NO!" He didn't know yet what he had to fly with. But above everything else racing through his mind was, "Fly the airplane. FLY THE AIRPLANE!" Paige Whitney hadn't taken his hands off the wheel. The captain took the controls from him and scrambled for his headset. Between them, they got the power back on and the nose up.

They were 48 seconds into the crisis and McCormick knew they had real problems. They would have to declare an emergency. Normally, you're reluctant to declare one, knowing that aircraft will be held, re-routed, told to change or maintain altitude—whatever is required to clear a path for the crippled plane. And you can expect to be greeted by fire engines, ambulances, and other emergency equipment on landing. You like to play it low key if possible; but when you do have a genuine emergency, the only responsible thing to do is declare it.

"Ah, Center, this is American Airlines Flight 96. We got an emergency."

But they were still in business. Whitney said, "I think its going to fly."

But what *did* they have to fly with? The crew's eyes flew over the dials and indicators, trying to figure out the precise status of the flight controls, engines, hydraulics, instruments. In an emergency, a pilot finds his answers in his instruments. Isolated from his plane, he can't see it. The only noises he hears are cockpit noises: throttles slamming . . . warning horns. His bristling array of switches and dials are his only reliable source of information, and he focuses on them with compulsive intensity. Like doctors feeling for broken bones or diagnosing an illness, the crew began comparing notes and checking out the systems.

While the first tentative tests of the airplane's integrity were being made, the flight engineer—who controls and monitors many of the systems—was going through every emergency checklist in his manuals, trying to identify the problem. But in a multi-failure situation like this it takes time and a lot of knowledge to accurately troubleshoot.

Still not knowing what he could rely on—or even if he could make it—McCormick worked out his emergency landing procedures with air traffic control. They had responded instantly to his initial squawk with *"American 96. Roger. Returning back to Metro?"*

Metro meant Detroit. Back into the clouds and the weather.

"Ah . . . negative. I want to get into an airport that's in the open."

He thought of Wright-Patterson Air Force Base in Ohio. They had lots of runway and barriers to stop a plane. But could they stop a jumbo? Metro was close and familiar. "I know the Detroit approach like the back of my hand. Good clear approach, no obstructions, and 9,600 feet of concrete, strobes and all." The decision was made to return to Detroit.

The complexity of the cockpit does not alter the

fact that, essentially, you fly with only a few basic controls: elevator, rudder, aileron, and throttles. Throttles control the plane's power, elevators control it in pitch, while aileron and rudder permit the pilot to change direction—to roll the plane and make coordinated turns.

After the shock of decompression, the crew's first reaction had been to keep the airplane under control and to get the power back on to stay on top of the cloud. Numbers 1 and 3 engines—the engines under the left and right wings—had responded OK; but number 2 —the engine mounted in the tail—had not. They tried the elevators, but they were heavy, and the airplane's response in pitch was sluggish. The nose was still dropping. Jammed rudder was causing the yaw to the right. And to counteract the yaw and rolling of the plane, they needed a lot of left aileron.

To lighten the elevator forces, to make it easier to keep the nose up, Captain McCormick "pickled in" some stabilizer trim. The stabilizers—the large horizontal tail surfaces to which the elevators are attached —respond powerfully but slowly. Captain McCormick detected no response at all. He looked down at the indicator and could see no movement. He then reached for the manual stabilizer trim—the backup to the electrical trim system—but the "suitcase handles" were not functioning; part of the pedestal on which they were located was broken away. All this told him he had lost stabilizer control; he would not be able to trim off the elevator forces to get the nose up.

He did not know that the electrical trim was, in fact, working properly; it was the indicator that was inoperative—a fact that was to complicate his landing. Because he was new on the DC-10, he had, perhaps, not yet learned to recognize the "size effect" on control commands; response took longer.

He had to get the nose up!

He remembered something he had practiced at the flight academy in Fort Worth. You could use the power from the engines to help control the airplane in pitch.

Because the rear engine is *above* the aircraft's center of gravity, its thrust will shove the nose down; with engines 1 and 3 *below* the wings, below the center of gravity, their thrust will push the nose up.

The rear engine had been sitting in flight idle since the instant of decompression, but it appeared to be still running. If he shut it down, reducing any nose-down movement it might be creating, it might take some of the load off the elevators. He ordered number 2 shut down, and thought he felt the elevators respond a little better, though they were still very heavy. It must have been wishful thinking. For some of those "shiny new-looking cables and wires" that had been severed when the floor collapsed had already caused the tail engine to shut down.

He applied power to 1 and 3 to bring the nose up. But he needed them, too, for his severe directional-control problem. The engines could help straighten them out and help the ailerons control the roll to the right. By a basic principle, if the right engine thrusts harder than the left, it will push the nose to the left. So, by bringing up the power on number 3 or reducing it on number 1, they could reduce the yaw to the right. It would take some of the load off the ailerons. This asymmetric thrust was going to have to help steer them home.

They were getting things under control, but something was inexplicably wrong with the rudder. McCormick was getting confusing cues. With the rudder pedals jammed left, they should have been yawing left. But they were yawing to the right. Why? They had two engines, asymmetric thrust, jammed rudder, limited ailerons, no stabilizer and reluctant elevators. To get back to Metro, Captain McCormick was going to have to ease the plane around the turns as if she were a crotchety, lame old lady.

"... *Our turns are gonna have to be very slow and cautious.*"

"*Understand.*"

The controlled voices of both captain and controller disguised the desperate effort at both ends.

48

He started his long, slow turns, alternately retarding or increasing thrust on numbers 1 and 3. "After twenty-eight years, I'm back flying a DC-3!"

As they began to make their vectored descent to Detroit, a call came through to the flight engineer from one of the stewardesses, with the first hard news of damage. There was a hole in the fuselage, part of the cabin floor had collapsed, and they needed help to get out the two trapped stewardesses. The captain gave Burke permission to go, though he wanted him right there where he was.

Burke got up and grabbed for his hat on the cockpit door. It was gone. He searched for it. It was company policy to wear a hat in the cabin, something the captain insisted on; and the need for it was so deeply ingrained that, even in extreme crisis, he could not let passengers see him without it. A crazy irrelevancy, perhaps, to be hunting for a hat while two stewardesses hung in a hole. But it would have been a spontaneous response. And who knows if, in crisis, the sight of that symbol of authority—like the plumed helmet of a medieval knight —might have cast an aura of order over brewing hysteria. He was still hunting when another call came in saying that the girls were safely out of the hole. The captain was relieved not to have lost his flight engineer. They had an emergency landing to prepare for.

It was time now to tell the passengers what was going on. McCormick came on the PA and drawing on nearly three decades of experience in cool modulation, made an announcement that was a classic of under-statement—even for pilots. His passengers hung on every word as if he were Churchill making a wartime address and remember it as having begun with "I apologize for the slight inconvenience, ladies and gentlemen . . ." With a calm verging on boredom, he told them that the plane was under control, that they would be making an emergency landing in Detroit because of "a problem." New reservations would be made there to get them swiftly to their destinations.

"We pretty well knew we had a problem when the

ceiling caved in," Brad mused to himself. He was clearly going to miss his Buffalo connection.

The black lady sitting by the right-hand window started crying and shouting "HALLELUJAH!" through her tears.

With the help of a male passenger, Cydya and Carol Stevens had managed to pull Bea and Sandi out. For Carol, it was an unforgettable introduction to flight— she had graduated from the American Airlines Stewardess School less than a month before. Cydya gathered all the girls at the service center for their landing briefing. They would have approximately ten minutes to prepare.

Passengers were moved again, this time toward the exit doors. For Cindi Breloff, it was the third move; and as she ran to her seat, her legs were shaking. A boy next to her took her hand, fastened her seat belt, and told her they would make it. The girls went up the aisles with bags collecting shoes and glasses. Don Innes slipped his glasses in his suit pocket. Margaret Innes's cut-glass pitcher was moved to the center of the plane. Brad had the presence of mind to tie his shoelaces together and, like Don Innes, slipped his glasses inside his suit. They were an attentive audience as they were taught the emergency landing position and were directed to leave by emergency chutes, to move away from the plane the moment they hit the ground, and to observe the buddy system. They waited for what seemed an eternity as the final 23-mile turn was executed. As they descended rapidly now, Cindi "really thought it was over," and "strange thoughts about my personal life kept going through my head." Brad heard the engines reduce power and saw the slats—the leading edge flaps—deployed. He pointed it out to his frightened seatmate as a promising sign.

The cockpit crew was not so confident. They were trapped by immutable laws of flight. McCormick was now relying on his engines for much of his control—his pitch and heading—and had to keep a lot of power on to keep the nose up. But the more power he put on, the faster he went. He would have to reduce his speed dramatically for approach and landing. *You have to be slow for a landing*. But as you reduce speed, the nose of an airplane tends to go down, and, without the stablizer to trim the nose back up, he could go into an irretrievable dive. He did not know how slow he could go without losing control. Or if he could even get everything into landing configuration—"down and dirty."

It was time to start slowing and setting up for descent, deploying the slats and flaps that would slide out to give him the extra lift he needed to keep the plane airborne at lower speed. But the crew had no idea what would happen when they extended each of these devices or what kind of control problems they might experience. McCormick ordered Whitney, "OK, give me the slats, but if I tell you to get them off, get them off RIGHT NOW!" At 220 knots, the slats worked fine. Then he asked for 15 degrees of flaps, inching them out while gradually slowing the plane.

They were on final approach. The recommended stabilizer-inoperative landing speed was 145 knots; but with no rudder to steer with on the runway, McCormick wanted it slower than that. He slowed to 160, and at that speed, was still able to hold the sink rate to no more than 600-to-700 feet a minute. If they descended any faster, they would fall below the glide slope and crash. But 160 knots was too fast for landing. Energy goes up proportionately to the square of the speed; and even a few extra knots sends the energy that must be dissipated on the runway spiraling up. At 160 knots, they could throw everything they had into slowing down—spoilers, thrust reversers, brakes—and still go hurtling right off the end. At 160 knots they would be eating up the runway at 270 feet per second. He tried pulling off a little more power, slowing to 150 knots. But the sink rate dropped to 900 feet a minute . . . to 1,000 . . . 1,200 . . . 1,400!

Now, for the first time in the flight, Whitney showed excitement. He called out the sink rate as if he were calling out the final seconds of his life. "1,600 . . . 1,700 . . . 1,800!" McCormick applied power and went back up to 160 knots. Whitney breathed again. They would *have* to come in hot and rely on brakes. BRAKES! *They* were actuated by the rudder pedals, and the left rudder pedal was jammed so far forward that the brake was difficult to reach and could not be moved. Whitney had identical rudder pedals, and his were jammed too. There was no left brake; and if you used the right brake alone, it would pull you off the runway in the direction the yaw was already pulling them.

And he couldn't count on full reverse thrust either. The thrust reversers—responsible for the thunderous roar heard right after landing—direct the exhaust gases so they spew out in the opposite direction, slowing the plane. He could not put both number 1 and number 3 into maximum reverse thrust and still maintain control. He would still need asymmetric thrust to help maintain directional control. The spoilers—the flaplike devices on the upper surface of the wings that deploy at touchdown to break the airflow, destroying lift and creating drag—still worked. But they couldn't do it alone.

THEY WERE TOO FAST! The captain gave the brace command.

Cydya looked up, saw heads popping up all over the cabin, and hollered "BRACE!" It was echoed down the cabin by the other girls. Margaret Innes, with her arms clasped under her knees, her head down as close to her knees as she could get it, now made her Act of Contrition—"just in case." The cabin went silent.

Brad watched the whole landing.

They came in at 160 knots, yawed about 5 degrees to the right. Even with both pilot and copilot pulling back on their control columns, McCormick had to squeeze on a little more power to help flare the nose up and break the rate of descent. But the nose was still down so much farther than usual due to their high approach speed, that McCormick suddenly thought, "My God! My gear's not down." Pilots know what height they are above the runway when their mains hit; but in this flatter attitude, his cues were all fouled up. "I don't have any gear!" A few moments later, he felt the wheels touch. It was a smooth landing.

They had 7,700 feet left. At that speed they'd devour it in less than 30 seconds. "Then all hell broke loose. The automatic spoilers came up and I jerked the power off and went for the reverse thrust levers. I applied full left aileron and was waiting for the reversers to come in. We started for the right side of the runway and I felt for the first time I had lost control of my ship." He yelled for Whitney to give him all the power he could on number 1 and tried the nose wheel to turn her back. But it had no effect.

Charged with unspent energies, the massive vessel tore off the runway, still doing nearly 160 knots. Grass spewed up. Taxiways and runways came at them—a nightmare; hitting their raised concrete edges hard could snap off the nose gear and start progressive disintegration of the plane. McCormick tried to ease the nose up as he whammed over them.

Passengers were rattled and jarred as the plane hurtled on. It was now heading directly for the terminal building. For those with their heads up, this was the most terrifying phase of the entire incident.

After what seemed like miles of terror, the plane began to pull back toward the runway. Reverse thrust on number 1 was taking effect. Flight 96 came to a stop 1,000 feet from the end of the runway, and almost back on it. McCormick yelled out "SHUT 'EM DOWN!"

The soggy ground and bumpy ride may have saved the flight, the friction dissipating energies that might otherwise have been reserved for a fiery crash at the end of the runway.

Fearing fuel leaks, the pilot had ordered an emergency evacuation; and passengers raced to their positions at the exit doors. Yellow slides were deployed and inflated. The stewardesses yelled "JUMP!"

The slides were precipitously steep. Exiting on the right side, Margaret Innes hit the ground with her heels and pitched forward on her stomach. A young man grabbed her hand and pulled her across the wet grass to safety. She looked back and was struck by how huge the plane looked. She would retrieve her pitcher later, in perfect condition. Her friend, Katherine, in her late sixties, jolted her back as she landed. Don Innes, exiting from the left side, landed on cement and blistered his hands trying to brake his slide. The Italian couple refused to jump and had to be pushed. With her baby in her arms, the black girl slid with a grace and dignity that amazed a dentist from Detroit, a fellow passenger. As Cindi Breloff ran from the plane, the soft wet ground felt good to her feet. Later, she would look back with good feelings on "the closeness, the willingness to help each other," on the calm and cooperative way in which they had all shared the imminent prospect of death.

Brad couldn't see the slide until he was right at the door. As he waited his turn, he thought, "There's no way old Brad's gonna jump unless there is something to jump into." He later made a recommendation to the National Transportation Safety Board that stewardesses say, "Slide!" or "Jump into the chute!" to reassure passengers that there is something there. As others hopped around on the wet grass in one shoe, Brad had on both shoes. And his glasses. But he would never see his bag again. The escort luggage had been swept out of the cargo hold with the coffin, raining suitcases on southern Ontario. Though most were retrieved, Brad's was not. "My efficiency was my undoing."

When the passengers were all off, the crew made a tour of the plane and examined the hole where the cargo door had been. The door had torn away from its silver skin, leaving the metal sheathing rolled back from the door opening like the lid of a sardine can. They slid down and joined the thankful survivors. They had all survived the Windsor Incident. And McCormick still hadn't blown a tire.

But Brad wouldn't get back to the office now until the next day. Though the black woman was vocal in saying, "It's my first flight, my last flight, and I want my money back," he had no hesitation in flying on to Hartford. When he reached Pittsfield, he went directly to the office. After dinner that night, when the children were in bed, he told his wife what had happened. "She took it all very calmly, I thought."

It was the kind of story he might have told his friends Tom and Fay Wright in a letter, or during one of their occasional get-togethers. They had kept up their friendship since the San Jose days in the early sixties, when they had all swum, barbecued, and talked around the same apartment house pool. Now that Tom had been transferred to England, he didn't see the Wrights as often, but had had some good letters about their life in England, their children, the differences in shopping . . .

He would never know whether telling them would have altered their decision to take a Turkish DC-10 from Paris to London two years later.

Brad Reed had flown the dress rehearsal for the crash that would kill his good friends.

Chapter Five

"Could You Check
The Lists, Please?" ...
The Ones Who Waited

THERE WERE NO precedents for anything this big, this
global in scale. There was no appropriate rite for the
final passage of 346 souls.

The crash sliced through the full spectrum of human
activity and relationships: marriages being celebrated,
or salvaged; people fed up with winter; men fed up
with their wives traveling with their lovers; excited
families; phony names; hearty sports fans; lonely
individuals. . . .

It struck families in more than twenty countries—in
Brazil, Britain, Canada, Morocco, Turkey, France,
New Zealand. . . . It hurled the numbing shock of death
at Kansas. And at Berkeley, California.

These were deaths that were not expected as in war,
or old age. This was a brutal truncation, an unacceptable squandering of life.

Like the rest of the world, Stephen Mitchell blundered into the news. After a gin with friends, he headed
back to Heathrow, sure that Prudence's plane would be
arriving soon. He switched on the car radio. The new
Charlie Rich song was on again. "Hey . . . did you happens to see the most beautiful girl in the world?" He
wasn't a romantic, but songs had always been able to
expand a feeling or sharpen a memory for him. The

mellow rock beat rolled on as he drove. "I stood alone in the cold gray dawn, and knew I'd lost my morning sun. . . ." The announcer cut in with the first snatches of news: ". . . *airliner has come down in the Ermenonville Forest about 15 miles north of Paris . . . thought the airliner might be Turkish . . . believed there are no survivors. . . . If . . . this figure of 334 is confirmed, this will be the worst air crash ever . . .*"

It was as if he had been shot. His car careened off the road, but he retrieved it and kept going, head pounding with shock. "I knew at once that Prudence was on that plane; I had no feeling in my mind that she might have escaped. I held out no hope." But he had to make sure. When he got home, he checked the answering service. His first contact with her had been by phone. He could still hear her voice from Paris the night before. He prayed there would be a message now. There was none. And then the phone rang. One of his office colleagues saying, "Just wanted to set your mind at rest. I wasn't on that plane that crashed. I didn't go to Paris after all."

He didn't tell her mother, Mrs. Pratt, until late in the evening, when he had absolute confirmation that her name had been on the list and that there had been no survivors. He had already endured an endless day, but he drove the 50 miles to her home in Kent because he had to tell her personally. She was delighted to see him at the door. It meant that Prudence would be just behind him. Mrs. Pratt had no idea that Prudence had even been in Paris. When she saw Stephen's face, and he said, "I have some very bad news to tell you," she knew instantly. "Prudence was on that plane, wasn't she?" Stephen drew on the control he had learned from his parents' deaths, but held Mrs. Pratt as she wept.

Britain, too, blundered into the news of the crash at Paris—news that throughout the day tumbled out in garbled surges followed by terrifying blocks of silence. As the first incomplete flashes came on radio and the first pictures of the still-smoking scene came on TV as a jarring intrusion on afternoon tea, a network of anxiety spread from husbands, wives, and parents to brothers and sisters, children and grandparents, to fiancés and close friends. By late afternoon, people all over England hung in a limbo of dread. Summoning characteristic stoicism, they tried to ease each other's fears and *find out*. Families made tentative, then concerned, and finally frantic contact, blocking each others' phones as they checked and cross-checked. "Did he say anything to you about being late? It's not like him . . ." "I thought she might be spending the night with you in London before catching the coach home tomorrow . . ." They began to phone Heathrow, BEA, friends in London who might check for them, or any airline contacts they could think of, trying to find out. Telephone lines were jammed. And busy signals were the unbearable response to the growing need to know "was he on that plane that just crashed?" "Could you check the lists, please. I know they couldn't possibly have been on the plane, but they are late, and the family's getting a bit worried, you know . . ." If they did get through to the airline, there were no lists at first, nothing tangible to check against for relief or confirmation. "Just give us your name, please. We'll call you back."

They got into cars, taxis, buses and gathered together to wait by the telephone. Some headed for Heathrow. By midafternoon, hundreds of people were waiting at the airport for news. Some, *knowing* they had someone aboard the plane, had flown to Orly on the next plane out.

At Heathrow, frustration was building, and there was little release. At first there was no passenger list. When Turkish Airlines' Paris office had asked BEA to open up its accident center at Heathrow, names did begin to come through. The BEA staff took down the passenger list from Paris and the requests coming in to the airport, and tried to coordinate the two on huge blackboards. Where possible, names were listed by sex, nationality, and religion. But, because of the strike, the list was hopelessly inconclusive. Phones rang. Chalk scratched. And the center ran out of blackboard.

The British Airport Authority knew all those worried, milling people had to be put somewhere. A Turkish crash with BEA passengers was not the responsibility of the authority, which simply rents space to the airlines. The plane had still been under French air traffic control when it crashed. It had not been handed to Heathrow at "halfway across, captain"—the decisive point, midchannel, where homebound English sea captains traditionally turned the pictures of their Calais mistresses to the wall and exposed their wives' loyal faces. Too, the airport's efforts to prepare for the era of the wide-body planes were being poured into operational improvements—strengthening the concrete aprons at terminals 1 and 2, extending and raising the height of the piers, enlarging the gate rooms. Contingency planning for massive grief and human confusion had not been given priority.

A VIP suite for visiting ambassadors was opened up. Families were shuffled into the Kingsford-Smith suite, and those who didn't pace were eased into big white vinyl lounge chairs. Trolleys of food and drinks were rolled in. People came and went, with an estimated flow of between five and six hundred in the afternoon. The airport's Church of England chaplain, Rev. Ben Lewers, came and chatted with families, trying to help them cope with death.

Clearly untrained to handle the shock of bereavement, airport officials plugged in a televison set, an act that is still branded by many as "inhumane." Though motives were probably good, the effect was brutal. Wives and parents, crowded together in the sterile elegance of the lounge, watched as reports came on, hoping to see a familiar face being given hot tea by the Red Cross. But it was the ghastly, wasteful slaughter of war; a level of destruction alien and incomprehensible to anyone who had not been in battle. Police in smoking debris. Close-ups of their faces, anguished, grim. A leg? Stretchers. Men carrying clumps wrapped in blankets. Lifeless desolation. A death terrible beyond the most awful speculation. TV brought their son's intestines to them on a plate. Civilized sensibilities recoiled.

When a newspaper photographer moved in for a tear-jerking close-up of grief for the Monday paper, a man lashed out at his camera and broke off the flash attachment. The scuffle was quickly calmed. And though the papers reported the fight as part of a scene of chaos in which heads were being beaten against the wall in despair, relatively few let their anguish pour out. The English hold death privately, and the fortitude glimpsed in orderly queues at bus stops glowed clear in disaster.

The isolated episodes of striking out were vividly described in the press. But there was no one at Heathrow to recognize them as a predictable response to death. None of England's trained bereavement counselors were there to explain that one of the things grieving people do is lash out at whoever is closest.

In Bury St. Edmunds, rural distrust of foreigners added an extra dimension of pressure. But it built more slowly than at Heathrow. Watching television that Sunday afternoon, the Savidges felt free of involvement with the crash. They saw two men carrying a blanket of remains. Later, Mrs. Savidge would remember the blanket and think, "It could have been my son's body." But at the time, she was confident that he was safe in Paris with the rest of the team. When their daughter's boyfriend said, " I wonder what Robert's doing now?" Mrs. Savidge thought she knew. She always knew Robert's schedule. It was about three o'clock. "I should imagine they are now running out on the field for the game."

Rugby was one of the few things that could have pulled the boy to Paris. His heart was in England, and in the land. An honor graduate of an agricultural school "for working farmers, not for gentlemen farmers in soft hats and brown suits," Robert had announced at the age of six that he would be a farmer like his father. His father had never forced it; it was a life of muddy gum boots, pigpens, and few vacations. But Robert had never veered. Now, at nineteen, he was assistant manager of a large estate outside Bury. The family dream was to have a farm of their own, for his father was a manager, too, of someone else's estate outside Bury.

In an England buffeted by shifting values, Suffolk attitudes were clear and strong. Drawn from hard experience with the world beyond Suffolk, they were imprinted young and held for life. "I would never buy a Japanese car," Jim Savidge said. "I wouldn't give 'em that much, and I don't care who hears me say it." The Suffolk Regiment had been captured in Singapore in 1943 "before they'd fired a shot," had been imprisoned, and many had died. He still had a letter written from the camp by a "dear friend who still suffers very much." When his sister had bought a Toyota "my wife thought I'd gone berserk. And I'm very near as bad with the Germans. I wouldn't give 'em an inch. I think they'd do the same thing again if they had half a chance."

His convictions were both Suffolk and rural, and he would stick to them. Like his son. For both, life's focus was the land. Farms were still productive and the soil good. Even rugby would not keep Robert from his obligation to it. Spring planting started Monday morning. And he would be home for it.

But the phone started ringing. People had heard about the crash. "What time was Robert coming?" Had they heard from Robert? "No." Why should they? But they began to worry. All over Bury, the pressure was beginning to build. "You keep waiting. . . . You don't know. You just live in a vacuum." Jim called the Bury police. They were all friends, but when they took a long time to answer, he burst out with "What the hell are you playing at down there?" They could tell him nothing, but promised to call as soon as they could.

By now, they should have heard a car door slam and seen his huge form moving up the walk. He always warmed up the house when he came home from work or a game, curly hair tousled, looking like a big friendly lion. "Our boy's a homing pigeon. He'd 'a' been home by now."

Very late in the evening, they heard a car drive up to the gate. But it was late now. They looked out and saw two figures hovering about, hesitating. One of them was a friend of Robert's from the rugby club. He lingered at the end of the lane, but he didn't come in. Jim Savidge knew why. He was the teammate the club had assigned to bring the official news to the Savidges. Savidge had never seen anyone "so, shall I say, *dejected* in my whole life." He knew it was as painful for the lad as for himself. But he couldn't wait any longer. He walked out to the gate, to meet the tear-glazed eyes of a boy who couldn't yet cope with his own desperation, much less a father's. "All right, boy. Come on in and have a cup of tea."

He was dead, their only son. Not on the land he loved. But across the Channel. Somehow—but why? —their boy had been snuffed out. You couldn't compare loss, of course, but the widows could marry again. You could never replace a son.

For Noni St. Amand, the fears hadn't begun until next morning. Her fears for Fay Wright. Fay had come into her life at just that point when both, prosperous young matrons living abroad with their families, had been lowering the shoulder bags full of Pampers and canned Similac and lifting their eyes to look at their lives. The jet plane had produced it, this contemporary corporate nomadry they were all part of. It sounded so great in the letters you wrote back home. But it lacked the colonial's six-week sea voyage for adjustment. It was so mobile that social scientists could scarcely stop it long enough to give it a name, this inchoate new subculture weaned on airports and alien tongues, and growing in size. But Fay, sensitive to a problem few other even saw, and so *intense* about life, had seen it and cared about its effects on families, on children, and was trying to understand, to help.

The Monday car pool was late, and that wasn't like Fay. Judy, the other member of the tight triangle, had called Noni to find out if she'd had any word from Fay.

You counted on the car pool. It simplified life a

little; and life for American wives abroad was never simple. In the international divisions, corporate husbands shifted from one post to another every two or three years. Exchange the acrylic pantsuit for an indigo veil, and you were just another nomad mommy moving the kids and the camels along to a new watering hole in the Sahara. Breaking camp was always a strain, no matter how many times you'd done it. The responsibility would fall "at one end or the other." You either stayed behind, sold the house, and packed up; or you went ahead to a foreign city, facing alone the frustrations of a strange language, finding an apartment, new schools for the kids. And car pools.

This one was working out well. Judy and Fay were on the same route to the American School. And systematic Fay would have called if there was going to be some delay. Judy had already called her house, where the Japanese *au pair* girl had mumbled something garbled about "not back, you know, that plane." She was no help. But she had got Judy thinking. "Noni, you don't think . . . ?" And Noni had snapped back with, "No, no. They're in Spain . . ." No connection.

But Fay was the one who was always there. She was the one who'd turned up to help Noni unpack a year and a half earlier, when she'd arrived from Rome, though Fay herself wasn't settled. When Tom Wright had been posted to London to help open an international banking office Fay hadn't just found a flat and moved in. She and Tom had bought an old house, torn it apart, and returned it from a rabbit warren of rundown flats to a stunning private home. Fay had run all over London choosing faucets, tiles, and towel holders, but never forgot to give the workmen their afternoon tea, jollying them along. Nobody else bothered. But that was Fay.

They could be on a thousand flights. But a strange, inadmissible fear was beginning to take hold of the two friends. They started making a few calls, just "to have it negated." Judy called BEA, was given their emergency number, and was told she'd have to wait. There were ten calls ahead of hers. She then reached a friend at BEA and asked her if she could try to check the passenger list to make *sure* there were no Wrights on it. The friend said she'd call back. Noni called Tom's office. Yes, they had heard from him, and he would be delayed. She phoned Judy in relief. But there was still this fear. And the *au pair* girl was still no help. She called a TWA friend to see if there was any way they could have got from Spain to Paris. The friend said that, yes, last time BEA had had a strike, passengers *had* been diverted to Paris.

They buoyed each other up by phone while they waited for the call from Judy's friend at BEA. "We kept talking to each other because we were a triangle. We were together." At 10:45 that morning, Noni picked up the kitchen phone. It was Judy, and her voice was breaking. "That was it." Their names were all on the list.

"How do you describe shock? It's like you yourself are in the last moments before going, because you remember, in those first few seconds, everything." Fay putting in the squares of grass at the house. Fay locking herself out, getting stuck halfway through the window, and calling her later, laughing, "I've just pulled a Noni!" Going out to tea with Fay in hat and gloves, giggling like girls "playing the English lady bit." Fay talking to her shopkeepers on Finchley Road. Fay, with her ecological passion, building her own compost heap. ". . . All these things. And then, Fay no more.

"You keep seeing the faces of the children . . ." Karlaine's and Jackson's and little Sherry's. And Tom's. He'd worked terribly hard in the new job, traveling to Latin and South America, to Poland and Mexico. He'd roughhoused with the kids and taken them to the zoo whenever he could, but had had so little time for holidays with his family. Wives learned quickly that work came first. Trips and home leaves were regularly canceled or postponed. But now that Tom had been made managing director he had taken a week off in Spain. It was to have been a happy renaissance for the family.

Noni felt a desperate need to touch home base. She talked to friends of Fay's on the phone, and they cried together. None of them had known each other long; they had learned to make friends cautiously, but fast. Even children learned to look swiftly through to the "inner person." Far from hometowns, they became a family, a close interdependent tribe of expatriates.

The American School in London was the tribe's long house, its YMCA and community center, a spiritual Welcome Wagon for new arrivals. Overnight, it had become a house of grief. Nine children had been killed. Two families had been wiped out—the Harts with their three children, the Wrights with their three. Dr. Wayne Wilcox, the charismatic cultural attaché at the American embassy, and his wife had been killed with their two oldest children, leaving two behind as orphans. Ronny Smith had gone to Turkey with his friend Bob Hart and would now receive his second-class scouting award posthumously. The school's scout troop number 401 had lost three scouts. The Harts were the only family who should have been on the Turkish plane—they'd been on a "Breakaway" weekend in Istanbul.

On Monday morning, stories of near-misses and tragic ironies flew through the school. Teachers and students functioned like sleepwalkers, going through the motions, paralyzed by the shock. But classes carried on around the nine empty desks. The school had to stay open. "The family unit had been threatened . . . the kids had to have some place to go." They could not look to the mainland for comfort; for though they thought of the States as "home" and looked forward to going back to college, they would often find themselves aliens there. And they could not expect the British to close around the American grief. They all clung together at the American School and planned a memorial service. There had to be some collective release for the confusion and fear, some familiar and reverent focus for the sorrow.

Fay had been so concerned about the kids the multinational corporate life had spawned. It was a life-style made possible by the jet plane; and though still evolving, it had already produced a subculture of young people who were caught—like half-breeds—without a culture of their own. Sociologists were beginning to call it the "third culture," and it had become the subject of much of the thinking and talking Noni and Fay did.

For the third culture child, the family was far more important than for the mainland child. "What kid in the States would write to his father three or four times a week, big long letters?" Families holidayed together, did everything together. But marriages were under great pressure. Absence, ambition, the loneliness of a foreign land. When homes broke up, as they often did, the children turned to school as home. And the children, having spent most of their school years overseas in isolation from the language, after-school jobs, corner drugstores, and television programs that bond stateside kids, were often rootless and insecure. They grabbed at friendships. They would come home from school the first day and say, "Mommy, I want you to meet my *best* friend." The school offered every facility a child could want. But could a gymnasium offer a clear sense of identity? Noni and Fay had talked so much about these things while racing each other to see who could help the most. But you couldn't catch Fay.

Noni couldn't bear to have their shared momentum stopped. "Fay, we weren't finished yet!"

Did they feel anything? Were they conscious when they hit? In Berkeley, California, Mrs. Wright, Tom's mother, could not lift her mind from that preoccupation. 77 seconds. She woke from nightmares in which they had all been conscious at impact—Tom, Fay, and the three children. She was haunted by the experience of the children on the way down. Were they screaming, terrified, not knowing what was happening? She had counted out the seconds and it seemed an awfully long time. All she had to draw on were her own terrible images of what a crash must be like, her own instinctive fear of falling, erupting in the nightmares. She tried to find out from anyone she met who might know. She asked the pilot on the flight to England after the crash, and he reassured her that they would not have been conscious all the way down. But she feared he was just being kind.

In London, Stephen Mitchell had had nightmares about Prudence. Projecting his own lifelong terror of flying into his visions, he saw her as one of the six who had been sucked out of the plane at decompression and thudded into soft dirt nearly 12,000 feet below. He knew she wasn't at a high enough altitude to have blacked out and saw her falling, conscious, with the fields and buildings that had looked like charming toyland miniatures moments before racing up toward her, starkly real. He read the rumors that screams had been heard in St. Pathus.

In Los Angeles, the venerable old judge who would handle the massive court case that grew out of the crash shuddered at "the terror—the *terror* that must have come up in some of their hearts. They *knew!*" His personal vision of that terror would hang before him throughout the case, inspiring his massive compassion for the dead, driving his efforts to speed payments of damages to the sorrowng families who had sued.

In Japan, Hideo Goto responded to word that the bloodied hood of his son's parka had been found by reconstructing his own touching scenario. "My son witnessed a few passengers thrown out of the aircraft immediately after a violent shock and sound that followed a collapse of the floor of the airplane. His instinct told him that it is to be a crash. Also he thought he should try to survive. He grabbed his coat on the shelf and put it on. He even covered his head with the hood of the coat by tightening the string—still some time to go ... He thought about his parents, his girl-friend, and many other friends he had, and at the same time, he said farewell to all of them with a great regret and terror. He tried to crouch his rather tall body, holding his own head. Then he waited and waited for ... a possible safe landing. All he did was in vain at last. The blood stains inside the hood show how much he wanted to live and how loudly he shouted for his father and mother."

Hollywood had given most people their frame of reference for disaster, painting a picture of screams, pain, and people tearing at each other in greedy panic ... of moments of high heroism and, at the end, hands grasped in eleventh-hour expressions of love. The vision had been promoted on film by everything from the fall of Sodom and Gomorrah to the sinking of the *Titanic*.

Unfortunately, the bereaved families, too, drew on the same sensationalized vision that had been spread by the catastrophe genre in movies, books, and television. No one really knew. The forest, though an abattoir, was at least comprehensible. But the 77 seconds were a synthesis of unknown terrors. They held a grisly, macabre fascination. Though survivors of catastrophes abounded, the press had seldom probed beyond the physical sensations—What did you see? How did you get out?—to ask, "What were your emotional and psychological responses to the threat of death?"

Necessarily, catastrophes have generally been viewed from the outside, through the eyes of appalled witnesses describing screams and white flashes. Yet, for the first time in history, there is documentation on the experience of death from people who have been pulled back from "the other side" by sophisticated machines. There is a testimony of those who survived the Windsor Incident—the dress rehearsal for *Paris*—who, in conditions initially identical to those of the Paris disaster, faced the prospect of death calmly. And there is a handful of specialists—physiologists and psychologists—who, in hypothetically "flying" fuselage number 29 down, may come very close to the actual experience of the last 77 seconds.

But it was simply speculation. It did not replace the glazed lack of comprehension, the hovering uncertainty. There was no massive disaster unit that could be activated by the push of a button, no worldwide laws to cloak the agony with order, no soothing old ceremonials for death by air crash to free the survivors to get on with life.

But there was, in one small corner of England, a town, a company of people who were coping heroically with the impact of the crash—an ancient town that makes visiting Americans ache for roots. Bury St. Edmunds had lost eighteen men in the crash—all members of the Bury St. Edmunds Rugby Football Club.

The crash had devoured an irreplaceable elite of healthy, well-educated young men—for rugby, though not quite the "class" game it was, is generally learned at "public" schools and refined at universities. All had been involved in agriculture, the base of Bury's comfortable self-sufficiency.

And now there were ten widows, eight pairs of parents, and nineteen children to be looked after.

Bury responded with an enveloping display of community that in America's transient suburbs is only a dim memory from the frontier. By Sunday evening, the day of the crash, surviving officials of the club had met at the home of former club chairman Bill Hakes to plan the club's response and put it into effect. Simultaneously, team captain Chris Tilbrook set up an emergency office in his home—an office that would continue during the crisis as a coordinating center. He was motivated by more than his club responsibility. He had lost his brother Mike in the crash. And a sixteen-year-old boy had died using his airplane ticket. Chris had originally planned to go to Paris, but when his back had been injured in a recent game, he had given his ticket to young Nick Jones, a keen member of the club's junior Colts team.

A member of the club was assigned to look after each family. Most of the men knew instinctively which family they would go to. The years of playing together had built close, almost kin, ties; and the lost affection was now eagerly spilled out onto the stricken families. First, they headed out to do their hardest job: the agonizing task of telling their best friends' wives and parents that, after desperate hours of hope, it was now official. Then they hovered around, taking days and weeks off from work to help in any way they could.

A flow of information was essential. The club installed two direct phone lines to Paris: one to the Ministry of the Interior and the other to the British embassy. Bury would never have the sense of isolation from news that so many others would feel in the next few months.

Of the group that had gone to Paris, only three were alive. They had missed the plane. And they—the last from Bury to have seen the eighteen alive—went around to tell the families about the circumstances of the flight, about the fun they'd had together in Paris, and the good spirits of husbands and sons as they'd left for home. The trip to the Continent was always a great event for the club. They had had such a great time in Germany and Bordeaux in previous matches that there had been high excitement over the Paris trip. Rugby and its friendships had meant so much to the men; there could probably have been no happier prelude to death. The three confirmed it as they did their grim rounds.

Within twenty-four hours of the crash, the mayor of Bury had launched a disaster fund to aid the dependents. Within an hour of his announcement, collecting boxes appeaed in shops all over Bury. A stream of people, even pensioners, started dropping by the borough offices to contribute a few pence . . . a pound or two. . . . Within the next few weeks, all of Suffolk had responded. A fish-and-chips shop gave its proceeds from lunchtime sales, serving potatoes donated by a local farmer; school children, the local milkman—even an old English sheep dog—hiked 15 miles for the fund; an RAF rugby team churned through icy water on a sponsored swim; farmers gave bullocks, pigs, calves, lambs, and a fat cow for a benefit auction at the Bury market; a pop group gave a benefit concert; and volunteers stood in the chilling rain to collect on the street, warmed with hot drinks from Boots the Chemist. Two streakers sold their dignity for the cause. Whist, bingo, and a grand ball swelled the fund.

The Eastern Counties Rugby Union started its own fund, and all member clubs—Bury's friendly rivals —organized benefit matches. The union's secretary, John Motum, had barely missed the plane himself. He had been in Paris to watch the international, and on Saturday morning—the day before the crash—he and his wife had "wandered around the city and along the banks of the Seine with Bryan Ellis and several of the other Bury lads." They had been traveling with the official English party and, sixty strong, couldn't get seats on the Turkish plane. They had caught a Pakistani plane several hours later.

By the first day after the crash, hundreds of people had been mobilized to help. But Bury St. Edmunds was quiet. Bells had been muffled. Flags had been lowered to half-mast.

When Sue Ellis drove through town that day, the flags at half-mast struck her. Until then, it had been *her* loss. Now, suddenly, it was a much larger loss that had touched all of Bury and the surrounding villages, perhaps all of England. Feeling part of something bigger than herself helped.

Her husband, Bryan, known as "Number One," had been chairman of the club. And she knew that "if he'd been alive, he'd have gone dashing round." So she did what he would have done. She drove around to see as many of the widows and parents as she could. And though her doorbell and phone were ringing nonstop, she found time that night to fill out the government pension forms. The following night she gathered the families at her home for a meeting, to see how they were getting on. "They were all superb. All OK. Shopping still had to be done. You had to carry on just as before . . ."

When she'd married Bryan in 1961, the club had made her its first woman member. And now she had joined fellow members in doing her duty, in a way she could never have foreseen.

Almost two weeks later, she was in St. Edmundsbury Cathedral—the small cathedral that is the only building that remains of the original abbey compound, the cathedral in which she and Bryan had been married. Now, preparing for the memorial service, she was arranging white gladiolus, chrysanthemums, and green leaves in a pedestal urn that flanked the altar. On the other side, Beth Kirpatrick, a widow, too, of a former chairman of the club, was arranging the green and white club colors into a massive spray of flowers. No one had gone to a florist, for the Bury Flower Club had helped mothers and widows make their own sprays and wreaths for the service that would be held on March 17, just two weeks after the crash. There were reports of a big memorial being planned in France, but that was still vague. This was something real they could do, while the loss was still raw and acute. A tangible gesture of love. As they manipulated the stems, great feeling poured through their hands, reaching across to their lost men. "It helped," Sue remembered.

The club had made contact with every former member it could track down. And by the day of the memorial, the old boys were pouring into town from all over Britain.

The ancient town of Bury St. Edmunds had come to say goodbye to its dead. Shortly after 3 P.M., more than 2,500 people started moving toward the cathedral, many walking across the rich green grass that carpets the old abbey where the nobles had met in 1214 to draft the Magna Carta. Though the great arched nave and transept had been reduced to a flinty stubble, the clattering old barons still seemed to hover around Bury St. Edmunds. Seven and a half centuries after Magna Carta, the town was still drawing strength from the sense of civility and order, of human dignity, of the coming together for mutual help that had been hewn, then, out of medieval violence and uncertainty.

The cathedral filled and overflowed. Twelve hundred moved next door to St. Mary's Church to watch the service by closed-circuit television. The entire congregation stood as eighty family mourners walked in from the cloisters, young widows holding their children's hands.

Three members of the Racing Club of Paris carried in a huge round wreath and laid it in front of the altar. Its rugby team had been scheduled to play the Bury team on the afternoon of the crash. At news of the crash, the Racing Club of Paris had become part of the extended family that was closing in around the shattered families.

Whenever a widow or parent flew to Paris for the grim task of trying to identify belongings, a member of the Racing Club was there to drive, to interpret, to help. And now they stood in the cathedral, mutely determined that the canceled game would be played against a new Bury team before the year was out, and that the teams would meet for a memorial game each year from then on.

Bury's sister town in France—Compiègne—joined Bury in its grief. A letter of condolence from its parish priest was read. A town with the same proud antiquity as Bury and just 25 miles from the crash site, Compiègne would provide another haven of help and sympathy during the anguished visits that must be made to France.

Hundreds of rugby men stood in the cathedral, the straight-backed old boys and the sobbing Colts, confirming bonds that transcended any rivalries on the playing field.

Rugby Football Union is a vast family. Two weeks ago we lost some sturdy young limbs from our family tree, but the branch which is Bury will survive and perhaps grow stronger because of the terrible experience . . .

The chairman of the English Rugby Football Selectors had spoken for them all. The cathedral was filled with a sense of belonging that went back a thousand years. Through tears, parents and widows could look out on a sea of loyalty and support.

73

"You are not alone," the bishop had said.

The ceremony was followed by a tea at the Corn Exchange. The Corn Exchange had been an important part of Sue Ellis's married life. Bryan had been a corn broker, buying and selling Suffolk's famous wheat and barley. And though most of his business was done from the office over the telephone, he had still come to the Corn Exchange at 2:30 every Wednesday afternoon. He had sat in his assigned pew and fingered samples of grain brought around by the farmers in little brown bags. Originally, it had been brought around in linen bags. But that had gone years ago, as had the real importance of the trading done in the Corn Exchange. Yet the tradition persisted. Like the traditional Rugby Ball at the Corn Exchange, the club's major social event. Those had been happy times.

Pelted with memories, she caught her breath as she entered the Corn Exchange. They were all there—the schoolmasters, the wartime buddies, rugby men from all the other clubs, relatives, old friends. And the old boys . . . from all over England, from as far as the north of Scotland. The standoff halfs and prop forwards who'd torn up the field with the team in the fifties and sixties were helping the team now to play the toughest game of all. Sue was overwhelmed by "the support they were giving us all by being there."

It helped. Ties, love, attention. But the eighteen from Bury would never be back. In an impact that had leveled a small valley of trees and sent up a pall of smoke that reminded observers of Hiroshima, the eighteen had been wiped out. They had not died *for* something. They had just died. Pointlessly. And they could never be replaced or forgotten.

Later, Sue Ellis sat in her cosy, low-ceilinged old house where a fire, walls painted the color of glowing coals, and mellowed walnut chests and tables gave off the classic ambience of the English country cottage. She'd tried to prolong Bryan's presence, make his absence less final, by giving both of her children a framed picture of their father and by setting one up on the mantle. A bottle of Scotch was there in the cupboard to warm and thank friends who dropped by. But the chill was always there.

England took the brunt of it. But the tragedy reached out with icy fingers and touched thousands of people all over the world. As the appalling news spread out by wire service, embassies, newspapers, and telephones, the survivors gathered up their grief and began the lonely vigil with death.

"It's just . . ." In Berkeley, Fay Wright's father shrugged his shoulders, "sad." His eyes brimmed with tears as he repeated it, pouring anguish and futility, and even some gentle compassion for those who might have caused the crash, into the word. "SAD." It ended as a sob. And his fingers shook as he closed the scrapbook of pictures of his daughter and three dead grandchildren.

There was no global perspective in the hundreds of homes trying to grapple with the macabre unreality of what had happened to loved ones on a flight they weren't supposed to be on, in a forest they'd never heard of. The structure of life had been brutally altered, and it would take years of delicate, quiet, inner adjustments to bring it back to normal. It was a bleak and essentially personal ordeal.

Bury St. Edmunds had not reached out to comfort the world. It had closed ranks around its own. The entire town, with its gloom and gray stone and bare skeletal trees of late winter, had become a memorial for its own eighteen men.

Chapter Six

They Must Do Their Best

THE SITE

FIRST, THE MEN had come on chunks of twisted metal scattered randomly on the snow—a shock in the peaceful forest. Then, peering through the partial screen of pine trees as if through giant fingers, they were gripped by the enormity of what they were about to experience. In moments, they knew, they would have to rush into a still-smoking charnel hell to hunt for life—the first and only priority right then. And for the young gendarmes, it was only duty and military discipline, prodding them like bayonets in the ribs, that kept them from paralysis and complete loss of nerve. None of them would ever forget it.

Nor would Lannier.

Like Napoleon viewing the carnage of battle from his horse on a commanding hilltop, Chef d'Escadron Jacques Lannier viewed the wreckage from the small rise of land he'd chosen as his headquarters. As chief of the gendarmerie—the police—in Senlis, he had become commander of a piece of terrain as thoroughly devastated as any French battlefield.

The first call had come at 12:45, within 4 minutes of the crash; he and his gendarmes had speeded to the site, the first cars finding the crash site within 17 minutes of the call. A tall, imposing man who carried his dark uniform with de Gaullian dignity, Lannier had inspected the site immediately and would be able to recount it all a year later, with every detail intact.

The plane had slashed a swath half a mile long and 100 yards wide over a shallow valley broken by rough extrusions of rock and soil, and small natural trenches created by some ancient rending of the earth. From a helicopter, none of the grisly debris was visible—just bright white and silver bits tossed like confetti over the entire area. But on the ground, the destruction was *incroyable*. It was truly *la Grande Catastrophe* that would be engraved on a monument in the forest. At the east end of the site, a row of trees had been neatly topped as the plane made its first contact with the forest that would devour it. The trees had been clipped at a gentle angle toward the crash, forming a path that would prove an early clue to investigators who, with the help of the Flight Data Recorder, would determine precisely the angle of descent. Irresistibly, eyes traced the path that pointed like an arrow to the hump of rock where the hull first hit.

The trees were a shock of awareness that the plane had been *almost level* when it crashed. They made the mind race to the agonizing question: "Did he almost make it?" Clearly, the plane had not been in a spiraling nose dive. Did the pilot have some control?

Although thousands of trees had been snapped off, many had survived the impact to act as rigid spikes shredding the plane as it came through. Now the stumps stood like crude, blackened coatracks, their short sheared-off branches hung with ghastly ornaments —shreds of clothing, bits of shiny aluminum, and human parts. Trunks bristled with metal shards impaled deeply in the young trees.

As the horror imprinted itself on Lannier's mind, every lung and finger was filed for visceral recall later on: the intact heart found on the blood-spattered snow . . . the torso that fell from a tree, hitting a young fireman and making him retch . . . the huge rear engine and ninety-five bodies catapulted together to the far end of the site . . . the woman's hand found clutching the hand of a child . . .

Lannier cast it all in a mathematical mold. And in

the months that followed, he would describe with the satisfaction of a man who has done a good, soldierly job how many sacks of shoes they'd collected, the more than a million pieces of wreckage, the twenty thousand pieces of human remains—an average of fifty-five pieces per person. Horror by the yard. Reducing it to numbers was the only way he could handle the emotionally unacceptable volume of death he was obliged to process. He could not turn away from it. Where the investigators could absorb themselves in the technical detective job; where the lawyers could sublimate shattered flesh into a name on a legal brief; where families could hang on to wholeness in their minds; where consular and government officials could come, lower their heads in respect, and leave, Lannier had to face it directly for seventeen days in his headquarters on the hill.

Word came in late that first afternoon that six bodies had been found in St. Pathus, 9 miles away. The gendarmerie of Meaux had taken charge, and the bodies had been transported to the Institut Médico-légal in Paris for examination. The six bodies, the only ones found relatively intact, were crucial to early establishment of cause; they bore no burns or fragments suggesting an explosion. The bodies held no toxic or radioactive elements. Vital as they were to the investigation, the discovery had been deeply unsettling from the human point of view. A young Oriental had been found intact, hands neatly by his side as if waiting for burial; others had been grotesquely torn and twisted, a breast torn off. Fantasies of the unimaginable journey of the six who had fallen, impacting like meteorites into the freshly plowed earth, became the common nightmare of St. Pathus and of the surviving families. Rumors persisted that screams had been heard as they fell.

The door, found the day after the crash, had been identified at first simply as "structure" and been rushed to a hangar at nearby Le Bourget airport where the wreckage was being examined.

On the third day, March 6, the Japanese had arrived, and what Lannier witnessed that day moved him deeply. They had lost forty-eight people, thirty-eight of them fledgling corporate executives on a European tour. The sad little group of priests and parents who had flown in from Japan walked past the hill, down into the valley, and into the midst of the rubble. There they put up a table, covered it with a white cloth, set it with the ceremonial banners, fruit, flowers, and candles that are part of the Buddhist death ritual, and prayed at their makeshift shrine. Personally, each family mourned the loss of its son with aching compassion. But, as Japanese, they had raised the shrine in the midst of the bleakest devastation as a symbol of thankfulness for the self-renewing bounty of the universe. Though karma had already been released back into the universal flow of energy, it was essential to Japanese tradition either to bury the dead at the site or to return the remains to Japan for burial. And to find the spot, if possible, where each had died. Parents sifted through the debris, trying to find mementos of their sons. The father of the boy whose bloodied parka had been found stood in the devastation and played and sang a NO song that evoked Zen spirits and samurai warriors. He sang a wedding song, a choice he could not explain to himself.

Lannier had watched in disbelief as one family, after prayers and meditation on the site, walked directly up to a large, bruised tree at the far end of the site—the spot where the engine and so many bodies had been hurled—and laid flowers at the base of the tree. How could they have known that the body of one of the Japanese had been found smashed against that very tree?

Lannier worked ferociously at the site for seventeen days to the din of vehicles shunting, helicopters clacking overhead, men puffing by with their plastic sacks, and radios erupting in static bursts. Nearly sixty vehicles of all kinds quickly turned the light dusting of snow to mud, as they shuttled between thirteen centers set up the very first day to help. The hauling away of debris, begun March 8, took thirteen days. Three hundred men were immediately assigned to the crash site. At first, men searched the wreckage for bodies, belongings, and the vital voice and flight data recorders from the plane. By March 8, both recorders had been found and all victims removed from the site. Stretcher parties, mute with shock, had moved along the forest's trails. Additional men were keeping back the crowds stalking the periphery of the crash, pressing through the pines for a better view, and then staggering away dazed as the sight had its impact. Every man they could find had been thrown into the smouldering valley—all of the gendarmes from Senlis and neighboring towns, a transportation regiment from Senlis, firemen, the Red Cross. But they weren't nearly enough, not with the Sunday drivers converging on the forest as they had heard the news on their car radios.

Hundreds of people strolling in the forest paths had also sensed the site and homed in on it like sharks after blood. How had they all found it so quickly? A number had seen the plane come down into the forest. Others had heard the accelerating aerodynamic scream. At impact, they'd heard the plane explode with a thunderous noise; they'd seen a cloud of smoke "like an atom bomb." But after that, there had been no more sound. No more smoke or fire. But the crowds moved toward it.

Through it all, in contradiction to its grim function of identifying the dead, Lannier's office was lusty with life. Though Lannier learned to handle color photographs of the disemboweled bits and pieces, fingers in trees, as easily as if they were family photographs, and evoked General Patton's "God, I love war!" as he strode the crash site, he seemed to revel in his civil mission as commandant of the gendarmerie of a rural arrondissement. Though he was a man trained for war at Saint Cyr, France's West Point, since coming to Senlis in 1966 he had brought a gentle note to the woods of l'Oise, setting up a permanent cavalry post to survey the massive forests. Horses had disappeared from the French gendarmeries by 1935, and their revival was such a success that other cavalries had been set up at Fontainebleau, Chambord, les Landes . . . His compassion for all life was confirmed in his just-published book on the prevention of cruelty to animals. A framed testimonial to his efforts on behalf of animals from the French equivalent of the SPCA hung on his office wall, next to the antique weapons collection—the pistols, ax, the brutal mace, and bayoneted rifle.

Since he lived in the gendarmerie building, his office was as much a personal study as an office of the local commandant. It faced on a garden where early hyacinths and pink daisies bloomed, and where a gardener invited spring birds by cleaning out a small tiled pool. A great life-confirming beanstalk of a plant, big and vigorous like Lannier, had thrust up beyond the window and was now headed off across the high ceiling.

Pictures of Lannier on horseback gave a sporting look to the room. A big friendly dog lay on the floor. And off-duty in casual dress—in white turtleneck sweater, handsome brown plaid jacket, twill slacks, and Sherlock Holmes pipe—at forty-five, Lannier had the virile charm and the robust articulateness of a well-bred country squire.

"When we first began, experts thought only ten bodies could be identified," he said. But France had given identification of bodies a very high priority. Legal proof of death was needed to liberate life-insurance policies and to institute wrongful death suits. It also gave families the final blunt fact of death, the symbolic lurch forward on the slow, painful road from shock and denial of death to acceptance and, eventually, adjustment. But it could not be issued simply from a name written on an airline manifest. Proof was required. And proof could be had in two ways: by conclusive identification of physical remains or by inferring identification from belongings found in the wreckage. The first would be done at the Institut Médico-légal in Paris. The second would be done in Senlis and would require investigative work as taxing as any the aeronautical engineers were doing on the shattered hull.

Remains were being rushed from the Chapel of St. Pierre as soon as possible to the refrigerated vaults at the Institut. Personal belongings were being taken to the gendarmerie, and piles of clothing to a small church a few blocks from the chapel.

In the gendarmeries, the charred and twisted artifacts were meticulously grouped on wooden tables. Watches, wallets, passports, photographs, rings, jewelry were grouped and lined up in rows. In the abandoned old church, tattered garments were heaped up on several banks of tables—like a squalid rummage sale. Lannier knew they would have to bring families over for the painful job of trying to identify belongings. But that would be the second line of identification. First, he and his gendarmes would work on the clues they already had. And these were pitifully few. Not one suitcase had been retrieved. Some of the baggage belonging to the nearly two hundred British who had boarded in Paris had been flown over to London on a later plane, to speed departure. And not one identifiable shred remained of the bags loaded in Turkey.

Women's handbags—those gold mines of information —had been demolished. And of the thousands of helpful pieces of paper—drivers' licenses, credit cards, letters—most had been destroyed or damaged beyond usefulness. A great number of letters found at the site had seemed promising, but they were found to be part of a mail shipment aboard the plane. Useless to Lannier.

There were desperately few names to use as a starting point. The airline list had arrived after three days, but did not provide proof. Merely a rough guide. And the pressure to identify would build daily. Identify! Lannier was already beginning to sense the impatience of the English, the urgency of the Japanese. Groups of gendarmes from Orly were permanently assigned to help.

There was so little hope of success. But they would begin.

They tacked a big piece of paper up on the gendarmerie wall, gridded it with lines, and wrote in four

82

headings: *Nombre. Identité. Domicile. Observations.*
They started printing in anything they could find. They
crossed things out. Changed spellings. Started to build
up a crude list. As with children learning to print, every
word was an agonizing achievement.

    1 LERENDU Robert André 23-8-39 a Orval
    6 BITTON Tamar mars 1942 . . . Casablanca
. . . passeport 2 photos 1 enfant . . .
    9 TAKEO Shimmi 25-8-51 . . . Osaka (Japan)
. . . passeport . . .
Senlis would do its best for France.

IDENTIFY!

One hundred thousand autopsies since 1932. Political
assassinations. Brutish murders. Charnel houses full of
bones and quicklime. Deteriorated flesh fished from the
Seine. He had finally turned from it all and, since 1970,
had spent much of his time building new limbs for
people severely damaged in accidents. He now rehabili-
tated the living.

But he could not turn from the DC-10. The miniature
red rosette he wore in his lapel, the Croix de Guerre,
was an honor that carried with it an inescapable obligation. An obligation to France.

He leafed through his own textbook on forensic
medicine. And the pages flipped easily, as if from habit,
to a photograph of a Mayan stone sculpture of a skull.
The sun's corona radiated out from it in roughly carved
spikes. Beneath was a quote from La Rochefoucauld,
the seventeenth-century moralist: *"Le soleil ni le mort
ne se peuvent regarder fixement."* He read it often.
"Neither the sun nor death can be looked at directly."

Professor Léon Dérobert sighed. He must rejoin his
staff. How long would it take?

On orders from Peter Martin, solicitor for Turkish
Airlines' insurers, the large London undertakers J. H.
Kenyon, Ltd., had loaded three hundred coffins aboard
a specially chartered plane. The day after the crash,

they had been flown to Orly, shifted to trucks, and moved out in somber procession along the highways to the Institut Médico-légal in the heart of Paris. But when they arrived, they were greeted with the French equivalent of "What the hell is this? Get them out of here!" Angry at what they thought was British interference, the Institut had phoned the British consul, Macadam Clark, who could only sputter diplomatically, "I know nothing about it, but I'll look into it."

The French, it appeared, had a monopoly on the supply of coffins for mass disasters in France; unknown to Martin, they must be ordered through a company called Pompes Funèbres Générales, a name that throbbed with the sound of muffled drums and ceremonial grandeur. "And," a British consular official said, "it was a trial test by Kenyon's. They *knew* you couldn't bring them in. They've had experience with other French crashes—Nantes, for example."

The coffins did an about-face. The trucks lumbered them back to the airport, they were loaded aboard, and delivered ignominiously back to England. But Martin negotiated for two hundred of them to be kept on hand for "next-time," an order he placed with the sad expectation that somewhere, for some airline, they would be needed. Easter, the beginning of the crash season, would be here in a month.

The French did not need Britain's help, either, with the identification of remains. Professor Kenneth Mason, professor emeritus of pathology at the University of Edinburgh and former head of the RAF's crack forensic medical team, had been sent to Paris after being called out of semiretirement for the Paris crash. But he too was hustled home.

One of the great men in the field, a man termed by some the "mad scientist" of forensic medicine, Professor Léon Dérobert, had been assigned to the job. Dérobert combined the skills of a surgeon and pathologist with an artist's eye and the deductive powers of a master detective; he moved in on cadavers to help Interpol solve murders, to identify a bloated corpse dragged from the Seine, or to make a philosophic assessment of the moral and legal rights of a human body.

This was his twelfth major crash. And like all the professionals involved in the case, he spoke a language of crashes—a terse shorthand of place names: *Nantes. Brussels. Staines. Karachi. Boston Harbor. Grand Canyon. Everglades.* Simply places on a map to the uninitiated, these names were the touchstones of aviation, the measure of its condition. To the men of the relatively small club of crash specialists, each word evoked a world of meaning—of something lost, but something learned.

It was *Bahrein . . . The Azores . . . Orly* that had taught Dérobert to walk the fine line between pressures to release the bodies for burial as soon as possible and the need to identify all they could. At *Cairo*, he had been able to identify only four of the fifty-two dead. In the 1956 Rome–New York crash at Orly, all thirty-three found in the debris had been identified within three weeks. That crash had been "rich with learning" and had taught him the value of organized cooperation among embassies, airlines, families. Within five days, dental charts, X rays and completed questionnaires had been rushed to him from Turkey, Italy, and America. From teeth, bones, pregnancy, measurement, clothing, passports, he and his staff had done the job fast and efficiently.

On examining the plastic bags brought in from Senlis, he knew this would be more like *Cairo*, and he had been forced to make the dismal prediction that probably only a handful—perhaps twenty—would ever be identified by remains. Bodies had been torn apart like dolls in the hands of monsters. And again, the destructive forces of a crash appalled him.

The positive energies of flight did become monsters when their mission was thwarted and they turned back against you. At impact, wild energies were released, crushing, twisting, deforming the wings and fuselage. Survival depended on how much energy the structure could absorb before it was torn apart, transmitting the excess to the people trapped in the hull.

Already Dérobert could sense the global clamor to IDENTIFY! But like Lannier, he was determined to be scrupulously thorough. He worked with a thoroughness that had become compulsive after a macabre experience he had had in 1949 with the Super Constellation crash in the Azores. He had described it to an amazed Lannier. The crash had killed a famous French boxer, Marcel Cerdan, and a Japanese violinist. It had also killed the husband of a friend; and when the widow asked Dérobert to examine the remains sent to her in a coffin, he had obliged. He had found three legs in the coffin. Shocked at how bad identification procedures were, he had vowed that he would never put anybody in a box unless he knew who it was.

Since 1932, he had done one hundred thousand autopsies. His own forty years' experience were backed by a history of classic techniques of examining, preserving, reconstituting and identifying bodies that had been evolving since the time of the pharaohs. He had augmented resin, paste, and sawdust with computers and microscopes. But he still called on the legacy of work done by pioneers like Alphonse Bertillou and Ambroise Pare, whose faces stared up at him from the heavy, round bas-relief portraits he used as paperweights on his desk.

Dérobert had done his own pioneering work on the reconstruction of skulls. Using wax, he built up a face over the facial bones, letting the bones dictate what the face might have been. By rebuilding faces, having them photographed, and circulating the photographs, spectacular identification results had been achieved, particularly in criminal investigations. His was not the cosmetic reconstruction perfected in American undertaking parlors to shield families from the unpleasantness of death. His purpose was to assign specific human identity to anonymous skeletons. There were stories of his heroic and successful efforts to identify French freedom fighters killed during the war. The reconstruction techniques he had perfected in rebuilding the face of René Duguay-Trouin, a famous corsair of the eighteenth century, were legendary.

The techniques would not be used on the DC-10 victims. There were few skulls. Now, he would rely on other, standard identification devices. Fingerprints. Teeth. Fracture records, for all old fractures leave a scar detectable in X rays. And bones. Bones can tell age and height. Tissues and blood are of limited use. Pigmentation can be a guide to race and blood can give type, but they are crude guides to firm identification.

Fingerprints and teeth were the first, most important lines of identification. And embassies had been put into action acquiring records. In England, Kenyon's was collecting, processing, and forwarding the records.

Of all the countries involved, only Japan and Turkey could provide fingerprints. Japan cooperated on all requests with a vigor motivated by the traditional requirement to identify and properly bury all of the victims. If only all countries could provide fingerprints, Dérobert thought. But compulsory fingerprinting smacks of faceless documentation, of invasion of privacy, of insidious Big Brotherism. It is resisted in most countries. As with buying life insurance or writing wills, anything done in conscious preparation for catastrophe seems, to many, a confession of fear. An invitation.

Dental records were more readily available. And again the *professeur* remembered the Rome–New York crash. Then he'd been called at 1 A.M., had acquired the manifest list from the airline, ordered all dental and fracture records, and with the help of embassies had most records within twenty-four hours.

Here, the manifest was a mess because of the BEA strike. There was no neat list of families to contact. Embassies were getting what they could; and as records arrived, physical characteristics were being fed into a computer in the hope that they would match up with characteristics of the remains.

The "mad scientist" had tried to organize some orderly international system of exchanging and filing dental records, but nothing had come of it. You still had to *hope* for cooperation. And now, twenty-two ... twenty-four countries!

The job was a discouraging climax to a professional lifetime of piecing together shattered vessels. A few miles away from the Institut, the technical investigators were piecing theirs together by tacking bits and pieces onto a frame of wood and chicken wire hastily mocked up in a hangar at Le Bourget airport. They were flying parts to Switzerland and America for examination. But *their* mission had been simplified by the identification of the cargo door.

Dérobert had 346 individual missions and too many missing parts. He had good microscopic equipment, refrigeration, computers . . . But he was not a magician. And the environment was depressing. His laboratory, built in 1921, was so shabby and out-of-date that he was embarrassed to show it to visitors.

But he could turn away from it and from the pressures of anguished families to the handsome library, or to the large amphitheater where eager medical students hung on his words. Or to his office, where the only reminders of death were the red-bound volumes of traumatic medicine; and where a lavish palm fanned out, filling the corner to the right of his desk, and a shiny-leafed rubber plant grew even more lustily than Lannier's, up and over the panoramic windows that looked out on the eternal fluctuating silver of the Seine. The suavities—the clipped fringe of white beard that framed jaw and chin, the superb gray suit with stylishly wide lapels, the broad intellect that could put the "bits and pieces" into historical and literary perspective— were not those of a mad scientist. They expressed a man of great accomplishment and dignity. This was not some Transylvanian conjurer with a ghoulish bag of tricks.

At his gray desk, he was the distinguished *professeur* of the University of Paris, director of the Institut Médico-légal, author of perhaps the thickest and heaviest textbook written by any of the distinguished men who would be drawn to the DC-10 case, and recipient of the Croix de Guerre.

How long would it take?

Chapter Seven

Waiting ... Waiting

"I GOT A CUFF LINK. That's all I got," Shirley Backhouse said defiantly. She wore it around her wrist on a gold chain. But it wasn't enough. Not of a man who had been so extraordinarily alive. She wanted her husband buried.

But, like others, she had been frustrated by the unsatisfying responses to her string of Telexed and written pleas for information to both French and English officials. When would burial be? Was identification complete? Shocked by the lack of help, the idea of a "disaster group" to help with the human issues "next time" was beginning to take shape—a group that could function like the shipwreck squads that spring into action when the maroon goes off, signaling a wreck and drawing people instantly from their normal jobs to the emergency. There were hopes growing, too, for a memorial in the forest, but that would take organization, consensus, money. And there was no way to make contact with each other, with the families scattered all over England and the world. The Foreign Commonwealth Office would not supply the list of families.

For Shirley Backhouse, the frustrations were intensified by the swift truncation of such a vital life. Steve's motto had been "Life is for the living and get on and live it." He'd thrown that motto at them so often, spurring his family on to optimism and good spirits if they ever flagged.

"An absolute fanatic on physical fitness," Steve hadn't "hung up his boots" until he was forty-two, playing actively for the Davenport Rugby Club until a year before the crash. His energy was unquenchable. She could still feel it everywhere. Every time she passed the picture of him lined up with his teammates for the 1953 team photo, she was inside the clubhouse again, an excited eighteen-year-old, looking out the window at the fantastic man she'd met on New Year's Eve two weeks earlier. It was their first date, but she'd responded instantly to his energy and his exuberant personality. The intense feelings that would bond them for twenty-one years were already there. For nineteen years of marriage it had been "a great partnership with lots of tears, lots of laughs, and lots of love."

There had been bad times. When they found out that Kary had broken her back and was going to have major surgery, Steve had whisked the family off to Gibraltar for some sun, without telling Kary what she had to face when she got back. She had spent five months in a plaster cast from neck to toe, and Steve had been at her bedside every night until the lights were turned out in the children's ward. "We kept each other's spirits up when the other's looked as if it was flagging. But then, that is what a family is all about, isn't it?" Their world had been consumed by Kary's illness that summer of 1970. Even if they had known, it would have meant nothing to them that that same summer a manufacturer in Long Beach, California, was having trouble, too. With a cargo door. While Steve was sitting by Kary's bedside, a cargo door had violently blown out in a pressure-vessel test of fuselage number 2 of a giant new type of aircraft. Four years later, Fate would hand Steve his ticket for a trip in fuselage number 29. He would finally meet energy even greater than his own.

The Backhouses, and all the other families of the DC-10 casualties, experienced normal grief, shock, anger, fear, vengeance, and desire for redress exaggerated by the horrible nature of those deaths, and by the nagging, growing suspicion—as information about the crash began to spill out—that it might have been avoided. Hungry for facts, they read and reread reports that a cargo door had been found, linking this crash to a history of well-documented door problems on the DC-10 and even to a chilling dress rehearsal for it two years earlier over Windsor, Canada. Was it true? they agonized. Did "they" know about the problem? Could "they" have fixed it? As anger and frustration built, they began to want to make the authorities . . . the French . . . McDonnell Douglas . . . feel the sting.

The British press made it hard to keep peace with death. Within a few days of the crash, John Godson, a writer of books on aviation safety, had speculated on the part of the plane's structure found in St. Pathus. He remembered, as Chuck Miller had, another piece of structure that had fallen off a DC-10. A door. And a coffin. He had been researching the Windsor Incident for a book he was already planning on Douglas and the DC-10, and was struck by the parallels. The first to implicate the cargo door and place blame on the U.S. government and McDonnell Douglas for not heeding the warnings of Windsor, Godson went on radio in London.

The media were slow to pick it up; they were still after other explanations—terrorist sabotage, or an exploding engine. But on Sunday, March 10—a week after the crash—the *Sunday Times* of London let go its first major volley in a campaign to get at the truth of the DC-10 crash. In a front-page story headlined "Warnings Ignored about Doomed DC-10," they introduced British readers to the Windsor saga and "the peephole that looked into death," documenting the responses of NTSB, FAA, and McDonnell Douglas to *Windsor*, explaining AD's and Service Bulletins, government and industry's devices for correcting problems. Graphic sketches showed the peephole, the handle, the latches; planes in profile with the cargo door flying off and the floor collapsing; and the flight path of the doomed plane. Though the technical inquiry was still in a preliminary stage and only the investigative teams

had seen the door, the *Sunday Times* had no difficulty
in defining cause. On line ten, readers were told that
"the door burst open because of a design fault." There
were no grays in the area of guilt, either.

The American National Transportation Safety
Board recommended modifications to the DC-10s
in service and production after the Windsor Incident. But last Sunday, nineteen months later, the
most important of these modifications had not
been made to any of the 130 DC-10s in service.
And production of the model is going ahead un-
interrupted at the Long Beach, California, factory
of the manufacturers, McDonnell Douglas. Not
until last Wednesday—three days after the Paris
crash—did the American Federal Aviation Administration make some of its earlier *recommendations* about the rear cargo door into firm orders.

The *Sunday Times* had found its villains and would
hammer Douglas and the FAA with increasing vigor
over the months to come.

With the *Sunday Times'* commitment to the story, a
sequence of events—as apparently irreversible as the
events initiated by the blowout of the cargo door—was
put into motion. Like the Pied Piper, the press played
the tunes that would dance England away from its own
laws to a country beyond the seas where laws looked
greener. Like the children of Hamelin, England seemed
almost hypnotically drawn to the music. There was no
way of measuring whether, in ridding the land of rats,
England might be stripped of something essential to a
nation trying to hold confidence in itself—faith in a
value system that, however imperfectly, still expressed
the English soul.

It was almost as if Britain had been premediatedly
primed for the crusade by three previous crashes,
Munich, Staines, and *Basle.* Munich, more than fifteen
years earlier, had wiped out Manchester United, the
country's finest football team, putting the nation into

mourning. The pilot had fought and won a lonely, ten-year battle to clear his name, teaching the lesson that, at times, justice could only be achieved by crusades. Then, after the 1972 crash of a BEA Trident at Staines, a leading American aviation lawyer, Lee Kreindler, had participated in the public inquiry, an unprecedented event that planted the seeds of American-style product liability suits against the manufacturer, and made the British question their own low payments for death. When, a year after *Staines,* 104 were killed at Basle, Switzerland, most of them "moms" from a Somerset village, air safety had become a social issue, with angry families eager to sue the airline and the French and Swiss air traffic controllers for "wilfulness and reckless-ness."

The press crusade for *Paris* began by arousing public anger. There would be no respite or escape for families torn between the needs for truth and for peace. For them, and for the builders, insurers, and owners of the airplane, it was the beginning of a nightmare.

Had all those passengers been sacrificed to greed and corporate power? . . . To a damn door! The theme, picked up by the *Guardian,* the *Observer,* the *Daily Express,* the *Evening Standard,* the BBC, was spreading across the country.

The headlines didn't let up. "Jumbo Safety: The Fatal Decision." "DC-10 Inquiry Points at the White House"—a story of scandal and compromise with air safety that reached right into Nixon's Watergate-rent offices. It made the waste and the waiting for news even more unbearable. Families waited . . . and waited.

Macadam Clark knew the horror the French were dealing with. This crash was "not only the worst ever but they were chopped up in little bits." But "you couldn't just say that flat out from a humane point of view." His office, and the foreign Commonwealth Office in London, the FCO, tried to use "the phraseol-ogy that seemed right at the time, depending on the psychology of the people at the time . . . as much truth as possible without more hurt than necessary." But no phraseology, delicate or indelicate, was forthcoming until the middle of March.

Most endured the wait for identification and burial plans with what Clark described as "heroic patience." Others wanted to know what was going on; but their attempts to find out met with the same lack of communication they'd felt on the first day when all the phones to Heathrow were jammed.

That first week, in Bury and all over England they waited for the announcement of funeral plans. The extent of the mutilation had not been made clear. On March 7, a poignant Telex was sent to the British ambassador in Paris by the brother of a young man who had died, asking "is it possible for me to travel to Paris and view the victims with the hope of identity?" By next day, they all knew. The official word had come through from France. In Bury, rugby club captain Chris Tilbrook made the announcement from the emergency headquarters in this home. "No bodies are able to be identified so no one will be required in France for identification purposes." It was news. But such shattering news!

What would happen now? Individually, families phoned, Telexed, wrote to French and English authorities asking for information as Shirley Backhouse had. With no way of coordinating efforts, many private little blitzes were launched. Nor was there any way of coordinating help that was offered. Four days after the crash, Axbridge, the Somerset village that had lost all the "moms," tried to offer its help and experience to the families of DC-10 victims. They called Heathrow, but were rebuffed with "We've finished with that. We're no longer dealing with it." Told to contact Turkish Airlines, they again received no reply.

An eighteen-year-old girl who had lost her parents in the DC-10 crash, and was now trying to take over her mother's sweet shop alone, could have used the comfort of the 180 Axbridge families who had organized themselves into a disaster unit after the Basle crash. But they couldn't find each other.

The nation's first official communication—a March 14 form letter from Mrs. V. E. M. Hartles of the Foreign Commonwealth Office—came by a grisly backdoor route, as an enclosure in a letter from Kenyon's, the undertakers.

The French authorities will need another two weeks to complete the identification process but they fear it will be impossible to make positive identification of more than a small number of the victims. . . . The French propose to organize a ceremony for the burial of the unidentified dead in about three weeks' time. . . . Meanwhile, the way is now clear for them to travel to Senlis to identify personal effects, etc., and to make and sign statements for the French authorities. . . . Everyone going to France can be certain that the British embassy in Paris will do everything possible to assist them.

The letter urged a "fairly constant stream of up to seventy families a day." Reading it, Stephen Mitchell tried to imagine how they intended to control and coordinate the "fairly constant stream."

On the same day the Hartles letter arrived, the manager of Turkish Airlines for the United Kingdom and Ireland wrote a moving letter of condolence to each family; a shorter but similar letter from the airline's general manager in Istanbul followed ten days later.

Like Mrs. Hartles, Peter Martin had been waiting to act the moment he had anything to report. As solicitor for Turkish Airline's insurers, he had shouldered the responsibility of handling much of the complex human aftermath. Simultaneous with the Hartles letter, he wrote to solicitors, quoting from the same French communiqué. He had some helpful information on death certificates: a step had been taken to ease the acquiring of the death certificates so desperately needed for life insurance, government-paid widows' pensions, and the probate of estates. He explained that the

Principal Probate Registry had agreed to accept as evidence of death a certified true copy of the definitive passenger list that the would deposit with the registry. He did not yet make an offer to start negotiating claims.

But at last there was something to hang on to. A tentative date for burial. The firm knowledge of death and the fact of burial had become overwhelming preoccupations for those who had had no word of identification. Trying to confirm burial date, calls and Telexes poured in from all over England to the British secretary of state, Mrs. Hartles, the French ambassador in London, the British consulate, the ambassador to France, and the French authorities in France.

But diplomatic pressure on the French could not speed up the appalling job. Lannier and Dérobert did not feel that the English were making their job any easier; had they had fingerprints like the Japanese, many more identifications could have been made. They were able to identify thirty-three of the forty-eight Japanese by forensic means. The unavailability of some dental records destroyed the main line of identification. But for Lannier, it was the garbled list caused by the British strike that made his job most difficult. And the lack of British cooperation. He had been able to connect a picture of a baby with the name *Hobe* on the list. But was the baby aboard? Even when they were able to establish that the name was not *Hobe*, but *Hope*—Francis Hope, a well-known journalist for the *Observer* and one of the most publicized victims—they still didn't know whether the baby in the picture was alive or dead. Lannier despaired when Mrs. Hope would not come herself, but sent one of her husband's journalist friends. How could *he* identify a baby's picture? Lannier asked for Mrs. Hope's statement in England, but it was not until a month later that he received word that the baby in the picture was living. "Until then, I couldn't *prove* that there was not a baby, too, dead in the crash." Consumed by his own job, he could not know that Mary Hope may have been too preoccupied to realize how important her help was to Lannier's work, that she was preparing to file a complaint against McDonnell Douglas, asking the courts to make her suit a $125 million class action against the company. Her suit would carry the case to California and give the British one of the first tangible opportunities to release the pressure. To strike back.

Lannier only knew that pressure from the British was building on *him*. Misspellings plagued him. Collier, one of the English models, appeared under four different names. He had thought FESTEW, M., was British; but the only clue they could find was a student card from the University of Zurich for a PFISTER, R. Could Festew really be Pfister? He phoned the Swiss consul in Paris, who found that a professor at the University of Geneva by that name had a missing son. When last heard from, the son had been a teacher at a driving school in Vienna. The father rushed to Senlis, and among the thousands of objects he found the card of a Directeur École de Pilotage Automobile—the director of a driving school. He had found his son.

How did you handle the Englishwoman who demanded to have her husband buried in the cemetery near her French home, when there was no body to bury? No matter how often she besieged the British consul in Paris, or how many papers took up her cause, Dérobert could not forget the *Azores*. He could not simply dump remains into a box. The woman finally received her coffin. Humane, perhaps. But was it right?

And the unknown—who was he? Would they ever know? A Britisher, a male, Lannier believed, had been listed as "Mrs." on the ticket and appeared to be traveling with a male companion. That was not surprising. A plane crash, like a suitcase suddenly spilled open on the floor, revealed the human tastes and frailties not always apparent on the surface. But why had he boarded the plane, then got off and sold his ticket to an unknown as had been reported? Would anyone ever miss *l'inconnu*?

Almost every case was as difficult as these. And yet the English pressed for firm dates. They *must* come to Senlis to try to help.

The flow to Senlis began. Peter Martin assigned the job of making travel arrangements to Pickford's travel agency whose branch offices blanketed the United Kingdom. Four members of each family would be paid for. With great efficiency, and at considerable cost to Turkish Airlines, Pickford's orchestrated the flow of people from towns, cities, and farms all over Britain—in fact, from all over the world—by plane, ferry, bus, train, and car to the medieval village that had now become the goal of perhaps the most painful pilgrimage ever made. From the collection of effects at the gendarmerie and the tables of clothing at the old hospice, shoes, wallets, rings were recognized. Even the discovery was a relief, for it meant that now they had confirmed what was already really known and would soon have a death certificate.

A note was found in the handwriting of one of the Turkish stewardesses, Semra Hidir. It was her shopping list for gifts she planned to take home to her family— a scribbled testament to the generosity of a pretty nineteen-year-old who was already the largest single supporter of her family and who kept only a small allowance from her own paycheck. As a Turk, she had been part of a code of family love, bonds, and obligations so strong that her death drove her father to attempted suicide and severe depression. With Turkish families showing a depth of grief equaled, perhaps, only by the Japanese, and far more emotionally displayed, the torn scrap of paper would have the power to bring her father and her family to tears for many, many years to come.

Harold Barrow of Polegate and his married daughter, Sally, were able to identify his wife Gene's rings. Gene had won her trip to Turkey by her success in the winter's sales drive of Pippa-Dee, a lingerie company that sold its robes and nighties at evening coffee parties in private homes. Three rings were all neatly together;

they must have been taken intact from her left hand. They found the ring from her right hand, too, but it had been crushed. Sally reached out numbly for the rings, functioning as if in "a dream . . . it had a remoteness about it." When they went home and told the two younger girls about the rings, Theresa, for the first time, told the family that whenever she tried to think of her mother, all she could see was her left hand. They all looked at each other and shivered. For all four had had the same experience. It was her hands, especially her left hand, they had all reached out for in their minds. None had ever thought of hands as a symbol, but realized now that they were "something you hang on to very tight . . . a link between people." The rings were proof of death. But Harold Barrow had had little uncertainty—on the day after the crash, Thompson Holiday's agent in Istanbul had confirmed that he had seen her board the plane. Her body would be identified and sent home for burial in a cemetery near the Barrows' half-timbered home. He would have the comfort of taking red roses to her grave.

Stephen Mitchell went to Senlis to try to find some trace of Prudence. She had not been identified. A man from the British consulate, not knowing that he was there in any capacity other than a family solicitor, took him aside and whispered, "They were mincemeat—they were taking heads out of trees." Stephen winced and went back to the tables of torn and bloodied clothes. He searched the rows of jewelry, looking for the ivory heart and the gold initial *P*. It would be irrefutable proof. But it was also something he wanted to keep. They hadn't had time yet for wedding rings, and it had been a symbol of their affection and commitment. He couldn't find it. Finally, he spotted her social security card, a token of her stay in the United States where she had gone hoping, he secretly suspected, to become a movie star. And his car keys. He wiped the dirt of the forest from the keys, and pocketed the few bits of proof he'd found. It gave him little sense of finality . . . or peace.

Chapter Eight

The Litigation

FROM THE FIRST DAY, Shirley Backhouse knew she was a widow. Steve and four friends from the Davenport Rugby Club *had* been on that plane. With two teen-agers and a baby at home, she was thrust into the chairman's seat of Steve's insurance company. Straight-backed and handsome, dark hair pixie-cut, she had the presence and style to carry it off, to pretend that she didn't still hear his voice and *see* him in his wrinkled old leather chair in the study. She tried to "get on and live life" as Steve would have wanted her to. But there would be no sense of finality until she'd seen him buried.

Several of his friends had gone to Senlis for her and had identified the gold cuff link, one of a pair her parents had given Steve on his fortieth birthday. But the Institut had not been able to identify his body. There were no dental charts, nothing to send to the nine dentists waiting at Kenyon's to fill out the forms that would be sent on, coded, to Paris, then decoded and delivered by hand to the British embassy before being delivered to Dérobert and his forensic team at the Institut.

Shirley Backhouse knew nothing of the procedures or politics of international identification. It was the further violation of whatever remained of a vital man that disturbed her. "I knew he hadn't been identified, but whatever was left of my husband, I didn't want it being messed about in Paris. I wanted it buried. I wanted *him* buried. There has got to be something *final*. A lot of people felt the same way. You had to finalize it or you could never get out of it."

The fact was that by March 20, only seven bodies had been positively identified, none of them British. The authorities, Mrs. Hartles in particular, could only pass on what the French told them; and the French, following their own meticulous investigative and identification procedures and the international accident procedures defined in ICAO's Annex 13, were chary with news. They preferred silence to premature or misleading information. In Senlis and at the Institut they worked frantically. By March 23, thirty-five had been identified; but it was predicted that no more than fifty ever would be. By April 15, there were seventy-five identifications, a triumph in light of the early despair. But the British were not being given a daily count; they had no organized way of dealing with their desperate need to be told everything that was happening, and particularly to get confirmation, one way or another, that there had been identification and remains would be sent home, or that a date had been set for the mass burial for the unidentified. Mrs. Hartles responded to all queries with whatever information she could get from Paris; but she did not open a tearoom for distraught families, nor did she give out the list of families so that they could contact one another. There was growing need to make contact and no way to do it.

Her first letter had given Shirley Backhouse hope, had helped snap her out of her numbness. Now there was the prospect of burial. But as the weeks went by, and there was still no confirmation of the burial, and still no word on Steve, she began to stir inside, to want to fight the silence. She wanted to fight "the whole lack of communication that started from the time I rang up the airport." On April 3, Mrs. Hartles's second form letter reported that the burial ceremony would be held in three weeks in Thiais, a cemetery very close to Orly airport. Three weeks more! And in the shadow of Orly!

By mid-April, only twenty-one bodies had been sent back to the United Kingdom, and Steve's was not one of them.

Coming suddenly and explosively alive, she started drafting a petition to oppose both the site and the apparently endless delays. She would take it to the French embassy in London. The elegant, raised chin of the chairman of the board tilted up even higher in defiance of bureaucratic impotency. The petition was taken around to all the pubs, to the rugby club Steve had belonged to, to friends, neighbors, and relatives. Hundreds of names were scribbled on. But she wanted more names, more of the DC-10 families to join her.

In London, a petite young widow had more quickly gathered her frustrations and anger together and released them on a different target. The crash had snuffed out a brilliant husband at the brink of high achievement in journalism. Francis Hope had been the *Observer*'s European correspondent, had published a book of poems, and had been writing for the *New Statesman* when he died.

"I felt a rage about his life being unfulfilled. . . . I felt a senseless fury against what one would have called Fate in another time . . . for Polly [her baby] not to have him is daggers in the heart." In a technological age, Fate was not an adequate answer.

Mary Hope read reports of faulty cargo doors and gross negligence and committed herself to getting at the truth of the crash. You couldn't physically assault the Long Beach hangar where the plane had been built, attacking it with fiery catapults and fingernails—not in a civilized world. But you could pour your anger into words, into legal language, and hurl a massive legal action against your foes. You could hit them in the stomach, expose the viscera through *discovery*, the mandatory spilling forth of all the files and documents and memos that had documented the birth of this new plane. And through *depositions*, discovery's oral phase, when the men who had designed, built, sold, and certificated the plane would have to sit through tough interrogation by plaintiff attorneys, having the facts pulled out, one by one, like cactus needles. But only in American courts. In aviation cases, discovery—the production of documents and depositions—was a consolation prize for those on the plaintiff's side who had no access to the crash site or to the essential information held by manufacturers and investigative teams. They were the basic means by which American plaintiffs got at the facts.

On March 18, Mary Hope filed her $125 million lawsuit against McDonnell Douglas. Although the demand was later raised, it was initiated as a $1 million suit on behalf of her and her baby, with the request that her suit be made a class action that could be joined by all the families bereaved by the crash. It was filed in California, the home of the DC-10 and of the highest settlements and jury awards for product liability, personal injury, and death cases in the United States. She wanted people to join her, to help her get at the truth.

With leaders like Backhouse and Hope, there were potential avenues for release. Able to articulate the feelings of many—the need for fast resolution of identity and burial, the need for a more responsive bureaucracy, for better disaster planning, for some meaning from the deaths—they lacked only a platform.

It was the press that provided the most effective platform. The press became both reporter and service agency, rousing anger with stories on the alleged scandals, on one hand, and offering a vehicle for venting the anger, on the other. They instructed the public on compensation and the Warsaw Convention, the international treaty that limited claims against the airlines. They explained class actions. The *Observer* invited next of kin to write in with support for the formation of a group to handle human problems. The *Sunday Times, Guardian, Observer,* and *Daily Telegraph* all carried Mary Hope's plea for others to join her in her cause; they gave the name of her American lawyers, Speiser and Krause of New York.

The BBC, treating the case as a consumer issue,

became the prime conduit for communication between families. Assigned to the DC-10 story, David Graham produced a series of programs in which the BBC, playing the consumer's advocate, critically explored the human, legal, and technical aspects of the case, and offered suggestions for action. Gary Ryan, who had lost his only son in the crash, had his petition of opposition to the Thiais site for the burial ceremony aired with his telephone number. Shirley Backhouse gave an intense presentation of her frustrations. And Mary Hope told the "Nationwide's" television audience:

> I've been advised by lawyers—American and English lawyers—that I and all the other people concerned in the crash can get more compensation by suing the manufacturers of this aircraft in America than by going through the British courts. In any case, we can't sue McDonnell Douglas in the British courts. They have to be sued in California. . . . I just feel that we can get some sort of meaning out of a disaster like this by trying to, first of all, stop such a thing ever happening again, which maybe we can by taking this action, and also by bringing both financial and some kind of spiritual comfort to all those who are, like me, bereft.
>
> My name is first on the list. But . . . anybody can join me in this from this minute onwards. I want as many other names with me in this as possible. . . . We must all act together on this.

A former English honors student at Oxford, she appeared intelligent and sincere; her concern for the legal rights of other English families, genuine. Already whipped up to a readiness to act, many of those watching came away with the impression that the class action was already a fact, an impression compounded by newspaper coverage of the suit. On all sides, legal action was being encouraged. Newspapers were now briefing the public on the inadequacy of Warsaw, and on the low expectations under British damage law.

In the House of Commons, Trade Secretary Peter Shore announced that "the legal personal representatives of the people who lost their lives in the Turkish DC-10 airliner would be wise to seek legal guidance on compensation and insurance at the earliest possible moment." The same message was echoed by Lord Beswick in the House of Lords. Thirty families contacted the BBC to join Mary Hope in her cause. More were contacting solicitors, inquiring about the class action.

From local pubs to the House of Lords, the shock of the Hope suit forced a frantic reexamination of the whole question of compensation. In a letter to the BBC, a man from Buckinghamshire spoke up for the quavering structure of damages being imperiled by the *Paris* case. He asked the questions many Englishmen were quietly asking themselves:

Do you think it is right for parents to receive a monetary award for the *death* of a child or of children? Do you think that *nondependent* relatives of a bachelor should be awarded money for his death? Should sorrow or grief be mollified by money? Is hysterical sympathy to be the yardstick by which loss of a dear one is to be measured? Do you realize that compensation does not descend like manna from heaven—it has to come from someone else's pocket, and in the end air travel passengers must foot the bill.

He ended with a solemn caution to the BBC.

I do think you have a responsibility to proceed with due care and caution not to work up what I can only all sympathetic hysteria. Please let cool calm common sense rule the situation together with a proper respect for British law, based as it is on equity and justice—equity and justice to *all* parties concerned.

Countering this traditional stance, the BBC did an exposé on the current market value of death by air crash. The settlements were scarcely bonanzas. A father had received only five hundred pounds—roughly $1,200 dollars—for the death of his single son, a typical payment for a nondependency case. A widow with two children had received five thousand pounds. How long could a widow live on five thousand pounds? A man who had lost his wife had received three thousand pounds. In a crash near Manchester, where seventy-two people had been killed, more had been paid by insurance companies for the lost plane than for the people who had died. The BBC asked the loaded questions, "Are aeroplanes really worth more than people? Are we in this country showing a callous lack of care for the families of those who died in this way?" They did not mention that damages paid for the thousand Britishers killed in air crashes in the past ten years were ruled by the same English legal principles as death by automobile, or any other kind of accident; that if there were inequities, they were inequities that went far beyond air crashes. In fact, car crashes in England each year killed seven times as many as the usual *world* total for commercial air crashes of 1,000. A single earthquake could kill 5,000 and be quickly forgotten. But air crashes have always had an impact wildly out of proportion to numbers killed. This mystique made it hard to hold balance and perspective. But the fact was that whether by air or automobile, deaths were being recompensed with sums no family could live on for long.

The Hope action and the press coverage put enormous pressure on the solicitors who represented families of DC-10 victims. The Hope suit flouted Warsaw, the international treaty England had signed, circumvented English law and led British citizens off in quest of something noble-sounding but completely unfamiliar called a class action.

Since the first week of the crash, when it was already clear that this was a very special plane crash, families had been contacting solicitors, asking advice. Many of the solicitors were from rural counties and had no experience with aviation law. They knew little of the Warsaw Convention. They could only translate the deaths into the legal terms they knew and search Lord Campbell's Act for the relevant sections. Now, they scurried for copies of the Carriage-by-Air Act and for *Shawcross and Beaumont on Air Law*—the aviation text Peter Martin had edited. They read and argued the Warsaw Convention. Suddenly aware, with the Hope bombshell, that they had been cast into something historic—a case that could ultimately alter British and international aviation law—they were increasingly concerned with their clients' rights, and with their own abilities to protect them.

As solicitors searched the law, families waited.

Chapter Nine

The French

MERE CHANCE HAD MADE this a French crash. The DC-10 was an American-built plane, owned and flown by a Turkish airline, loaded mainly with British, with less than two dozen French aboard. The flight had been simply passing through Paris. But it had crashed on French soil. And tradition and Annex 13 dictate that the country where the crash occurs conducts and controls the inquiry.

Very quickly, France and its methodical bureaucracy had begun to cast a white sheet of dignity and order over the shambles, calling into play procedures and techniques refined over hundreds of years of high civilization, fitting the chaos into a neat legal framework.

The French were not, however, to be rushed or pushed. Their Code Napoleon was a matter of great national pride. Far more than a punitive tool, it was a mighty moral force—a receptacle of national wisdom, training and molding its citizens as parents train a child. French law, like Lyons silk, was an expression of culture.

And France had a buoyant tradition in flight to uphold. The Montgolfiers' balloon had sailed majestically past Louis XVI's courtiers at Versailles. Penaud and Gauchot had patented an amphibian monoplane with retractable landing gear twenty-five years before Orville Wright's first flight. French pilots had pioneered flight across water and deserts; the gallant exploits of Antoine de Saint-Exupéry and his fellow pilots, flying the suicidal mail runs across the Sahara, were still being relived in the Vielles Tigres, the club in the Bois de

Boulogne where the few surviving "old tigers" still misted up over memories of sandstorms and murderous camel-driving Moors.

Its national airline had survived the nickname "Air Chance" to build a creditable safety record. The French were currently building the hot Mirage fighter to compete with American fighters for huge NATO contracts. They were leaping into wide-body competition with the Airbus, the A-300, built by a three-country consortium; and sharing, with England, the prestige and financial drain of the Concorde—the supersonic commercial transport that would go into scheduled service to Rio de Janeiro in 1975 and, in May of 1976, would cut commercial transatlantic flights to four hours.

France had had the unpleasant task of cleaning up the crash of the first supersonic airliner, Russia's TU 144 at the Paris Air Show, in the same vicinity less than a year before. Now, the world's largest crash and the biggest aviation inquiry of all time had come, uninvited. It would be a terrible drain of time, money, personnel, France was being put to the test. And she would do her best. The French way.

The French legal system, as any Frenchman will quickly point out, is very different from the American or English. And the Paris crash bared its structure very clearly. First, it invested the local judge with full authority to conduct the inquiry and to recommend criminal prosecution, if he so decided. In theory, even the minister of justice dare not stay his hand, though in practice, the discreet hand of Paris is felt. It was a gift of power to the provinces that would have been the despair of Louis XIV.

In France, judges are not elected; and they are not all middle-aged ex-lawyers. Often they are chic women in their late twenties who have spent up to five years in university studying law, and a further two in magistrate's school. A *juge* is not solely a judge in the American sense, but also a magistrate on the local level. Senlis's two judges were young and female, and one of them was *enciente*—pregnant.

In the DC-10 case, the all-powerful *juge d'instruction* should have been appointed from one of the two resident judges. But as it was felt that experience was needed, a judge from the nearby town of Beauvais, Jean Helle, was appointed *juge d'instruction*. His mission was to find out *who* was responsible and then to decide whether a criminal or civil prosecution was required.

Helle instantly launched a two-pronged legal effort. First, to find out what had caused the crash, he directed a massive technical investigation—the Commission d'Enquête—to be conducted by the Ministère d'Aviation Civile, headed by René Lemaire, chief of the French Inspectorate General for Civil Aviation. The investigation was divided into five manageable and logical parts: Group 1—wreckage; Group 2—history of flight; Group 3—cargo door; Group 4—human factors; and Group 5—digital flight data recorder. With the discovery of the cargo door the day after the crash, the ill-fated door had earned its own group.

The first organizational meeting of the commission was held on Tuesday, March 5, at 9 A.M. at Le Bourget, less than forty-eight hours after the crash. There, all the investigators—French, Americans, Turks, English—were assigned to their groups. In an accident almost instantly classed as nonsurvivable, Group 4 would have little to do. It was the findings of Group 3 that the plaintiff lawyers would be hungriest for, but all would be kept in strict secrecy. Ultimately, the findings and conclusions of the technical investigation would be published in the *Journal Officiel*—the "French Report" that would be waited for for more than two years.

The highly secret results of the second, and quite separate, penal (or judicial) investigation would never be published. Although the *juge d'instruction* in Beauvais directed it, and was the one who must decide if there would be criminal prosecution, the investigation would be discretely supervised from the ministry of justice in Paris by the vigorous and elegant Christian Le Gunehec, that ministry's Directeur des Affaires Criminelles et des Graces—a Gallic Robert Kennedy in his defense of civil justice. Charged with determining if criminal acts had been committed, and working at first on the possibility of bombs and Middle Eastern terrorist plots, this investigation would be aided by the police from the Ministère de l'Interieure—the French equivalent of the FBI. The *juge d'instruction* would stay in constant touch with the departments working on both investigations; and all would defer to his orders and instructions.

Apart from the major diversion of legal power to Beauvais, Senlis remained the physical center of the DC-10 activity. The town looked a more appropriate setting for *Les Miserables* than for a jet crash involving high technology, corporate power, and more than twenty embassies. According to Lannier, "Half of France's medieval movies are shot here." You could expect to see peasant thieves being hauled in wooden-wheeled carts through the narrow cobbled streets, or the Three Musketeers galloping under the stone archway that is the entrance to the ancient walled part of the town. Short-haired engineers from Long Beach, coming through with their briefcases and their talk of "redundancies," "psi differentials," and "failsafe systems" were alien.

They were certainly from a different world than the *procureur de la République* in Senlis, the man charged with being society's advocate in the case—a man profoundly ill at ease with the event that had intruded itself into his orderly world. As the people's prosecutor, it was to him that the *juge d'instruction* would send up his recommendations on the need for criminal prosecution. And it was he who would prosecute.

For Léon Gourraud, as for Lannier, life had changed dramatically with the crash. Normal duties had had to be shunted aside. But he seemed less ready for the task than the ebullient chief of the gendarmerie. A neat, nervous man who looked like Sigmund Freud, the *procureur* of Senlis favored long contemplative silences in his conversations. He sat in an ancient bishop's palace built on Gallo-Roman ruins, in an office rich with eighteenth-century detail, yet hung with a disturbingly moribund air. With an Oriental rug covering parquet floors, and a gilt mirror and classic Greek sketch topping an ornate marble fireplace, the room—and he—seemed frozen in time.

He would have to wait until the *juge*'s inquiry—a very long process—was complete before he could make the decision that would focus the eyes of more than twenty nations, and of his superior in the ministry of justice, upon him. A painfully cautious man, he deliberated over the making of even a phone call as if it were a Supreme Court decision. He lacked the confidence of men who take "the royal route" to the position of *procureur* by studying at L'École Nationale de la Magistrature at Bordeaux. He had gone back to school at thirty to earn his position the hard way. And one suspected that he would not be eager to seize his historic opportunity; that when the time came, he might welcome more than a little help from Paris.

If he did ultimately decide to prosecute, it would make stunning headlines. But it would be largely an empty exercise. Of the possible defendants in the case, only one—the Algerian baggage handler who had closed the cargo door at Orly—lived in France. The others: McDonnell Douglas, Turkish Airlines, the U.S. government, and General Dynamics (who, as the French would soon discover, had actually built the cargo door as subcontractors), could not be forced to stand trial. And France had no extradition rights.

He was not idle while waiting his moment. He was charged, too, with the task of issuing the death certificates, the 346 required *jugements déclaratifs de décès*. It would be his responsibility to accept or reject all the evidence of identity that could be mustered from all sources, and to sign the two-page documents confirming death. These would then be sent to the consular authorities, who would send them on to the families. The *procureur* would be busy.

"But the *juge* is the center of all investigation," he said. And as he said it, he ground his fingers in a circular motion on his leather-top desk until his fingertips turned white with the pressure.

PART II

What Happened?

Chapter Ten

The Size Effect

TO THE DUTCH engineers, it was inescapably the door. They had tried to convert everyone. But, like Cassandra, their prophecies had been ignored.

In his office in Amsterdam, Hendrik Wolleswinkel was first confronted with the potential dangers in widebody jets. He was the youngest of the triumvirate within the Netherlands Civil Aviation Authority, the RLD, whose responsibility it was to certificate any new plane, of any nation, that was to be owned and flown by a Dutch airline. It was precertification studies of the 747 that had begun to raise his fears.

A lean, dark-haired and handsome man in his midthirties, he had sat at his desk playing with pencil and paper, toying with numbers. He had played with the new dimensions, with volumes of air, with floor strengths. He worked in a drab bureaucratic environment—pale green vinyl floors, gray-flecked walls, gray metal desk and file case, old radiator under the window. But his mind was intense and alert. And he quickly grasped the alarming fact that *engineers were not designing adequately for the larger hull size*. Criteria was being met. But criteria itself was not recognizing the "size effect," the dynamics of the dramatically larger volumes of pressurized air that would fill the big planes. They were designing pressurization and venting systems that would allow planes to survive only a very small hole in the shell. And holes could and did occur—from bombs and midair collisions; from cockpit windshields being shattered by birds; fan blades from a disintegrating engine flung through the fuselage; doors coming off.

Numbers leaped out at him. If a plane's dimensions were doubled, air volumes would be *cubed*, filling the plane with *eight times as much air as before*. If the shell were punctured, causing sudden decompression, there would be vastly greater volumes of pressurized air pushing to escape through the hole. If a hole occurred in a cargo hold underneath the cabin—from a bomb or door, perhaps—the air in that compartment would rush out to equalize pressure with the ambient air outside. The air in the cabin above the hold would try to rush out, too; massive volumes of air trying to escape would press down on the cabin floor with the weight and urgency of rampaging elephants. *Pressure differential*—the difference in pressure between two adjacent bodies of air, separated by a floor, a fuselage shell, a bulkhead—was a fact of life in any pressurized aircraft. But in the new wide-body breed, it could be lethal. If the pressure differential between the hold below and the cabin above was great enough, the floor would collapse. They *must* design for it.

But how? Floors could never be strong enough to withstand a high differential; they couldn't be built like trestles or tanks. Catastrophic pressure differentials were normally prevented by letting air escape through venting holes between compartments. And it had to be able to escape fast. To prevent floor collapse, air in the cabin had to escape *almost as fast as the air below was escaping through the hole in the fuselage*. If the hole was large—evacuating the air in the hold almost instantly—and the vents were small, the frustrated air, rushing at the vents like a stampede, would simply burst through the floor. Air was a fluid; it could bottleneck. Only so much could go through at a time.

The vastly increased volumes of pressurized air in the cabins of wide-body planes, enclosed like caged hurricanes, would have to be given more avenues of escape, more venting between compartments. Though what good would venting and strong floors do if a large door came off at maximum altitude, sending the vital oxygen masks streaming toward the hole, out of passengers' reach? Doors *must* be failsafe.

But doors were not the main concern of the Dutchman. It was bombs—terrorist bombs. Bomb holes could be large. *Yet they were designing only for small holes. Venting as if it were the 707 or the DC-8. And worse, they were still routing vital control cables through the floors, floors that could collapse.*

Wolleswinkel could see that "aircraft were complying with and even exceeding existing regulations at the time. But the mistake was that authorities responsible did not recognize that with wide-body aircraft, there are things you can't extrapolate from experience." He and his colleagues appreciated the engineering dilemma facing the designers. Where could you put more venting? And could you, in the 1970s, design for every eventuality? Every potential kind of hole? In an uncharacteristic burst of fire, Wolleswinkel threw his arms in the air, and said, "How can you design for a *BOMB?*"

Venting holes between the cabin and cargo holds were usually put around the periphery of the fuselage at the edge of the floor. But in the wide-body planes, the increase in linear dimensions around the periphery could never catch up with the larger volumes of air. For the volume of air would always increase at a dramatically faster rate. You could not simply riddle the cabin floor with holes and grills, for they could be blocked by carry-on luggage, seats, passengers, and lavatories; or they could weaken the floor. Yet venting was largely the key to the size effect problem. The aviation industry was being confronted with a new kind of problem: The *need* to vent was outstripping the *ability* to vent.

By the late sixties, the size effect on structure had become a major concern of the Dutchmen.

They were only three, but they were dedicated men

117

—Nicolaas Schipper, chief of the Airworthiness Bureau; Casper Falkenhagen, director of the Aeronautical Inspecton Directorate of the Netherlands Department of Civil Aviation; and Wolleswinkel, Falkenhagen's young deputy director. Among them, they had served Dutch aviation for eighty-three years, dominating the certification and airworthiness of Dutch aircraft since World War II.

Somehow, sitting in their low gray buildng on the edge of Amsterdam's Schiphol airport, they were often able to see the problems more clearly than were the men at the drawing boards. A small organization, they had been forced to become generalists, free of the "tunnel vision" that afflicts those engineers who never have the chance to look beyond one very small aspect of a very large problem. But would anyone listen? They were a handful of men from a small country. Smallness was, as Wolleswinkel knew, "our strength . . . and our weakness." But they would try.

The crusade had begun publicly in November of 1970, when Schipper made his now-famous statement to ICAO's Airworthiness meeting in Montreal, a statement that has come to be respected for its prophetic vision. But at the time, it had little impact. His comments were not on the agenda. They were not recorded. Nobody was talking about pressures and volumes. Except Schipper, Falkenhagen, and Wolleswinkel.

At a less public level, they asked Douglas to do some testing. And in 1970, Douglas had begun limited research on vents, floors, and pressures.

When, on March 1, 1972, KLM applied to the RLD for certification of the DC-10, the concern of the three men increased. The long-range model, the DC-10-30, would give KLM the capability of flying nonstop and fully loaded from Amsterdam to Curaçao, and from Amsterdam to Anchorage, Alaska. Pilots were eager for its sophisticated cockpit. It would have a computerized inertial navigation system that would, when programmed by the punch of a few buttons before take-off, take over after lift-off and "fly" the plane unaided to the threshold of the Anchorage airport. KLM wanted, needed, these capabilities. The RLD had finally certificated the 747 because some of its controls ran through the ceiling; *from a control standpoint its safety did not depend on the integrity of the floor*. But the DC-10, with its control cables all routed through the floor, was a classic example of size effect ignored, and "we decided to concentrate our attention on it." They were under extreme pressure to put their stamp of approval on the plane, for KLM had already ordered six DC-10s, part of a mass order of thirty-six placed by the consortium of airlines KLM belonged to. This group, known as KSSU, consisting of KLM, Scandinavian Airlines, Swissair, and UTA from France, had announced the purchase at a meeting of the International Air Transport Association, IATA, where the world's airlines meet and regulate their routes and fares. It was a dramatic announcement that had effectively knocked the L-1011 out of continental Europe, for the powerful southern European consortium, ATLAS, decided soon after to go with the DC-10.

KLM not only wanted the plane it had bought certificated, it wanted to be the first in the consortium to fly it on intercontinental routes. To speed the process, a special multination certification group, consisting of the Netherlands, Scandinavia, Switzerland, and France, was formed to share the job, as it had for the 747.

The Dutch took responsibility for decompression and structures, and as they did their studies on the DC-10, the RLD was not happy with what it saw. They wrote and talked to the FAA, which had certificated the plane in the United States, saying, "You are waiting for an accident to happen." But the FAA argued that experience *so far* showed no need for new requirements. The three Dutchmen tried to whip up concern among KLM's consortium. They staged a summit meeting in Paris with KSSU, Douglas, and the pre-certification group to discuss "accidental pressure loss." But it was hard to get coordinated support in pressing for door/floor/vent changes in the DC-10. The Swiss and

Scandinavians said, fundamentally, that they were not in a position to take a strong stand because they were contractually bound to recognize the FAA's certification criteria. Most of the world, after all, accepted FAA criteria without question.

When the door blew out over Windsor, Canada, in June 1972, the Dutchmen stepped up their campaign. Twice they flew to Long Beach to talk about "sudden decompression," and they wrote a letter to Douglas opposing the proposed "fix" to the door. Wolleswinkel spoke for the RLD in Washington that December, the month when the clamor to certificate the DC-10 reached a crescendo. It was the month KLM took delivery of its first DC-10.

The planes were now a fact—massive, multimillion-dollar symbols of the economic imperatives pressing down on the three men. KLM was in a race with its "pool partners" to be the first to New York with its DC-10s. Crews were feverishly being prepared for flight. Instructors trained at Douglas's training center at Yuma, in the Arizona desert, were training KLM's pilots at Lufthansa's training center in Tucson, Arizona. Pilots were being run through two weeks of ground school and ten days on the simulator at Schiphol airport.

If the RLD did not certificate the planes, they would sit on the runway unused, intolerably expensive ornaments to Schiphol airport. If they did certificate, KLM would fly a pressure vessel that did not have the integrity the three believed it should have. But "from the formal point of view, the Dutch view was rather weak. There was no violation of any specific requirement." And they were dealing in imponderables. *"You can calculate what safety measures will cost you, but you can't measure how much safety you are buying for it."*

They had tried to convert everyone, and failed. On May 23, 1973, the RLD gave final certification for the DC-10. KLM had already taken off for New York, becoming, on December 19, 1972, the first European airline to fly the long-range DC-10-30.

For the record, they wrote into their certification:

"So the RLD isn't happy with the present situation, but for this generation of aircraft, we have to live with it." They knew Douglas had done an unprecedented amount of testing on the new plane. KLM's experience with Douglas went back almost to the beginning of the Douglas company. And they had been told by Douglas that even if the floor collapsed, you could continue safe flight by use of the autopilot, because the *wires* for the autopilot went through the ceiling.

Too late, Wolleswinkel came to the conclusion that the claim was in error. Yes, the wires went through the roof. "But they overlooked the fact that *all hydraulics run through the floor* and if lost *will not respond to electrical impulses.*" The loss of hydraulics had brought planes down in the past, and had almost brought a 747 down at San Francisco in 1971 when a piece of angle iron from a runway approach light structure pierced the plane at takeoff, severing *three* of the plane's four hydraulic systems. The autopilot could activate and "steer" the hydraulic system. But you have to have hydraulics to move the control surfaces. And hydraulic lines could be cut by a collapsing floor. This had not happened in Windsor, but . . .

Wolleswinkel's first thought on hearing of the Paris crash was the safety of the Dutch fleet; an immediate check was ordered of all DC-10s being flown by KLM and by Martin Air, a charter company. He felt certain that their own planes were safe, for all but two already had the final improvement phase on the aft cargo door —a so-called closed-loop system, which was "the closest designers have come up with to a failsafe door." But a failsafe door was still not an adequate response to the size effect.

As sure as he was of the cause of the crash, he restrained himself from bitter triumph. "It's not wise to say 'I told you so.' " He was going to have to live with the aviation community for a long time and must keep the lines of communication open.

He laughed joylessly, "Next time they will probably listen to us."

Chapter Eleven

But How Would It Work in Moose Jaw?

BUT WOULD THEY? The brutal fact was that it almost always took a major crash to precipitate action. And even tragedy didn't always get things fixed, as Chuck Miller knew. Waiting in Washington for word from the GO team in Paris, he remembered the *Everglades*, the first and only fatal wide-body crash, until Paris.

On December 29, 1972, an Eastern Airlines' L-1011, Lockheed's wide-body, had crashed into the swamp 18 miles northwest of Miami International Airport. It had been a clear, black, moonless night. And until five seconds before impact the *crew had thought they were flying at 2,000 feet!*

The autopilot had been engaged to lighten the workload while the four men on the flight deck worried over the nose landing gear, trying to determine if it was down for the landing at Miami. And somehow, inadvertently, the autopilot system that holds altitude steady had become disengaged, and the plane had begun a gradual descent toward the ground. Preoccupied with their problems, no one had heard the one brief C chord that sounded to tell them they had descended 250 feet below their selected altitude; and the descent had continued. When, just before impact, the captain had exclaimed, "Hey, what's happening here?" it was much too late. The NTSB report found "that the probable cause of this accident was the failure of the flight crew to monitor the flight instruments during the final four minutes of flight and to detect an unexpected descent soon enough to prevent impact with the ground."

The Everglades crash had confirmed Miller in his conviction that even in the increasingly automated environment of the new jets "somebody still has to be minding the store," alert to the unpredictable emergencies that fell into the never-never land of "remote probability," but which *did* happen. The flight crew should be monitoring every inch of the flight, but in the real world they didn't always. Alertness had to be maintained. But how did you maintain it in the reassuring arms of your autopilot? Sitting in a friend's houseboat on the Potomac, watching landings at Washington's National airport, Miller had always marvelled at the high safety record of one of the nation's most hazardous approaches. It required planes to snake along the winding Potomac through airways clogged with departing and returning senators and bureaucrats. *It was safe because it was bad. It kept pilots alert.*

But worrying about keeping pilots alert begged the real problem, he felt. Pilots were marvelously competent men who had mastered a demanding and sophisticated environment; with doctors, they were one of a small group to whom people willingly entrusted their lives. But they were human. And there would always be an element of human error. Everglades had been an opportunity to give the pilot an aid that could overcome human frailty—a ground warning device that would blare out the alarm that the plane was dangerously close to the ground. The device existed. But the FAA did not follow up on Everglades by making it mandatory. It would take *another* crash—the dramatic crash at Washington, D.C.'s doorstep of a TWA 727 just before Christmas, 1974, in which a conflict over the meaning of the controller's orders had led the pilot into a Virginia mountain—to finally force the installation of the ground proximity warning device.

And Air Canada came to mind, another fatal crash in which lessons had not been learned. It had bared one of the most difficult and elusive problems in air safety: cockpit design that *invited* error.

An Air Canada DC-8 had crashed on July 5, 1970, outside Toronto's Malton airport, killing all 109 people aboard. The ground spoilers had been deployed in flight, bringing the plane down like a rock. Spoilers, deployed at touchdown, help settle the great weight of the airplane on the ground and keep it there, overcoming the tendency to lift up again; and flipped up in a vertical position, they help brake the landing roll. Once the gear was down ready for landing, there were two ways to activate the spoilers: by pulling the lever up as directed in Air Canada's flight manual, you "armed" the spoilers, which then deployed automatically on touchdown; or, by pulling the same lever back against a heavy force, you could deploy them manually upon touchdown. You could safely *arm* them in the air, but if you deployed them in flight during the last stages of landing when altitude and speed were too low to overcome the sudden loss of lift, it could be catastrophic. Safety depended on a strict routine, a rote system of arming or manually deploying that never varied. In the last few crucial moments of flight, you did not dare switch procedures.

According to the official report of the board of inquiry, this time Captain Pete Hamilton did. Instead of letting his first officer deploy them immediately on touchdown as he usually did, he wanted them armed in the air. At about 60 feet above the ground, he said "OK." The first officer responded automatically, doing what he always did. He pulled the lever back, sending the spoilers flipping up. The plane instantly plunged down at 25 feet a second, giving them less than three seconds to avoid a crash. Hamilton fought back by pouring on the power, yelling an appalled "No! No! No!" and by pulling back on the control column to initiate a missed approach. The first officer, realizing what he'd done, gasped back one of the most poignant final messages ever recorded before a crash. "Sorry, oh! Sorry, Pete." The plane banged to the ground, right wing low, ripped off an engine, and careened back up into the air, wing on fire, fatally damaged. The pilot, not knowing he had lost an engine and was streaming fire from his burning right wing, tried to circle for another landing. Three explosions ripped off most of the right wing, and the great crippled bird—one of the sleek workhorses of Air Canada's jet fleet—plunged nose first into the ground. Pete Hamilton, one of Canada's ablest pilots and former president of the Canadian Airline Pilot's Association, CALPA, had "bought the farm." It would have been easy to blame the crash on "pilot error" and close the file. But CALPA waged a fierce and successful battle to have a whole battery of causal factors cited, among them "a design defect . . . from a human engineering point of view" that allowed ground spoilers to be too easily deployed in flight and ambiguous flight manuals that had led to confusion among the pilots over how to safely deploy the spoilers.

But instead of responding to the Toronto crash by requiring that the spoilers be modified so that they could *not* be deployed in flight, the FAA had responded with a mandatory Airworthiness Directive that required cautionary rewording in the flight manual and a new placard near the spoiler lever that would say "DEPLOYMENT IN FLIGHT PROHIBITED." Terming the fix "ridiculous," a Canadian official said that the wording might just as well read, "DO NOT CRASH THIS PLANE." And on June 23, 1973, an Icelandic Airlines-Loftleidir DC-8 was near touchdown at Kennedy airport in New York. At 40 feet above the runway, the captain ordered "OK, arm them." The first officer pulled the lever back, deploying the spoilers. With the flight engineer shouting "NO! NO! NO!" the plane dropped and hit the ground tail first. They lost number 1 engine, a fire began, but fire-fighting crews extinguished the blaze. All 128 aboard survived, though many were injured, eight seriously. The placard had not prevented the very same mistake that had killed 109 in Toronto.

The Air Canada crash had fallen into the controversial area of "design-induced pilot error"—crashes caused by design flaws that invited human error, even from Air Canada's superbly trained pilots. Canada, with its sparse population scattered over half a continent, has a more intensive air communication system, relative to its population, than any other nation in the world. There, a small town will still turn out in freezing rain to light an airstrip with headlights when it hears a plane in trouble. Evolving from the extraordinary traditions of bush pilots who, stranded in the Northwest Territories, have been known to fly a two-ton German Junkers out to civilization with a propeller hand-carved from oak sled boards and held together with moose glue, its pilots are an elite whose safety record is so good that they are in demand all over the world. But in "design-induced pilot error," it was always easier to lay the blame on the pilot's shoulders than to lay it at the feet of the manufacturers and the government authorities who not only certificated the questionable design, but allowed it to continue to court disaster, sometimes for years. But were they really flaws? How "idiot proof" did an airplane have to be? And were pilots sometimes using the ground spoilers intentionally in flight to increase rate of descent, as some engineers suspected? These fundamental pilot/engineer conflicts could best be resolved by involving pilots at an early stage in cockpit and design and procedures. But they weren't always to the degree they should.

The NTSB had leaped onto the Icelandic accident, recommending, above all, that the spoilers be modified so that they could not be deployed in flight. But it was not until January 1974—just a little over a month before the Paris disaster—that an AD had finally been issued requiring a failsafe modification. The AD gave the airlines up to eighteen months in which to comply. Planes might be yanked catastrophically from the skies

126

by spoilers deployed in flight at any time up to mid-1975, five years after the Air Canada crash.

Placards had been the response to the Toronto disaster and they had failed.

The Everglades, the spoiler accidents—and possibly the DC-10 cargo door—had left too much room for Murphy, Miller believed. Murphy was the mythical author of *Murphy's Law*, which roughly states that if there is a way to do something wrong, someone will find it. Murphy was the human element in flight. The guy who forgot to put in the last rivet, who pressed the wrong button, who would find ways—even if it wasn't easy—to put things on backward or upside down. He was the mechanic who should have been an English teacher, a pilot with "finger trouble." It was commonly known that he could never be fully outwitted, but Miller was committed to stripping him of some of his voodoo.

So was Harold Adams, Douglas's legendary design engineer. With Adams' reputation for safety consciousness, Miller had been glad to know that he was the chief designer on the DC-10. Adams was one of the men who had helped give Douglas a global reputation as a builder of sound, safe airplanes. He was a living embodiment of the design philosophy set down by Donald Douglas when he started the firm in 1920. It was embodied, too, in a cluster of words Adams had made a litany at Douglas during his forty-plus years with the company: "dispatchability, reliability, maintainability." And "simplicity," if the complex and the simple would do the same job. An elegant design that wouldn't work under operational conditions was not successful. Or safe. He had demolished the theoretical perfection of a thousand young engineers' ideas with the question, *"But how would it work in Moose Jaw?"* He had always kept in mind the vision of a thick-gloved mechanic trying to unscrew a bolt in the 30-below cold of a Canadian winter. It was recognition of the human factor. Keeping Moose Jaw firmly in mind was also part of a philosophy of safety—of building safety into the design and operation of the machine from conception through every mile and hour of its service—that he had tried to infuse into every Douglas plane he had worked on. And he had worked on them all, from the DC-1 to the DC-10.

As the design of the DC-10 began, the basic commitments hadn't changed: You didn't go with radical innovation. You let a new plane evolve from the last one, using the tried and true where you could. You went with the simpler rather than with the more complex, if you had a choice. You didn't push the state-of-the-art. You took a conservative approach and built a sound, not a sexy, airplane. And you never forgot that building an airplane was basically using common sense and abiding by immutable physical laws. To hell with the mystique. Even the DC-10's sophisticated air-conditioning system was essentially a matter of warming, cooling, and pressurizing "a tin shack on the top of Everest in a 50-mile-an-hour wind." "In spite of its sophistication," Adams cautioned, "the DC-10 has to be a conservative, reliable airplane, not a monument to the inventiveness of its designer."

Nothing could have been a purer application of the Douglas philosophy than the use of cables and hydraulics to control the DC-10. Entering the business in the days of open cockpits, Harold Adams had been only two decades beyond the days when planes were little more than flying skeletons, with the bones—the struts and wires—clearly exposed. Strapped to the left wing, the pilot pulled or pushed his wooden stick, saw and felt the movement of wire cables that stretched between his hand the canvas-covered control surfaces just ten feet in front of him, and he experienced the direct and immediate response of his fragile craft, pitching up or down. When Adams started designing planes in 1929, the skeleton had been covered by a canvas skin, cables hidden in wings and fuselage. But a pilot could still glance out of the cockpit at the wings of his biplane, see the ailerons move and feel the wires that levered them, causing his plane to bank and turn. He was still in direct and primitive contact with his control surfaces and with the environment through which he flew.

Like a helmsman trimming his sails to the wind, it was the intimate collaboration between human will and natural forces that merged the two and made an inanimate craft an extension of man's power. It was the sensual, primordial experience of flight that is now only tribal memory to a transport pilot. For in a well-insulated, pressurized cockpit, far removed from engines, wings, and control surfaces, the pilot can no longer see, feel, or hear directly the myriad of cues that once gave him intimate sensation of flight and, in fact, helped him fly his airplane. The evolution toward more refined and powerful control systems has systematically removed the pilot, step by step, from direct sensing of the forces acting on his craft.

As forces on his control surface grew greater and greater with speed and size, engineers were forced to give the pilot more and more mechanical advantage to keep the physical force required for control within the capabilities of the pilot. They no longer made him move the entire tail surfaces or warp the wings. Instead of moving the entire vertical tail section, for instance, the pilot had to move only a small hinged section of the surface—his rudder. Ailerons were cut into wings. Rudders, ailerons, and elevators were some of the earliest aids to the pilot. Soon even *these* surfaces would incorporate small surfaces of their own—tabs and trims—to further lighten the pilot's load.

By the time of the famous early DC series—the DC-3, -4, -6—fragile wires had become strong cables that stretched from cockpit to tail, running hidden through the entire length of the cabin floor. But as long as there were cables directly connected to the vital control surfaces, there was still the old feel. The pilot pushed on the control surfaces, and they pushed back—a reversible system. Engineers had been forced to become more and more ingenious in amplifying the strength of a pilot into the enormous power required to move large control surfaces at the great dynamic pressures of the high-speed jets. Dynamic pressures are best understood by sticking your hand out of a moving car first at 10 mph, then at 50 mph. On a plane, the dynamic pressure at 500 mph is 100 times as great as at 50 mph—a function of velocity squared. Hydraulics were the answer.

With hydraulics, with boosted systems, the pilot had power steering, for a hydraulic system did most of the work, the pilot a little. Then, with fully powered controls, the hydraulic system did all of the work. The pilot still had cables, but the messages he sent down were now fed into servomechanisms that harnessed the power of the hydraulic system. Now, aerodynamic forces on the control surfaces could only push back on the hydraulic system—not on cables as before or on the pilot. It was a one-way street—an irreversible system.

But pilots rely on this feedback to provide important feel cues, cues that instantly tell them the size of the input and the severity of their maneuvers. So with irreversible systems came *artificial feel systems*—systems that would push back at the pilot in much the same manner as the control surfaces used to. It was easier flying. But every complexity brought new vulnerabilities. The hydraulic system could fail—from a break in the lines that carry the hydraulic fluid or from a failed pump. The fear of failure was real and was met by giving the pilot duplicate systems—redundancy —so that a backup system could be manually or automatically activated if the primary system failed. Redundancy, the *failsafe* concept, became standard design philosophy in the 1960s. When you couldn't have redundancy—in landing gear struts, for example—you designed for *safe life*, 100 percent reliability for the life of the plane.

With this complexity, flying a plane had become far more than controlling surfaces. Pilots were becoming "systems managers," responsible for and dependent upon a whole range of complex systems—mechanical, hydraulic, electric, avionic, pneumatic, environmental—

required for navigation, communication, passenger comfort, weather avoidance, abiding by aviation's myriad rules of the road.... To keep the workload within human bounds, engineers were assigning some of the job of controlling the plane to inanimate "brains" —automatic flight control systems that were almost the final stage in the systematic removal of the pilot from his original function. Gyros. Yaw and pitch dampers. Computers. Autopilots. Elevators moved. The rudder deflected. The pilot didn't even know.

Flight had gone from the hand on the stick to computers talking through electric wires to a rudder half a football field away. Engineers asked themselves: "If automatic systems can send signals by electric wires, why can't a pilot?"

By the time the DC-10 came along, designers had a breathtaking option. They could stay with cables and hydraulics or they could go "fly by wire." Not wires in the old sense, but electrical circuits that, through sensors embedded in the control wheel, would transmit the pilot's messages electronically to the servos—the mechanisms that controlled the hydraulically powered control surfaces. Light and flexible, the wires could be strung along the ceiling, anywhere, and by the late 1960s were the sophisticated way to go. Some military fighters and supersonic bombers flew by wire, but, still unwilling to completely sever the umbilical cord, had mechanical backup, the ability to continue to fly manually. The pilot wouldn't be able to fly his airplane very well, but hopefully well enough to bring it back home.

Even with the supersonic Concorde, with its highly sophisticated flight control system, they would still not completely cut the umbilical. Though it had most of the elements of a fly-by-wire system, it would not be until the space shuttle, and a new generation of fighters like the F-16, that the umbilical would finally be cut.

Pilots and engineers tend to have an inherent trust in things mechanical, less in things hydraulic, and least in things electronic. And since a wire can be cut and electrons can misbehave, a fly-by-wire system would be very

131

complex; and, most importantly, since faith in even highly redundant fly-by-wire systems was not great, the DC-10 would fly by cable. With hydraulics giving them fully powered flight. It was relatively simple. It was well within the state-of-the-art. It was proven. The cables would run through the floor in a straight efficient line from cockpit to tail.

To make the system failsafe, there would be *duplicate* sets of control cables going through the floor. The three sets of hydraulic lines would be run even farther apart and closer to the edge of the floor, near the supporting struts. An alternate set of controls—the autopilot—would signal the control surface actuators through wires running above the cabin ceiling. In case of the almost inconceivable failure of all three systems in flight, with the loss of hydraulic power, there would be an extra failsafe feature—a wind-driven electrical generator that would "drop out" into the slipstream to power the hydraulics and give the pilot enough control to land the plane. These were prudent decisions, the decisions you would expect from Douglas men—and essentially the same decisions that were made for the other wide-bodies.

Douglas engineers pointed out that, yes, the 747's cables did run through the ceiling—an apparently less vulnerable location—but only because a straight run back from its cockpit to its tail happened to be at that level. And they felt that it, too, had its vulnerabilities —to damage from large engine sections piercing the fuselage. Douglas would go with cables through the cabin floor, a choice that was proving successful in the -8 and -9. Did anyone ask if, with all control cables and hydraulics running through the floor—regardless of how widely you spread them—you truly had re- dundancy? With this new breed of pressure vessel, did tried and true approaches always lead to a failsafe de- sign?

This may have been one of the silent questions hovering over the emergency meeting called by John Brizendine, president of McDonnell Douglas, that Sunday morning, as soon as he could gather his key men together. There was shock, a sense of loss, an enormous amount of speculation. "To have all those people lose their lives, however it happened, it's a terribly difficult and traumatic thing." They'd built the plane to fly at least 60,000 flight hours. They had racked it through 120,000 flight hours of fatigue testing, simulating the loads and stresses of taxi, takeoff, flight, and landings for twice the promised working life of the plane. That done, they went on to test the plane to destruction, stressing it until the wings failed exactly when they'd calculated they would. Fatigue testing, in excess of that done for either of the other two widebodies, had cost $30 million, but they believed the structure of the plane could last, at the usual airline usage of 3,000 or 4,000 flight hours a year, for *thirty or forty years*. They had put an extra layer of pure aluminum on the skin to lengthen its life, at the cost of $12,000 per plane. They'd shot four-pound chickens at the windshield to test its strength and given the pilot an opening side window to look through in a rainstorm—all to achieve the goal of "building an airplane that's not going to cause the guy any trouble."

TC-JAV had flown less than 3,000 of the 60,000 hours they'd built it for. And now it was down in a French forest with the biggest loss of life in history. "Whether you feel responsible or not, it's a very heavy emotional impact." The DC-10 was their baby. A very big, important baby. Douglas's profitability over the next ten years was largely staked on it. Research and development costs alone had exceeded $1½ billion. The -8s, though still filling an important niche as a mainstay of jet fleets, would eventually be phased out of the world's fleets. Designed in the mid-fifties, they had been flying since 1958. And a lot had happened to the state-of-the-art since then that could only be incorporated in a whole new type of plane. Mainly, advances in engine technology permitted the construction of very large aircraft powered by only two or three highly efficient engines. Like the DC-10.

They were still making and selling the -9s, Douglas's second generation jet transport, and had just marketed a new "Stretch 9" that brought its capacity from the original 80 to 139 passengers to compete with Boeing's 727. The stretch capability was something Douglas was proud of. All their planes were designed so that you could extend the fuselage by inserting an additional section. The -9 had been stretched three times. Douglas could point out that Boeing couldn't stretch their 707 to the same degree because its tail would drag on the runway upon rotation. Rotation—that critical moment when the plane, committing itself to flight, rotates about its main landing gear, lifting the nose and dropping the tail—can cause a lot of sparks. Douglas designed the aft section of the fuselage and landing gear to allow them to rotate to steeper angles. But in spite of the -9's flexibility, it was still a small, self-contained, hometown aircraft, really the sophisticated successor to the DC-3. It was great for short flights in Europe or California, island-hopping in Micronesia, or for serving northern Canada's frozen towns. Air Canada has fifty of them. Eastern Airlines flies eighty-seven.

But the DC-10 was the one you hurled across the continents and oceans. The one whose pure size gave it sex appeal. It was Douglas's entry in the highly competitive wide-body market, along with Boeing's 747, Lockheed's L-1011, and the brand new A-300 Airbus being built by a consortium in Europe.

Wide-bodies were the prestige planes, and national pride demanded that every country, no matter how small, try to have at least one. With your 747 or DC-10, you could join the Big League, a fact eagerly exploited by developing nations ambitious for an image of progress. You could schedule one flight a week across the Pacific, put up billboards in Los Angeles and take full-page ads in *Time* magazine, and get enormous public relations mileage out of a minimum of planes and flights. Wide-bodies had become a basic weapon in the battle for tourists.

They were also very useful airplanes. And the DC-

10, with its range flexibility, had advantages over the bigger 747. Its long-range model, the DC-10-30, could fly from New York to Karachi nonstop, nearly 8,000 miles. The basic model, the DC-10-10, could sprint off La Guardia's urban runways with a full load of businessmen and have them in Chicago for meetings in 75 minutes.

The wide-bodies were quickly replacing the narrow fuselages that had carried us into the jet age—an age that Boeing had dominated with its enormously successful 707 and 727 series. The Super "Stretch 8" had been lengthened to 187 feet, five feet longer than the DC-10, and had reached the limits to which it could be stretched without passengers feeling they were riding in a well-appointed culvert pipe—what engineers call the "tube effect." Wide-bodies were a transitional stage in flight. Not as big a jump as from pistons to turbines, from propellers to pure jets. Not the symbolic breakthrough of commercial supersonic transports. But a quantum leap in size, with substantial improvements and changes in engines, structure, and systems. They were the third generation of jets, with the versatility to replace 707s and DC-8s on long-distance routes, and supplement the 727s and DC-9s on short-haul routes.

But the big planes cost at least $20 million each, depending on equipment and interior configuration. Turkish Airlines had bought their three for $62 million, including spare parts. And with airline incomes slipping as they were in 1974, reflecting a general recession, there were increasing signs of a trend to cut back on the variety of planes an airline flew and to stick with one manufacturer.

The pressures to get the -10 well established were enormous. Douglas had projected building 500, and now had 137 flying with 23 airlines in Europe, North and South America, New Zealand, Asia, and Africa. There were 69 firm orders and options on 45 more. Serious negotiations were going on with at least 10 more airlines. But they were still less than halfway toward the eventual goal of 500. Airlines would look beyond a single crash to the overall reliability; and they knew that "Douglas had this fantastic heritage and reputation and training." But the crash—with the kind of press coverage it would get because of its size alone —could hurt the image of safe operational experience so crucial to sales.

Before committing themselves fully to a wide-body plane, McDonnell Douglas had wavered for several years, while the 747 was being developed, waiting for feedback from the airlines to be sure they had just the right feel for what the industry wanted and was going to want over the next few decades. Just as the 747 had been the product of Pan American and Boeing brainstorming, American and other airlines had been chatting with the visionaries in advanced design at Douglas since the mid-sixties about the need for a larger aircraft. Was the 747 too big? They might fill it now on the Atlantic routes. But what if the market shrunk? "You don't take a sledgehammer to hit a tack." And you don't just design a nice airplane in isolation, build a mock-up, and invite the airlines over to buy a few. A new plane is as much an expression of the tyranny of the marketplace—down to the shape of the coatracks and the color of the seats—as it is a reflection of a manufacturer's design philosophy. It was no lucky chance that the DC-10 was able to take off on La Guardia's short urban runways, fully loaded, for Chicago. That capability was one of the prime criteria laid down by American Airlines when they invited proposals on a new plane in March 1966—an invitation that had whipped up a frenzy of competitive activity between Lockheed and Douglas and had spawned the L-1011 and the DC-10.

The dialogue between Douglas and American had been constant and intimate. Even before American's initial order was placed, the parameters of the airplane —speeds, altitudes, size, etc.—were being mutually defined. Detail design began with the stunning announcement in February 1968 of American Airline's order of 50 DC-10s—25 firm, and 25 on option, an unprecedentedly large initial order. The historic purchase agreement for $800 million was signed at a press conference at the Waldorf Astoria Hotel in New York. Then, just two months later, United Airlines announced its commitment to an even larger number—30 firm and an option on an additional 30. With that, the news was broadcast through the Long Beach plant that they had "Authority to Proceed" with the building of the DC-10.

American had placed its order first. And it would get the first airplane. But to keep United happy, Douglas decided to stage a dual ceremony at Long Beach on July 29, 1971. Looming behind the podium, the two huge planes sat glaring at each other, nose-to-nose. American received the keys to its plane first, with United getting its five minutes later. They roared into the skies almost—but not quite—together. American would always be able to say, "I got the first DC-10."

After six months of operational experience with the plane, American's president, George A. Spater, mixing his modes as aviation men are prone to do, announced that the DC-10 "is the best airplane that's ever come down the pike, in every respect. It will have long use in increasing numbers at American Airlines." To a degree, the DC-10 was American's baby, too.

And now the baby had crashed, killing 346 people.

The mission at Douglas was still the mission defined by Donald Douglas with the DC-1, and redefined by John Brizendine, the current president: "Every new airplane we build has to do more useful work at less cost; carry more payload farther at lower cost per ton mile or passenger mile."

Aviation is an industry that goes after achievement of the mission with single-minded dedication. Borrowed from the military, the term *mission* meant simply a goal to be accomplished. Missions, whether to return safely to base after an air strike on Hanoi, to fly from Paris to London, or to build a profitable superjet, could be aborted, jeopardized, compromised. But a failed mission earned no Brownie points, no matter how hard you had tried. It was a black/white concept that allowed for no diversionary back roads or philosophical meanderings. The point of a mission was to get from A to B. The mission of the DC-10 was to be better—to do more useful work at lower cost—than the -8 and -9. And, to be realistic, than the L-1011.

Harold Adams's art was the successful mating of Douglas's philosophies with the facts of life. The cost of building, flying, and maintaining a wide-body plane was astronomical. The DC-10 was going to cost American Airlines more than $1,800 an hour to operate. And sales would be lost or won on a few maintenance dollars saved, or a few extra revenue dollars earned with an extra passenger seat or a few more square feet of usable cargo space. The decision to go with outward-opening latch-type cargo doors in the DC-10 rather than with inward-opening plug-type doors, for example, had been made not only because the door openings were marginally too large for safe and proper operation of a plug-type door, but also because the airline required it for their containerized cargo system—a profit factor.

Suddenly, the mission was in jeopardy. Other crashes haunted the meeting at McDonnell Douglas. The British aviation industry had never fully recovered from the failure of the Comet, the first commercial jet transport. It had lost all public confidence during the desperate months when investigators were trying to find out what was making it disintegrate in midair. The violent and mysterious loss of two Comets had deeply shocked a public just being weaned from propellers. England's prestige as an aviation nation and the survival of commercial jet flight had been at stake. In a painful but courageous decision, the British government had moved in, grounded all Comets, and thrown all of Britain's investigative resources into the most intensive investigation yet mounted. In a remarkable salvage operation, the Royal Navy recovered 80 percent of the wreckage of one of the Comets, the one that had come down in 600 feet of water off the island of Elba.

An entire fuselage was tested in a water tank, put through the pressurization cycle not the limited number of times that had been thought sufficient, but thousands of times. Finally, after the simulated equivalent of 3,060 flights, a tiny metal failure at the corner of a cabin window had been detected. It was determined that the crashes of the two ships had been caused by metal fatigue in the fuselage—fatigue caused by pressurization required for flight in the hostile world of high altitude. Though these were strictly state-of-the-art accidents, almost impossible to have predicted in the trailblazing plane, all the public knew was that Comets had disintegrated into the sea. They didn't care that subsequent models were safe. And the Comet, though a good plane, was never a successful one.

Then there had been Lockheed's Electra, a turboprop; that transitional stage between propellers and jets that combined the complexity of the former and the power of the latter. There had been a series of crashes in 1959 and 1960, two of which were as inexplicable as the Comets'. A controversy raged over whether or not to ground the plane—a shattering blow to revenues and public confidence. It was not grounded. Pilots slowed the plane as they went through turbulence, and hoped the answer would be found. After months of intensive analyses and tests in an investigation that rivaled the Comet's in thoroughness, flutter—the whirl mode—was found to be the cause. The whirl mode, which coupled vibration of the structure that sheathes the engine—the nacelle—to a flexing of the wing, reached such an intensity that the wings were literally torn off at their roots. This flutter mode developed quickly and was usually catastrophic. Where the Tacoma Narrows Bridge flutter persisted for a day before failure, finally flailing like a whip, the Electra's harmonic vibrations ripped the wings off in 30 seconds. Mourning did not become this Electra. And though the engine nacelles and wings were strengthened and the modified Electra 2 went on to earn the admiration of the transport pilot fraternity, its aura of death hurt sales. Only 174 Electras were sold to the commercial market.

Now, the first crash of a DC-10. Not off in the Everglades, with many survivors like the only other fatal wide-body crash, but fully loaded. Under the eyes of the world. With all aboard dead.

It could be the bomb the Dutchmen had feared. Rumors were already flying. But if something had gone wrong with the DC-10 itself—the doors?—the world's fleets would have to be alerted instantly and the problem corrected, or the fleets grounded. The cause had to be found.

If it had been a terrorist bomb—or pilot error—any doubts about the DC-10 must be cleared away. Until now, the plane had an almost unblemished *public* record. No crashes. Some incidents: the bad one over Windsor . . . a passenger sucked out of a window in a bizarre accident over New Mexico when an engine fan disk had pierced the fuselage. But all new planes had bugs to work out during the first year or two of operation. There were no ADs yet, the Airworthiness Directive that is the official hand-slap of the FAA, which is issued if you had a serious safety problem. It had the force of law. And it was public. It could hang around the neck of a new plane like an albatross, adding drag to its image. Was it a door? Was it *Windsor* all over again?

Cause was still unclear. But, by the end of the day, Douglas sent a telegram to all carriers alerting them to check the cargo doors. Next day, disturbing word arrived from Paris: Wreckage had been found on the flight path, miles from the crash site. *It was a door*.

How could they have let it get through? Miller wondered. The National Transportation Safety Board had been created to perform a gadfly function, to prick the aviation industry and the FAA into ever higher levels of safety consciousness. As part of the Department of Transport (DOT), it sat in incestuous proximity to both the DOT and the FAA in the DOT's massive square white marble home at 800 Independence

Avenue. But it had been formed in 1967 as an independent body mandated to investigate nonmilitary crashes and incidents to find the all-important *probable cause*—which was increasingly found to be a series of interrelated causes—and to send recommendations up to the FAA for implementation. Legally, the NTSB could have sent its recommendations to any body it felt could take action. And Miller was not convinced that the FAA's punitive, regulatory route was the only way to prevent accidents. There were other ways—pilot cooperation, local action at airports. But "prevention through regulation" had become dogma. And the FAA did have the power to get things fixed. The NTSB, and Miller's Bureau of Aviation Safety within it, had not. But the blue-bound NTSB reports were respected and waited for with fear and anticipation by the aviation community.

The NTSB had had to fight fiercely to maintain its independence. Miller had been having in-house battles with what he interpreted as White House interference with his bureau's mission for two years, and they were still going on, taking their toll of his energies. A new general manager, Richard Spears, had been installed at the NTSB, and Miller suspected him of being one of a number of men slipped into agencies by the White House staff to provide a direct line of communication and influence. It seemed part of a disturbing trend to mute criticism of the Nixon administration. Oversight bureaus like his were having their budgets cut, their manpower reduced. The outspoken were being muffled. Long before Watergate, he was becoming convinced that a megalomaniac force was trying to strangle any agency that stood in criticism of the executive branch and the major agencies that were an extension of its power. Or was he wrong? Was he losing his perspective and judgment? Miller had finally been able to air his concerns at public hearings staged by the Senate Commerce Committee's subcommittee on aviation—hearings that spurred the drafting of legislation that would, hopefully, once and for all, depoliticize the NTSB by making the NTSB independent of the Department of Transport. Legislation was pending at the time of the Paris crash. But the pressures on him within the bureau were still building. Gadflys are not always popular. He had been very alone. Losing his temper with the board, and worse, losing confidence in himself. But how do you measure your own performance? Even now, in March 1974, with the Palace Guard crashing around the king, the clash with the general manager continued to be a constant tension, a conflict he could no longer leave at the office. He was beginning to take it to bed with him. And these chest pains on the tennis court. It was no good. Air safety was a religion with him. But did it demand martyrs? Did you take the pressure until you really blew? His wife had been urging him to quit.

And now, Paris. He had snapped to it, the complete professional. "In the safety business, we have a set of priorities that, in a catastrophe like this, superimpose themselves on everything else."

"I'm going to France," he told John Reed, chairman of the board, "unless you have some objection." Reed did not. So Miller and Walt Sweet flew out Tuesday night.

It was to be Miller's last major crash as head of the Bureau of Aviation Safety.

A stop in Boston gave them a good chance to get a quick refresher course on the cargo door. Locating a DC-10 and a cooperative baggage handler who set up a stand for them, they ran the door through its opening and closing cycle several times. They looked through the tiny peephole that was the result of one of the *Windsor* recommendations, a small window that let you look through the skin to see if one of the four small lockpins that slipped behind the latches was positioned correctly. The one visible lockpin was only an *indication* of a safely locked door, for the peephole did not let you see the only real proof—the latches properly hooked over the spools and the linkage properly aligned.

Obviously nobody on the peephole "fix" had taken Murphy into account, or asked, "But how would it work in Moose Jaw?" Impossible to view from the ground, the peephole demanded that a stand be moved into proper position. You had to have good eyesight and know what you were looking for; for the peephole was only one inch in diameter. Scrupulous viewing through the peephole before every flight *could* catch an improperly locked door and prevent disaster. But how scrupulous would lazy or rushed ground crew be? Miller asked the baggage handler, whose job it was to close the door, what the peephole was for. The man had no idea. He claimed it was there for the maintenance man.

Miller moved swiftly from concern to alarm. If a baggage handler for one of the major U.S. airlines didn't know what the peephole was for, what would happen in airlines with less rigorous training and maintenance programs? The -10 would soon be flying all over the world. He called Washington and asked for a spot-check around the country to see how well ground crews understood the door.

He checked with Walt Sweet on the status of the *Windsor* follow-up. As structures ground chairman on the Windsor Incident, Sweet had been assigned the job of checking up on the implementation of recommendations the NTSB had sent to the FAA. FAA response to the board's requests could, and did, range from the slapping on of the mandatory AD, which forced corrective action, to polite rejection. To make sure the board's recommendations did not languish as paper tigers, Miller knew there should be a specific staff activity to track the NTSB's safety recommendations. He had started a follow-up system within the Accident Prevention Projects Branch within a year of joining the NTSB. It was headed by Jack Carroll, a man he trusted. Its mission had been to put emphasis on something other than investigation—keeping an eye on the FAA; monitoring the data that flowed through the hands of his investigators to catch the events that, isolated, meant little, but, coordinated, could be seen as trends

143

that could become crashes. It would keep unfinished business like the cargo doors active and not allow it to fall into a somnolent dialogue that could stretch out over years. Too often, the NTSB, FAA, and the industry sparred with problems like sleepwalkers, letting half a year drift by between feints. Carroll might have sat in on DC-10 certification meetings if the branch had been allowed to flourish and kept the NTSB more up to date on DC-10 developments. But it had been starved for manpower and throttled by inadequate budget support; formally abolished by the new general manager, it existed now only as a dying vestige.

With that failure, the follow-up responsibility had been assigned to whatever man happened to be closest to a specific investigation. On *Windsor,* it was Walt Sweet who, like all Miller's staff, was swamped by a workload that had been increasing almost exponentially with the increase in size and complexity of aircraft. Inevitably, their product was suffering from "size effect." Sweet's last contact with the FAA had been on September 13, 1973, six months before *Paris,* when he'd had a chat with the FAA to assess the status of a major McDonnell Douglas study of floor strengths and possible venting, venting between the cabin and the aft cargo hold that would prevent the lethal pressure differentials that had occurred at *Windsor.* Acting on the board's recommendation, the FAA had urged Douglas to make the study. *The FAA man hadn't known what the status was but would try to find out.* Hearing nothing, the NTSB had made another query two months later but had received no response. That had been the last record of contact regarding the cargo door, prior to the Paris crash.

When Miller asked Sweet why he hadn't done a new evaluation sheet of Douglas's compliance, Sweet said, "It's under a stack of things on my desk, and I just have not been able to get to it." Miller knew it was true. In his opinion, Walt was one of the brightest and most competent people in the bureau. But with so many other pressures building up, the problem with the cargo door was simply not urgent enough *to work its way up to the top of the pile.*

Miller flew on from Boston convinced of three things. "The peephole was a ridiculous thing to expect someone to use. At least one crew didn't even know what it was for. And any locking system that depended on a baggage handler's intimate knowledge of its mechanisms was a hazardous system." His alarm would prove to be well founded. More than two years later the official French report of the Paris crash would state that neither Mahmoudi, the baggage handler who had closed the door of TC-JAV, nor the THY mechanic aboard the flight, nor anyone else had looked through the peephole. It was a procedure Mahmoudi had never done himself and did not understand. He had, he said, seen mechanics out with their torches peering in viewports, but, as a baggage handler, felt he should not interfere with engineering matters. The need for looking in the peephole had been made even more critical by the fact, revealed by the French report, that a lock indicating light had not been installed on TC-JAV as recommended by a Douglas Service Bulletin.

Miller's was the same concern the three Dutchmen had expressed shortly after *Windsor* when they wrote, concerning the adequacy of the peephole, that ". . . Douglas took great pains in writing clear instructions. This will not help very much, however, if your freight is handled by untrained personnel. This is a real operational problem that needs considerably more consideration."

They didn't know for sure yet that it *was* the door. It wasn't Miller's nature to come into a smoking wreck after the fact and shake fingers at the guilty. It was his nature, and his *job,* to keep incidents from becoming accidents. Prevention *was* part of the mission. *How had they all—McDonnell Douglas, the FAA, his own bureau, the airline—let this one get through? . . . After the warning at Windsor?*

Chapter Twelve

The Smell of Scandal

CHUCK MILLER HAD wanted to have one of his men present at all of the meetings monitoring the DC-10's development. But, with the coming of the new general manager, he had lost control of his bureau's priorities. And he had no manpower.

It had taken a serious incident—*Windsor*—to bring the developmental problem of the aft cargo door to the attention of the NTSB. He had not known that on March 3, 1972, a log entry for the DC-10 involved in the Windsor Incident had reported difficulty in closing the aft cargo door electrically. Or that, just two weeks before *Windsor,* McDonnell Douglas, in response to reports by three of the four airlines operating the DC-10 of failures of the electrically driven actuator to latch or unlatch the cargo doors, had issued a service bulletin to operators asking them to install heavier gauge wire to the actuator motor.

Nor had he known that there had even been a rehearsal for the dress rehearsal of *Windsor*. On May 29, 1970, during a pressure vessel test of fuselage 2 at Long Beach, a cargo door had been blown out as pressure inside had built, and the cabin floor had buckled then, too. The door had blown at less than 3 psi (pounds per square inch), which is equivalent to the pressure differential a plane would have reached at an altitude of less than 7,000 feet. That should have been the shock that propelled engineers back to the drawing boards for a profoundly improved door design and, beyond that, to a hard look at the larger problem of size effect.

Instead, the 1970 blowout had initiated a gradual, voluntary program of modification aimed at making the door failsafe. It *had* to be failsafe for certification. McDonnell Douglas had begun the four-phase DC-10 Cargo Door Improvement Program, which in itself seemed a recognition of imperfection, but that moved only by degrees toward a reliably safe solution. By a series of Service Bulletins, operating airlines were invited to make a series of electrical and mechanical "fixes"—repairs or changes—that only compounded a locking system so inherently unsatisfactory that it would later be described by a senior FAA man as "an inelegant design worthy of Rube Goldberg." It would not be until phase four that the door would finally be free of the possibility, the nagging fear, of human error in closing the door. And even the final solution—the "closed loop" system—was, like all the others, purely voluntary.

The closed loop was a locking system in which the closing of a vent door that permitted pressurization could be achieved only when the lockpins had moved behind the latches and the door was properly locked.

The improvements were issued as Service Bulletins, or SBs, the Douglas in-house directives used to notify airlines and production-line crews of any kind of change that was to be made. A Service Bulletin could alter the wattage of a reading light bulb or the design of a toilet seat, matters so peripheral to safety that a Service Bulletin did not carry with it a sense of urgency —unless specifically issued as an Alert Service Bulletin. Even then, it was only a suggestion, not an order.

The little vent door that went askew during the closing process at Detroit had been the first response—the small door-within-a-door that *should* never close and permit pressurization unless the latches and lockpins were in their proper, safe position. It was the change that had satisfied the FAA sufficiently for certification.

Miller knew that it was only with jet aircraft and

147

high-altitude flight that the reliability of doors had become so critical. Before, a door coming off or flying open was inconvenient and embarrassing, but not generally catastrophic, because the air pressure was approximately the same inside as out. And it had been difficult to break the "set" of the engineer and pilot minds that still saw doors as "just doors." *But with pressurization, doors had become the gateways to disaster.* With the air pressing insistently against the shell from inside, it had become vital to maintain the integrity of the pressure vessel in flight. All openings—doors, windows—were suddenly vulnerable.

Engineers had followed their instincts to plug the holes by doing just that. They had created plug-type doors and windows that were stuck in from the inside. As pressure built up inside, they were pressed even harder into the hole, like a bathtub plug, making the seal even tighter. But, as always with airplane design, there were tradeoffs. The plug-type door, which opened inward, took valuable, revenue-producing space, especially in the cargo holds. On large doors there could be sealing problems. And it lacked the structural advantages of the latch-type door.

Douglas had been using outward-opening latch-type doors for the cargo doors of its pressurized aircraft since the DC-6 in the early fifties. Opening out, they did not take up any room in the holds; and closed and locked, they became part of the stress-bearing structure of the vessel. Curved to conform perfectly to the shape of the hull, and secured by powerful latches, they became aerodynamically, as well as structurally, part of the hull. The tension stresses created by pressurization passed through the latches into the door, letting the door itself share the load. In contrast, tension stresses could not flow *through* but had to *circumvent* the plug-type door or window, concentrating stress loads around the openings, particularly at points of sharp curvature. Strengthening added weight. The Comet mystery had finally been traced to metal fatigue at the top of a window—a point of stress concentration.

Once you were committed to a latch-type door on the DC-10 there was no turning back; for it became an integral part of the structure, and the fuselage structure in the vicinity of the door was designed accordingly. You could not simply substitute a plug-type door. You had to live with it and hope you could correct any genetic defects. Mainly, you *had* to make it failsafe.

As Detroit papers dramatized the Windsor Incident with breathless detail and explicit diagrams of the door, McDonnell Douglas and American Airlines had come to its defense like protective parents. "There's no way the craft could take off if the hatch wasn't properly closed. There are too many safety devices aboard to indicate an open hatch. If those devices showed it closed, then it was closed," American's Walter Boyd was quoted as saying. A McDonnell Douglas spokesman said that the only way the jet could possibly have taken off with an open or improperly closed hatch would be if the hatch warning light in the cockpit was burned out. "But that's a very remote possibility." They admitted that there had been some problems in closing the doors. There had been some binding of the series of rollers, or spools, that are gripped by the latches like a fist clamping around a metal bar. But "we feel the problem has been corrected by the addition of lubricating devices on the latching mechanisms."

But tests made at Douglas under the eyes of the NTSB and FAA investigators had turned their statements into empty whimpers. Hidden under the skin, in the door's latching mechanism, was a design defect that had not been discovered in precertification testing. *It* was *possible, they found, to have the door appear closed, latched, and locked when, in fact, it was not.* If the door was operating correctly, the pressing of an electrical switch would close the door. Holding the switch down for an additional four to seven seconds would position the clawlike latches on the door around spools on the door jamb, linking the bottom of the door to the fuselage. Then, pulling a locking handle down slipped small lockpins in behind the latches. The movement of the lockpins and the lock tube to which they were attached tripped a switch that turned out the warning light on the flight engineer's annunciator panel. The closing of the handle also closed the little vent door, allowing the plane to pressurize. Unless the latches were fully engaged around the spools and the latching mechanism was "overcenter"—the act that truly "locked" the door—the lockpins could not be driven home, and the closing of the vent door, which was simultaneous with the movement of the lockpins, could not occur, preventing pressurization. It seemed to guarantee safety.

But the design engineers had forgotten Moose Jaw. Or Murphy. It was possible, by releasing the switch on the outside of the door a second or two too soon, to leave the latches only partially around the spools and the latching mechanism *not* "overcenter." Also, binding of the spools or insufficient power to the actuators could result in the same problem. But the most disturbing finding was that even though the latches were not fully closed, the locking handle could still be stowed by applying approximately 120 pounds of force, closing the vent door and letting you assume the lockpins were in place. The baggage handler in Detroit had done it with his knee. And inside, the force that should have pushed the lockpins in behind the latches had been deflected back into a flexible linkage of metal rods—the vent door torque tube and push rods that connect the handle with the vent door and lockpins—that had taken up the slack and tolerances, twisting or bending just enough to get the handle stowed. This deflection of the metal also forced the vent door closed and pushed a small striker against the cockpit light indicator switch, turning off the warning light. *The warning light—the flight crew's only indication of the door's integrity— gave them a false signal.*

The NTSB had blamed the "improper engagement of the latching mechanism" as the probable cause and had been able to explain the mystifying sequence of events experienced aboard Flight 96.

As the aircraft had climbed, it had pressurized normally. At 11,750 feet, the pressure differential acting on the improperly latched cargo door had built to 4.5 psi, a force of approximately 5 tons. That had been enough to push the door open and fling it violently into the 260-knot slipstream where, torn off its hinges, it struck the horizontal stabilizer—the tail.

The hole in the fuselage allowed the aft cargo compartment to depressurize in a rush of air that hurled out the coffin. And now, with too little venting between the cargo hold and the cabin to equalize pressure, the huge volume of compressed air trying to burst out of the cabin pushed down on the floor with 4.5 psi. The floor could only take about 3 psi. It could not take the load, and collapsed, taking three seats and the cocktail bar with it. The cabin air escaped, like a tire blowout, and peripheral air, equally wild to escape containment, rushed into the cabin from above the ceiling, knocking down the panels . . . from the other cargo holds, hurling the galley hatch open, bursting through the service lift door, and throwing up the dust and grit that collects in any cockpit, creating the brief sandstorm that had blinded the captain. The cockpit door blew open. Air, sand, and hats gushed into the cabin. Air from everywhere raced down the cabin to escape through the hole in the shell. And as the air rushed out, the pressure and temperature dropped, and water vapor condensed, forming fog. *Explosive decompression.* Alarming, but not lethal. Yet.

What had threatened the flight was the jamming and severing of the control cables that ran through holes in the floor beams.

After *Windsor,* NTSB member Isobel Burgess had flown to the scene and had come home shocked by the extent of the damage, and by the close call. A special meeting of the board had been called to act on recommendations made by the Bureau of Aviation Safety, and these were sent out within ten days. The board recommended that the door be modified so that it would be "physically impossible to position the external locking handle and vent door to their normal door locked positions unless the locking pins are fully engaged." Chuck Miller, concerned with the more serious problem of floor collapse, added a recommendation that Douglas undertake a *study* of more venting between the cabin and cargo hold to preclude catastrophic pressure differentials in case of explosive decompression. The board, aroused, went further and recommended that Douglas do more than a study, that they *install* adequate venting.

It would be expensive. The industry claimed it might cost $250,000 to retrofit each plane and would keep planes out of service while it was being done. Miller had fundamental concerns about the whole door/floor/pressure relationship in the DC-10; but, in the real world, he knew the major modifications would not be made. He was right; they were not.

But he assumed the FAA would issue an AD to force correction of the immediate problem—the door. The NTSB waited for the AD that never materialized. He still didn't understand why the FAA had let Douglas get away with simply a Service Bulletin on something so vitally safety related. If his bureau had followed up more vigorously, could they have forced the issue? Questions were always easier in hindsight.

The first response to *Windsor* had been the peephole —the one-inch diameter peephole, subject of Service Bulletin 52-35, with caution placards, stenciled on in English near the operating panel beside the door, beside the locking handle and beside the peephole. The placards told the operator not to force the vent door handle. One read: "CAUTION: VERIFY LATCH LOCKPINS ENGAGED." The placard by the peephole said, rather primitively: LOCKPINS ENGAGED—SYSTEM SAFE; LOCKPINS NOT ENGAGED—SYSTEM UNSAFE. Placards did not inspire confidence in safety professionals. And neither the peephole nor placards corrected the problem. They still left lots of room for Murphy.

Miller's awful fear now was that *Windsor* might have been a dress rehearsal for a tragedy that should never have been staged. If it *was* the door . . . then, in the Windsor Incident report his own bureau had produced, they had all held the script for *Paris* in their hands.

When Miller and Sweet arrived in Paris Wednesday morning, March 6, they made a courtesy call to the U.S. embassy, then spent the morning at the offices of the French civil investigative group, their Gallic counterparts. They listened to the air traffic control tapes, then Miller told them about *Windsor*.

Early in the afteroon, he and Dreifus visited René Lemaire, who, as chief of the Inspection General of Civilian Aviation, had been named president of the Commission of Inquiry—the *Enquête*. They were told that the cargo door found at St. Pathus was now being kept in the gendarmerie headquarters at Le Bourget airport, under heavy guard, but that the Americans might see it. Briefly.

Immediately, the entire American team rendezvoused at Le Bourget for a swift examination—men from the NTSB, the FAA, McDonnell Douglas, and General Electric, the builder of the engines.

The door had been broken into two pieces as it had been flung upward on its hinges against the side of the hull, and there was "much deformation of the door structure." But trained eyes had been able to pick up some startling information. The latches were *not* locked overcenter, and at least one lockpin was against the side of the latch, rather than behind it in the locked position. Like *Windsor*. And something important was missing: a small metal plate.

Bill Weston was the first of the NTSB team to spot it, and he told Doug Dreifus. The plate should have been attached to the vent door torque tube that, coupled with rigging adjustments, increased the force required to close the handle from 120 to 440 pounds, making it virtually impossible for the handle to be stowed by force, as the Detroit baggage handler had done. It should have been installed on the Turkish hull in the Douglas plant, before delivery. It had been the subject of Douglas's Service Bulletin 52-37, which had been issued three weeks after, and in direct response to, the Winsor Incident. Following hard on the heels of the peep-hole, it was a far more positive modification than a dollhouse window.

Could the support plate have come off in the crash? Eyes narrowed to the point where three bolts should have attached the plate to the torque tube, to see if they had been sheared off. There were no signs of bolts. There were no signs, even, of bolt holes. They had never been drilled. The plate had never been attached!

They did spot some mysterious file marks, though, where the plate should have been. Had someone started, then stopped? Why? And who?

That Wednesday night, the American team met to discuss the status of their investigation. Doug Dreifus had pulled Miller aside earlier to tell him about the missing plate. With Dreifus chairing the meeting, Miller sat back and waited for the McDonnell Douglas men to report on the missing plate. They didn't mention it. But he knew that "it's normal for people to get a little bashful about admitting what's wrong." He had done the same thing for Chance Vought when he went out on crashes of navy planes his company had built. They had put "a hell of a lot of blood, sweat, and tears into this thing," and with product pride and corporate loyalty so strong at Douglas, he was not surprised at the reticence, and saw no conspiracy in it. But this was too vital to hide. He began to prod a bit. A Douglas representative finally admitted that, yes, the plate was missing. The plate that *could* have prevented the door from being improperly closed.

In Washington, in the offices of the Senate Commerce Committee in the baroque Old Senate Building, Robert Ginther knew about the missing plate almost as soon as Miller did. A handsome young ex-TV newscaster who had been plucked from Seattle by Senator Warren Magnuson, the committee chairman, Ginther was the staff man who drafted new legislation and staged public hearings on aviation issues. His job, the job of all the

Senate oversight committees, was to watchdog the big government agencies to make sure they were operating within the laws passed by Congress. As counsel for the aviation subcommittee, he kept his eye on the FAA. Now he was making the phone calls that always followed a major crash. He needed to get initial reactions from the investigators as to the cause to get a sense of whether or not his committee might have to leap into action as public advocate of air safety. He got hold of the men in Paris, learned that there was a strong feeling that *Paris* was a carbon copy of *Windsor,* with which he was familiar. He was told about the missing plate. Instantly, he could see "the accident posed a very fundamental policy question in terms of our oversight responsibilities for civil aviation, mainly, *What had the FAA done after the 1972 incident to insure that such an incident would not occur again?"* He talked to Miller and began to call other contacts at the NTSB and the FAA.

He had touched a nerve. The NTSB had always welcomed and used the hearings as a way to blow their frustrations over their own powerlessness. But the FAA had not always been so talkative. Now, however, FAA men were pouring out a story of scandal, anger, and frustration as if he were their psychiatrist; as if they had been waiting for a way to vent it without losing their jobs. It was the decision to go with a Service Bulletin after Windsor that they wanted to talk about. "It was clear that there was a great deal of unhappiness in the FAA itself over the way this was handled. I think it was fair to say that most of the career FAA people thought that a serious error had been made when John Shaffer, then administrator of the FAA, would not go ahead with the AD." It would be an explosive hearing.

Politically, there had been a special agony to the Paris crash. It had been a humiliating, flagrantly visible failure of an American product abroad—a product that, with agriculture and armament, was one of the few positive elements in the rapidly deteriorating U.S. balance of payments picture.

Now, pricked into action by what was being learned

from the inside, by the numbers killed, by letters pouring in from a frightened public quickly learning a confusing new language of lockpins and torque tubes as they read the newspapers, the aviation subcommittee began to gear up for public hearings. The hearings would be televised nationally and well-covered by the press. Ginther kept in touch with key aviation reporters.

The hearings were scheduled for March 26 and 27, just three weeks after the crash. Noisy, crowded, and with old campaign posters still on the walls, the Commerce Committee offices now became a madhouse. With Ginther stage-managing, he and his small staff worked until 3 and 4 o'clock in the morning. They invited senior NTSB and FAA people for informal chats; got Arvin Basnight, head of the FAA's western regional office that had certificated the DC-10, on the phone; chatted with John Shaffer; lined up Douglas president John Brizendine as a witness. They would lead off with Chuck Miller.

"Our real mission at that point was to establish a scenario for the hearing; that is, structure the witnesses in such a way that the story would come out in an orderly, chronological fashion, and make sure . . . that the questions were posed in such a way that the answers would become part of the record.

"I knew exactly what the hearings were going to produce." Millions of Americans might think they were watching history being made spontaneously before their eyes. They would, in fact, be watching a ritual exorcism of institutional evil; a collective form of purge and catharsis that was part of the remarkable American capacity for self-reform. A mighty metal bird would be laid on the altar, slashed open, and its vital systems held up and made to yield answers, like the dripping heart of a young lamb. In our culture, answers were found not by looking inward or upward, but by looking into the guts of a machine.

Ginther and Miller knew that the disgust and anger could not be sustained for long, that moral indignation would have to be exploited fast. It is generally known that any improvements in safety that are going to result from a crash will happen in the first few months. The hearings would have to be powerful.

Miller knew he would have to be back for them. After two days in Paris, he sensed that, for him, the action was shifting to Washington, where things were moving fast. He must report his findings to the board and prepare to testify at the hearings. And though the French would not permit him to say much about the progress of the investigation, it would be an opportunity to get *Windsor* and his concerns about interference with the NTSB on the record. It would give him a national forum.

He flew back to Washington on Thursday. His departure from Paris shortly after noon was a scene from *The French Connection*. As he raced, late, to the airport to catch a Pan American flight, he had the driver pull up to a curb at the terminal and wait for a rendezvous with Doug Dreifus. Dreifus's infinite resources were being taxed to their limits getting customs clearances for a small package. He rushed to the rendezvous and stuck the package into Miller's hands.

As Miller ran through the terminal, he thought to himself, "Wouldn't it be stupid if someone thought we were a bunch of terrorists and decided to start shooting?" He made sure the Pan American agent was leading the way.

The Pan Am crew, knowing Miller's mission and having a stake in helping to get the precious little package back to the United States, held the plane for him. Tucked safely under his arm was the digital Flight Data Recorder that, on one-quarter-inch magnetic tape, held the flight record of the doomed plane. In Washington, he would slip it into the hands of one of his waiting staff—the next stage in the relay—and she would run to a Northwest Airlines plane, fly to Seattle, and deliver the tape to the manufacturer for readout. There, in Sunstrand's facilities, the four tracks of digital data would be translated under the supervision of NTSB, FAA, and French specialists, and returned in great haste and secrecy to the French. They would have the readout by Friday. Combined with the data from the cockpit voice recorder that the French would transcribe, this data would permit investigators to refly every foot and second of the flight.

As the Paris crash swept across the Atlantic to be examined by Congress and litigated by lawyers, the disorder of the forest fell away. The biggest, most complex, most potentialy significant crash of all time was being slipped into the system. And this new phase would scarcely be touched by the human agony of Ermenonville.

But in France, Lannier and Dérobert still cleaned up and tried to identify. All over the world, families were still numb and unsatisfied. For them, there would be no such ordered focus, no ceremonial release, until May, when they finally came to Paris for a unique and stirring event.

Chapter Thirteen

"Let the Earth of France Be Light..."

So FAR EVERYTHING was quiet. But as a thousand family members from all over the world filed into Thiais cemetery, murmuring together in somber little groups, Peter Martin grew apprehensive. He feared that the sight of one another might trigger the crowd, releasing the rage and frustration pent up inside over the last two difficult months. One woman screaming with sorrow or one jet roaring overhead might set off mass hysteria, send them tearing at authorities, at the flower-covered crypts that hid the coffins, at cameramen. They might attack the Turkish Airlines uniform or even each other, as latent national hatreds, too, burst into violence. He watched as they filed toward the seats set out on the large grassy plot.

Still actively concerned with the human problems on behalf of the airline, he had been working toward this moment for two months, and the concern had begun to build as the day drew near. It had never been attempted before. A global gathering of the bereaved for a burial service of the unidentified dead of a plane crash. The idea had taken root during the early chaotic days and had grown as the sheer, unprecedented enormity of the tragedy had been revealed. There had been a shared feeling among families, embassies, the French authorities, and the airline that this most terrible of all plane crashes must be marked in some special way. That the intolerable disorder of the forest must be met with a

159

powerful display of order if peace were ever to replace the inner turmoil; if dignity were ever to be restored to the dead. Individual grief had gnawed at the heart. If they could find the right collective expression, grief could gain nobility, as France, England, Turkey, America, and Japan had all learned at war.

There was never any question that, in crisis, a traditional religious ceremony was wanted, one that must somehow accommodate every one of the major faiths: Christian, Jewish, Buddhist, Muslim, Hindu. A form of service must be drawn up that would satisfy each group. And arrangements must be made to coordinate the gathering of more than a thousand people from twenty-four countries at a precise hour in a cemetery near Orly.

The delicate job of developing the service fell to the French Ministry of the Interior's Bureau des Cultes, the government's bureau of religions, and to its director M. Jouffrey. The logistical job, and the expense, of gathering the families at Thiais cemetery was Turkish Airlines', and their representative Peter Martin's. Both Jouffrey and Martin worked actively with the embassies.

Jouffrey's apparently impossible job was to satisfy the religious requirements of the five major religions and to let each say its piece in its own language within an allotted total time of one hour. There were three different Christian sects alone: Catholic, Protestant, and Orthodox.

For weeks, consular representatives carrying briefcases moved past the armed guards at the imposing Ministry of the Interior on the rue des Saussaies. For Macadam Clark the incessant meetings merged into a blur of "muftis, Parsees, and rabbis," as each hammered out "what his bit should be." Thrust into this crucible of ecumenism, the men debated the sticky theological questions with the intellectual zeal of medieval scholastic philosophers. They tussled over the sensitive hierarchical question of "how much time each should have to do his bit." Christian . . . 15 minutes. Buddhist . . . 10. Hindu . . . 5? Or 7? And in what order should they speak? The service was finally reduced to a precise

54 minutes, which seemed more a dream than a possibility.

A date was always uncertain. The English, hanging on hopes that there would be an early ceremony, could not forgive the French their lack of certainty. But the French had wanted as many identifications as possible before setting the date. And they had other countries to deal with. At first, the Japanese had pressed to have their dead buried in the forest at Ermenonville, though French law prohibits burial in a national forest. The Japanese had been relentless since the day of the crash in having their traditions satisfied and, though always polite and cooperative, had caused delays.

Martin called again on Pickford's, the travel agency that had coordinated all the travel arrangements to Senlis, to arrange transport and accommodations for the English. A golden yellow Tristar jet was chartered—Lockheed's wide-body L-1011. Many, terrified and appalled at the thought of flying the same sort of plane on the same route and to the same airport as the doomed DC-10, could not face the flight. For them, there was a special train and Channel ferries. Coaches were booked. He hired a Japanese travel agent to make arrangements for the many families who would fly from Japan. A tight-knit culture, they preferred to stay in the same hotel and to eat Japanese food together. Because of the great distance, they would stay for a week, with all bills, even taxis, paid for by Turkish Airlines.

One of the most delicate decisions that had to be made was whether there would be actual burial of the coffins of the unidentified remains at the time of the service. For families who had had no identification, the act of seeing the coffin buried had become an imperative. Shirley Backhouse "couldn't have a sense of reality" until she'd buried Steve. She was infuriated at word from Mrs. Hartles that the burials would not be held on the day of the ceremony, but would be held later, quietly, with no one present but embassy representatives.

The French knew what the burial would be like.

161

There would be approximately fifty coffins, into which the decaying bits and pieces of the more than two hundred still unidentified would have been indiscriminately tossed, with no possible way of associating flesh with a name. Holding the last of the human residue of Ermenonville, the coffins would be buried in a common grave at the northeast corner of the Thiais cemetery. The process of burial would be noisy, mechanical, and very long, with earthmoving equipment and workmen shoveling dirt over the layers of coffins. It was felt that the experience would be a scarring one for the families; that the burial of nameless coffins in that brutal way would give no more sense of finality to the deaths than would a dignified burial service.

Shirley Backhouse did not agree. She raged, too, at the word *symbolic,* which Mrs. Hartles had used in her letter describing plans for the service, and had shot off a Telex asking, "What is this 'symbolic memorial service' and 'coffins will be placed in the grave at a later time with due reverence'? This is not the type of burial we were informed would be taking place. I have had my *own* memorial service for my husband, J. S. Backhouse. As his widow, I insist on seeing the coffins placed in the grave and buried. We are standing by for an immediate reply."

For her, and for the other vocal spokesmen, anger was reaching a crescendo. She hated the idea of the service and burial at Thiais. "It's so near to Orly. To have the site so close to the airport where the plane took off is a dreadful thing. Someone with no insight at all has done this. Jets will be screaming overhead even during the memorial service. It would be inhuman to subject relatives of those who have died to this experience."

Families were roused by rumors that the monument would be placed beside an already existing one in the forest that commemorated ten people killed in an airship crash during the early days of flying. They wanted their monument as near as possible to the site of the DC-10 crash, for many felt that the "essences" of the dead were in the forest. Tension built as families waited every day for the confirmation of the date for the service. A family from Bury felt "the entire blame for lack of cooperation lay with the British embassy, who, as far as we could find out, were completely ineffectual and whose attitude seemed to be 'Oh, keep quiet, and perhaps it will go away.' "

Shirley Backhouse, with pressure building to the bursting point, lashed out at Mrs. Hartles as "the most inhuman person I have ever met." Mainly, she just wanted Steve buried. "I knew that he hadn't been identified. But at the same time, there has got to be something *final*." She finally blew. The date of May 9 had been announced for the service, then never confirmed. Desperate for a firm date, she began her campaign of telegrams and Telexes. Unsatisfied with replies, she drew up in rage and wrote her petition demanding a firm date for the burial service and opposing the Thiais site. The press picked up the story and broadcast her plea for more names across England. Calls and letters of support poured in. The phone and doorbell never stopped ringing. She had become a clearinghouse for others' frustrations, a spokesman "for all the things they couldn't say themselves."

A Jewish family wanted her to help them get consecrated ground. Gary Ryan and his wife called, supporting the petition and eager to start a committee to organize the monument. The monument meant so little to those who had had a coffin come home; but for the Ryans and Backhouses, it had become a towering priority. It would be all they would ever have to visit. Over the phone, they arranged the first meeting of an international committee, a committee that would disband as soon as a suitable monument had been raised in the forest, perhaps by the first anniversary of the crash. There would be a battle with the French over cost and the use of a French sculptor. But they would fight for simple Cornish stone, carved by an Englishman.

For the first time since Steve's death, Shirley Backhouse was feeling the fiery energies they had always

163

sparked in each other. In a chic suit and dark pillbox hat set firmly at the front of her head, she marched to the French embassy with her petition on April 21. She did not see the French ambassador. "More fobbing off," she thought. But she gave his press officer the message: "If you don't do something and get a definite date for burial, the French Revolution will have *nothing* on what the English will come across and do!"

The date was confirmed. May 9. Peter Martin's fortieth birthday. The massive plan that had been developing over the past two months was now put into effect.

In Bury St. Edmunds, the same encircling care that had supported the families from the beginning closed around them again. Only three of the bodies had been returned, and eighty mourners headed for France by train, coach, and plane. As they were shepherded from hand to hand, from Bury to Thiais, every worrisome detail was taken care of by the rugby club, by Pickford's, by Bury's sister town of Compiègne, by the Racing Club of Paris.

It eased Jim Savidge's passage to the land of his "brethren across the sea." He had been violently sick on the North Sea in 1938 and had never crossed the Channel. He had "no love of going to France." He and his wife were whisked by chartered coach to the Channel, ferried to Calais, and driven to Compiègne. The mayor of Compiègne had invited all of the Bury visitors to use the town as the stopping point on their journey, and the Savidges spent the night in the hotel of the quaint ancient town. It was like staying with old friends. After the big memorial service, they would return to Compiègne for an intimate memorial service in the Compiègne church. It would lack the polish and grandeur of Thiais. People would nudge each other with elbows as bits were forgotten and mistakes were made. But it would touch the Savidges deeply.

Sue Ellis had flown over in the golden Tristar and had been impressed with the dignity of their arrival in France. They walked to the Pavillion d'honneur along the same red carpet she had seen the British Prime Minister stroll on television just a few weeks before. Two soldiers stood at attention at the entrance to the circular building, and the flags were at half-mast. It gave her the same sense of a loss larger than her own that she'd had driving through Bury the morning after the crash. They were served tea and refreshments, exited out the other side of the building onto waiting buses, and were driven to Thiais.

As Stephen Mitchell had boarded in London, he had thought how ironic it was to see this sad, somber group filing aboard the festive plane, painted yellow and mauve to put package-tour travelers in a holiday mood as they headed for the sun. He had dreaded the flight.

A group of 1,200 mourners walked past stately rows of poplars and *marronniers* to the site of the service in the heart of the cemetery. Flags of the grieving nations were muffled in black. It was a chill but sunny day, and people, dressed universally in dark clothes, moved like a gray wash across the fresh spring grass. The dais was set up on a grassy knoll that had been rolled up over the white stone crypts that held the coffins, disguising the repository. The religious men ascended the dais, wearing the saffron, black, and white robes of their faiths. The Muslim priest flown in from Turkey had rushed, almost late, to the service, delayed by his flight. A Buddhist priest had come from Japan, wearing his white gloves and carrying the tambourine and stick that would sound at intervals through the service, unsettling the English. From India, a Hindu priest had come.

Jouffrey had begun to despair that they would all fit on the *estrade,* the dais. Each day as the numbers had grown, he would call and have the dais made larger. Twenty-five people filled it as the service began. As Ruth McClendon, American consul in Paris, saw the numbers moving onto the dais, she thought to herself, "This is going to be god-awful, and this is going to take three hours."

Stephen Mitchell was keenly aware that this was not *his* service. Prudence's coffin had come home. And he had felt a sense of release and finality at her cremation, as he had at his father's. He had come because he

165

sensed, by now, the pivotal role he would play in aviation's most complex piece of litigation. An irreligious man who found the robes and trappings of the holy men as "bloody silly" as the gowns and wigs of British courts, he had come as a lawyer. He watched with wry amusement as, one by one, a black-suited man would break from the unified block of Japanese, run to the broad center aisle, and snap a photograph of the group. The complete tourists, even at Thiais!

Shirley Backhouse went to the service still angry and bleak. "I felt very lost that day. Everyone had their personal grief. There was very little communication." She was disturbed by the Buddhist gongs. And she could hear planes. "As soon as it started, a hell of a jumbo jet went right over." But the rage was largely spent. It had been vented on the embassy. And she found herself being caught up in the words that were coming from the dais at this strange, sad, historic service, the service that was her formal good-bye to Steve.

"Let the earth of France be light for those which it embraces. France considers them as its own children." The words had been spoken with gentle compassion by France's senior transport minister. *"Let the earth of France be light for those which it embraces."*

Cameramen were stopped in their aggressive hunt for front-page anguish by the words, and tears rimmed their eyes. Stoic fathers felt themselves moved in a powerful new way that transcended the early harsh sorrow. A Muslim *hoca* chanted the haunting, lonely wail that comes from the minaret at sunset, reaching out into the desert. As Stephen Mitchell listened, the lawyer fell away and feeling welled up. He was in touch again with a lovely girl with red hair.

The voice of an Indian priest flowed over the crowd, speaking an English so strange that the Savidges could scarcely understand him. But it didn't matter. Carrying over the chill and impersonal graveyard, it was lyrical and full of love. He had begun with, "Dear brothers and sisters. . . ." To Jim Savidge, who had fiercely guarded his Suffolk loyalties from foreign intrusion, "it was incredible. Whether you were an Englishman or a

Chinaman, you could understand it." He was moved by the "sheer music" of the voice, "a voice that somehow was comforting *whatever* he was saying. Whether you understand it or not, the sympathy was there. . . . He gave you half a lift." Perhaps the Savidges could begin to bear Robert's death on Gallic, not Suffolk, soil.

It was going smoothly. There had been no hysteria. And the last words of the service had been said within the allotted hour. It had taken 54 minutes. But the next phase would be the most difficult part for the families. Mourners would move from their chairs and file past the flower-banked crypts. They would pass within feet of the coffins, but would not be able to see or touch them. They could only file by and lay flowers. It would be the moment of greatest stress, when the symbolic death of the service would suddenly collapse into the fact that wives' or children's flesh might be within an arm's reach.

Peter Martin watched closely. Several Turkish women threw themselves on the flowers, wailing with loss, and were helped from the crypts, weeping. The Japanese, holding pictures of the dead young men, moved silently, laying flowers. Someone had offered to take Shirley Backhouse's flowers from her, but she had held on to them firmly. She laid them herself at the base of the crypt. For her husband, Bryan, Sue Ellis had brought flowers shaped like a rugby ball. Worked into the flowers were the words *Number One,* his nickname. People sobbed. A few were held by the shoulders and gently moved away by women with red armbands. But control and dignity held. There would be no hysteria.

For the first time, Peter Martin relaxed, looked around, and experienced the remarkable event that he had helped to create out of chaos. Twelve hundred random people from all over the globe, most with no connections before March 3. They would all make their way home within the next few days and continue their adjustments in private family groups. But they had been inescapably bound by the same tragic event. The ceremony had focused on that unity. Now, regardless of color, faith, language, or loneliness, they all knew that

167

they shared the same grief. They knew, as Bury's widows and parents had known from the first few hours, that they were not alone.

The crash was not over yet. As a legal case, abstracted from the fact by lawyers who had never even been to Senlis, the momentum building in Los Angeles might continue for years.

Martin would continue to be involved in it, he knew, on an almost daily basis, until it was finished. The families, too, would not be fully released until the suit was over. But he felt certain that the service had been a great catharsis for them. Some of the most savage wounds would now begin to heal. It had been an unforgettable day.

The crash had occurred in the bleak late winter when the English, restless with the damp, drab weather, turn to the sun like plants—to Spain and Turkey. Now it was May. Martin noted that blossoms were just beginning to come out on the trees at Thiais. The British strolled back to their buses to eat box lunches. Some sat on the grassy square outside the cemetery. Families began to chat with each other, to exchange experiences with relieved amiability. And from the black and gray and grief, a curious, pleasant picnic atmosphere began to grow.

On his return to Bury, the rugby club captain Chris Tilbrook announced that "all we want to do now is forget."

On June 21, forty-three days later, the English and Turkish consuls in Paris stood silently by the gaping common grave at the far end of the cemetery, observing the burial. Heavy equipment had dug out the hole, and puffing cemetery workers heaved down the coffins and spread the dirt shoved over each layer by a bulldozer. The Turkish official left after a few hours. The British consul stayed for four, and it still was not finished. As he turned to leave, there were only two other observers left, the men he knew represented one of the British families. They would go back and tell Shirley Backhouse that Steve had been buried properly at last.

PART III

The Cost of A Crash

Chapter Fourteen

Pacing Off the Cost

THOUSANDS OF FEET had walked the devastation of Ermenonville. They had tramped through the stretchers; kicked the debris, searching for scraps of a son's clothing; come with cameras, looking for blood. They had paced off the site to measure point of impact and length of swath.

Peter Martin had paced off the cost.

As solicitor for the airline's insurers, he had tramped the site with the experts to get a preliminary grasp of what they were going to have to pay. It would clearly be the most expensive crash in history. There could be as many as 334 individual passenger claims brought by literally thousands of relatives and dependents. There could be a hull suit to replace the lost plane. Regardless of who was at fault—the airline, manufacturer, pilot, maintenance men—it was ultimately the insurers who paid. The London aviation insurance market. Lloyd's syndicates and the insurance companies—a society of men who, if they were to summarily cancel all policies, could paralyze international transport. Few ships would move. Few planes would fly. For taking off without adequate insurance coverage was a risk no airline would be willing to take. It was a risk heightened by the wide-body jets. The industry knew that the passenger claims from the loss of one fully loaded jumbo jet could, in one accident, easily exceed the entire amount paid out by Lloyd's after the San Francisco earthquake—$100 million. Insurers did spread the risk around by *reinsuring,* by selling parts of the policy to other underwriters, "laying it off" all over the world, creating a family tree that stretched out into an almost infinite number of branches, some of which curled back to the leader at the top of the tree. For a leader might often buy back portions of the risk from another syndicate far down the insurance tree. By spreading the risk in this way, there had so far been no risk so big that the market couldn't handle it.

But since the 747s had gone into service in 1970, there had been a certain nervousness at Lloyd's. An accident had been expected in the first year. But there had been no wide-body crash until the very end of 1972, when an L-1011 came down in the Everglades. And there, 77 of the 176 aboard had survived. There had been no test yet of the thesis that, with 400 people aboard, with the luxuriant growth of product liability and negligence suits in California, and a growing global eagerness to sue, the risk might be getting *too* great. Insurers could simply raise premiums to cover higher risks. But was there a limit to the premiums manufacturers or airlines could pay? At Lloyd's, they had discussed it over lunch in the Captain's Room, as they waited for the crash—the test—they knew would come.

Now it had come. On a Sunday, when Lloyd's of London's traditonal ritual of disaster could not be played out. The Room, modern successor to Lloyd's Coffee House where London's maritime insurance market was born over cups of coffee in the seventeenth century, was closed. The aviation underwriters, a nouveau breed created in 1911 with the writing of the first aircraft risk, were home with their families or out for Sunday lunch. The famous Lutine Bell was silent, the bell that is as symbolic to the insurance world as the Liberty Bell to Americans. It might have rung for the DC-10, sounding the one gong that signaled bad news, the reverberating gong that still made the most seasoned underwriter shiver. For the sound carried with it images of great sailing vessels smashed on the rocks . . . crippled steamers sinking in the China Sea with all hands and cargoes of tea, furs, silks, and copra squandered

172

and spilled into the oceans. The Lutine Bell had rung the death knell for the thousands of ships, captains, and crews that had been offered up over the past several centuries to the prosperity of the world's most impressive thalassocracy: the British Empire.

There was no red-robed speaker calling the aviation brokers to the caller's rostrum. No clerk from the intelligence department sitting at a lectern in the center of the room with a sharpened, ink-dipped quill from the swannery at Abbotsbury in hand, scratching the news of lost ships into the huge leather-bound Loss Book. No terse description of the crash posted on blue paper on the casualty board. No murmurs of shock and hurried consultation.

That would have to wait until Monday, when the Room's vast marble-columned spaces would fill with its traditional sounds of transactions, stamping of blotters, scratching of quills, flipping of pages of *Jane's All the World's Aircraft*. Then, the echoes would be softened by a sea of dark wool suits dressing one of the last legitimate bastions of British supremacy.

But the insurers had a second line of ritual, a far less public pattern of action that was put into effect the instant word of the crash reached London. Unlike the shocked families blundering into the news, they had a tight script to follow. On planes to Paris and in cars to Ermenonville, their lawyers and investigators sped to the scene to protect their client's interest. Faster than the much-publicized United States official GO team heading for the wreckage to find technical cause, they rushed to find out what the losses were and to do what they could to help. It is ironic that in pursuing the interests of their investors, they were one of the only forces organized to deal with the human residue, both living and dead, of a major crash.

Peter Martin had been one of the first to get underway. His wife, Elizabeth, called upstairs to tell him the minute she heard. "Peter, I've just heard on the radio that a Turkish Airline's plane has crashed near Paris with a large loss of life." Just two months earlier, he'd flown to Izmir to investigate a Turkish crash that had killed seventy-three. She guessed he'd be involved in this one, too. And there would be no Sunday lunch with friends today, as they'd planned.

Peter Martin's appearance, like his accent, had the stylish impeccability—the civility—of England at its traditional best. With thick dark hair brushed back, horn-rimmed glasses aiding the impression of lively scholarly interest in everything around him, he did not look a man turning forty. Or a man who tired sometimes of his role as a "glorified undertaker."

Beaumont and Son, the firm he had joined as a partner in the early sixties, were solicitors for many of the Lloyd's syndicates and companies that insured most of the world's aircraft and airlines. Flying out, day or night, to the Sudan, Thailand, India, Yugoslavia, he was one of that slightly specialized breed of crash-followers who brought whatever sense of order and continuity could be brought to the chaos and disorder that followed a crash. If a ceremonial form of aviation disasters exists, then Martin and the insurers, lawyers, and investigators who work together in the aftermath are its high priests.

Upon hearing of the crash that Sunday, he rang David Dann.

Dann, a sandy-haired man with ruddy complexion, square jaw, and the speech of an Oxford classics scholar, was claims manager of the Ariel Syndicate at Lloyd's, the lead underwriters on the Turkish risk. He and his syndicate head led the insurances on the Paris crash and would have to authorize any payments on behalf of the airline to the families of the people killed. He had already heard the news and had been trying to get in touch with Martin. Even on Sundays, Lloyd's communication system passes on information of losses to leading underwriters. Dann directed Martin to get on the first available flight to Orly.

He was not the only representative of insurance interests on that flight. He saw Jim Sommerville, an aeronautical engineer with Airclaims Limited, who would be there to report on the hull loss.

When Martin arrived at Orly airport he noted an unexpected calm. Apparently the airport hadn't missed a beat. Flights were leaving on schedule. People were checking baggage and buying candy bars.

There was one unhappy center of activity. In the small booth at the end of a long counter, at least a dozen girls of the Aeroport de Paris were busy with two telephones and the passenger list, helping with queries about passengers on the crashed plane.

He rushed to the Turkish Airlines' offices on the first floor. The offices were two small rooms, for Orly was not a major terminal for the Turks. It was simply a service stop on the way from Istanbul to London.

At Orly, the Turks were understaffed and under enormous pressure. Caught up in the largest crash in history, they found themselves with over twenty nationalities involved and hundreds of families to notify; and all they had to work from was an incomplete, inaccurate list prepared as last-minute passengers had shifted reservations and rushed aboard. Names had been hastily scribbled on some of the tickets when first issued with little attention paid to spelling or initials. And, adding to the chaos, immigration officers do not match passports with tickets; some passengers had boarded on tickets issued in other people's names.

Given the circumstances, Martin was impressed with what he saw going on. Officials of the Aeroport de Paris and policemen were crowding into the room, with journalists pressing in with cameras. But through the confusion, two young French girls, employees of Turkish Airlines, were painstakingly trying to put the passenger list into some kind of alphabetical and national order. *Hokiya* would be Japanese. And *Takashima,* too. *Temizkan,* Turkish. But *Wilcox,* English, perhaps. Or American? Or Canadian? And what of *Wormeer . . . Berg . . .Ortoogetyan?* There were gross misspellings. There were also assumed names, though the people working on the list couldn't know that at the time.

Martin did what he could to help—answering press questions, keeping the Turkish embassy up to date, struggling with the compilation of an accurate passenger list. But he knew he must help Sommerville and Clancey, another insurance man who had joined them, get to the crash site. Fast. And with permission. He tried to find the local chief of police, but he was unavailable on a Sunday afternoon. "Sunday is just about the worst day a crash can occur." He was assured, though, that he could get the necessary *laisser passer* that would let them get through the ring of gendarmes protecting the crash site the next morning.

Above all, identification of the dead and notification of the next of kin must take his attention. From what the police had already told him, it was going to be an impossible task, for the shredding effect had apparently caused mutilation beyond imagination and experience.

"I knew that families really do want to have the bodies of their family members brought back for burial or cremation, especially the Japanese, to whom it is a matter of religion to acquire the individual bodies of their dead." Overseeing the aftermath of crashes in India, Laos, South Vietnam, and Hong Kong had made him sensitive to cultural traditions and family feelings, and he tried to anticipate them. He placed a call to J. H. Kenyon Ltd., London's specialists since the 1930s in burying the dead from aircraft accidents. He knew Kenyon's kept a stock on hand of coffins specially constructed for transport of human remains by air. He doubted the French had any, and this would save time. He ordered the three hundred coffins sent to France. And he asked Kenyon's to activate their own highly sophisticated identification center, with its Telex room, codes, and specialists. They would start collecting dental records and other physical particulars and would send a team to Paris to work with the official identification group—if the French would permit it. A plane was chartered and the coffins moved out of London to Orly during the night.

BEA agreed to activate their accident control center at Heathrow—their Incident Center, as they preferred to call it—and put it to work chalking up names and presumed nationalities and religions on the big blackboards as they came in from Paris on the telephone . . . taking calls and feeding information to the families who

By strange coincidence, a few weeks before the Paris crash, British solicitor Bernard Engler photographed the commanding sight of a Turkish Airlines DC-10 at Heathrow Airport. He would later become actively involved in the litigation.
BERNARD ENGLER

This section of fuselage was the largest remaining section of the plane. JAMES ANDANSON/SYGMA

"Ribs" bared, a portion of the shattered hull rests like a great beached ship in the pine forest of Ermenonville. Impacting at nearly 500 mph, the plane was virtually shredded by the pines as its momentum carried it through one-half mile of forest. SYGMA

Early searchers were met with the site of stripped trees festooned with ghastly ornaments. PARIS MATCH

A large-scale rescue operation involving more than 300 policemen, firemen, soldiers, civil emergency squads and government investigators was in effect within an hour of the crash.
BAJANDE/RAPHO/
PHOTO RESEARCHERS

Commandant Jacques Lannier of the Senlis gendarmerie commanded the site.
THE SUNDAY TIMES/
KELVIN BRODIE

The destructive energies of the crash were appallingly evident at the far end of the site, where the rear engine and nearly 100 bodies had been catapulted. JAMES ANDANSON/SYGMA

A father prays at a spot he believes to be the site of his son's death. SYGMA

The suffering of Japanese families symbolized the global agony created by the catastrophe. With 48 dead, mostly single young men, families flew from Japan to search for familiar belongings.
SIPA

Remains and most personal effects had already been collected in plastic bags and rushed to identification centers.
BAJANDE/RAPHO/PHOTO RESEARCHERS

In a traditional Buddhist ceremony far removed from the technology of the DC-10, Atsuko and Takehiro Higuchi were married just a month before the crash.
PHOTOS SUPPLIED BY THE FAMILIES OF ATSUKO HORIYA AND TAKEHIRO HIGUCHI

Dreams and aspirations of the Higuchis and 344 others ended in this tattered heap of clothing here being ransacked by families trying to assist the French authorities in the desperately difficult job of identification. R. M. MEUNIER/SIPA

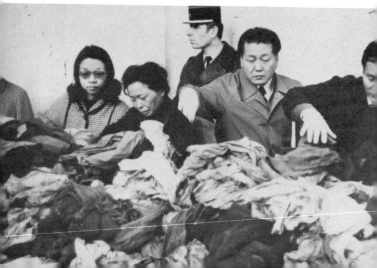

On May 9, 1974, a thousand family members were flown in from all over the world for a memorial service at Thiais cemetery, near Orly airport and site of the common grave for the unidentified dead. Holding a picture of her dead son, a Japanese woman kneels at flower-banked crypts. The unique and moving ceremony had been organized by the French, by Turkish Airlines, and by the embassies of the 24 nations involved in the crash. BAKER/SIPA

The American community in London received a tragic blow. Among the 15 adults and children killed was the Wright family from Berkeley, California. Tom and Fay Wright flank a senior U.S. Air Force officer and Queen Mother Elizabeth at a reception in London.

The house the Wrights renovated in London.

The Wright children, Jackson, Sherry, and Karlaine, were 3 of the 9 students lost from the American School in London.

In Polegate, Harold Barrow and his 3 daughters tried to adjust to the loss of wife and mother Gene Barrow, who had won her weekend trip to Turkey.

Prudence Pratt had been returning from a modeling job in Spain. Her fiancé, Stephen Mitchell, a London solicitor, became liaison between a large number of the British families and the California courts where their lawsuits were brought. Above, Stephen and Prudence. Below, a photograph from Prudence's portfolio.

One of many rugby enthusiasts aboard the flight was Steve Backhouse (left) from the Davenport Rugby Club. His widow, Shirley, shown below with her 3 children, became an articulate spokeswoman for the English families frustrated by the slow resolution of the identification and burial processes, and focused public attention on the unpreparedness of even advanced nations to deal with the human problems that follow a major aircrash.

Personnel of the HMS Ganges *embark on a sponsored walk for the disaster fund launched to aid the families.*

The ancient town of Bury St. Edmunds responded to loss of 18 playing members and officers of its rugby club with an inspiring display of help and moral support for the parents, 10 widows, and 21 children of the young men. Mace-bearers lead the procession from the cathedral where Bury's memorial service drew "old boys" from all over the British Isles.
EAST ANGLIAN DAILY TIMES

Among the dead was the club's chairman, Bryan Ellis, known as "No. 1."
BURY FREE PRESS/
H. J. AYLIFFE

Though five of these men would never take the field again, the club would play an annual memorial game against the Racing Club of Paris, the French team they should have played the afternoon of the crash. The five who died were Robert Savidge, Graham Levet, Brian Arthur (rear, third, fourth, and fifth from right), Richard Coult and Greg Rynsard (front, first and third from right).

The Racing Club sent this wreath to Bury's memorial service.
EAST ANGLIAN DAILY TIMES

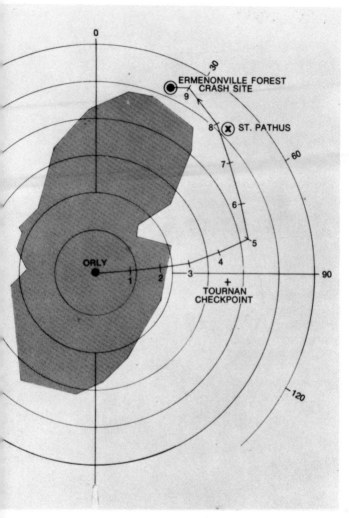

The last nine minutes, as recorded by French radar.

On news of the crash, investigators studied the flight path of the doomed plane and searched for the "black boxes" (left) containing the flight data and cockpit voice recorders which would enable them to reconstruct the entire flight. SYGMA

Investigation quickly focused on a small cargo door (shown below), recovered, with 6 bodies, from freshly plowed fields near the town of St. Pathus, nine miles from the crash site.

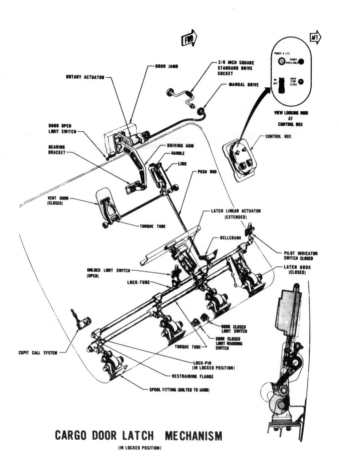

CARGO DOOR LATCH MECHANISM
(IN LOCKED POSITION)

A *is locking mechanism at time of Windsor Incident.*

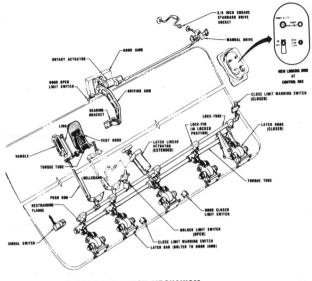

CARGO DOOR LATCH MECHANISM
(LOCKED)

B *is closed-loop system, now required on all DC-10s.*

C *is detail of closed-loop mechanism.*

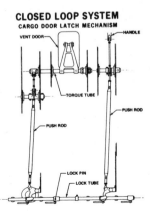

CLOSED LOOP SYSTEM
CARGO DOOR LATCH MECHANISM

The DC-10, powered by 3 high-bypass ratio turbines, each with 40,000 pounds of thrust, would carry up to 380 passengers. Donald W. Douglas, Sr., in dark suit and tie, supervises Cloudster production from the top of the fuselage.
MC DONNELL DOUGLAS

The global village is in large part a product of these 4 planes: facing page: from top to bottom, the legendary DC-3—of the 10,500 built, more than 1,000 are still flying; the DC-4, Douglas's first 4-engine plane, made transoceanic flights routine; the DC-6, with pressurized cabins, greater range and speed, led the explosive growth of air travel after World War II; the DC-7, last piston-engine plane of the DC line, had a 4,900-mile range, 400 mph speeds. Below, Douglas's first and second generation of jets, the DC-8 and the DC-9, first flown in 1958 and 1965 respectively. MC DONNELL DOUGLAS

The birth of a plane. Far more complex than its predecessors, Douglas's first wide-body aircraft was more exhaustively tested than any previous Douglas plane. Above, the wind tunnel test and structure proof test. Below, fuselage sections made in San Diego and wings made in eastern Canada are assembled at the Long Beach plant. MC DONNELL DOUGLAS

Nose to nose, the first two DC-10s are delivered to American and United Airlines on July 29, 1971, two months ahead of schedule. American, which placed the first order for DC-10s, received its gold key 5 minutes ahead of United. At the ceremony FAA administrator John Shaffer presented Douglas with its type certificate. The crash would bring critical scrutiny of certification procedures that had allowed the rear cargo door to be certificated as "failsafe." MC DONNELL DOUGLAS

Near-catastrophic failure of an American Airline's cargo door in flight over Windsor, Canada, did extensive damage to door area, control cables, and surfaces, presaging Paris.
NATIONAL TRANSPORTATION SAFETY BOARD

The -10's mighty tail, showing vital control surfaces, and containerized cargo system that influenced choice of outward-opening cargo doors. MC DONNELL DOUGLAS

For the defense: Above, James M. FitzSimons, New York law-yer representing McDonnell Douglas's lead insurers, the *Ariel* Syndicate at Lloyd's of London. Below, David Dann, *Ariel's* claims manager. BRITISH BROADCASTING CORPORATION

For the plaintiffs: Lawyers representing the largest groups of cases, Lee Kreindler, above, and Stuart Speiser, to his right, both of New York, and (lower left) Gerald C. Sterns of San Francisco.
above right: BLACKSTONE-SHELBURNE, N.Y.
bottom: DONALD JOHNSTON

John C. Brizendine, president of the corporation's Douglas division and former DC-10 program manager.
MC DONNELL DOUGLAS

In his chambers in Los Angeles Federal Courthouse, senior United States district judge Peirson M. Hall works through the mountain of legal paper triggered by aviation's largest and most complex piece of product liability litigation. In his eighties, Hall is noted for innovations that have streamlined the handling of complex transport cases. Though several defendants have been named, legal attack has focused on the DC-10's manufacturer, McDonnell Douglas Corporation. THOM ELDER

A LA MEMOIRE DES VICTIMES
DE LA GRANDE
CATASTROPHE AERIENNE
SURVENUE EN CE LIEU
LE 3 MARS 1974

The monument, raised at the site by an international association of families as a permanent reminder of the agony of Ermenonville—and of the frailties of men and their machines.

were still phoning and coming to Heathrow, desperate for word. Although BEA had no official obligation, they seemed to feel the moral pressure of the fact that it was *their* strike that had caused the crisis that had shifted some two hundred British passengers to the Turkish plane.

Next morning, Martin sped to the forest with his precious *laisser passer*. He had worked with the other insurance men before. Jim Sommerville was there to assess the nature and extent of the hull loss. The hull, the physical body of the DC-10, was insured for $20 million; its owners, Turkish Airlines, would claim that sum to replace the craft. Hulls were the source of terrible battles among insurers as the argument over who or what caused an accident reached crescendo after crescendo. If the insurers paid, they would watch for an opportunity to sue someone else, such as the manufacturer or subcontractor, to get some of their money back.

Vernon Clancey had been called in by the "War Risks" insurers, for if, as suspected at that time, the accident had been caused by a bomb explosion, they would have to pay for hull and passenger claims. Clancey was a renowned chemist and explosions specialist with Burgoyne and Co. Guided by Sommerville, who would identify the parts for him, Clancey would study them for the possibility of explosion. Martin's job was to clear the way through the police squads by explaining what they were doing. It was always a delicate task, for the insurer's men had no official status, and Martin's fluent French and diplomatic manner were essential to help the team get started.

From years of trudging through the ghastly abattoirs of crash sites, they had all learned to coat normal responses with a veneer of dispassion. As he followed them through the wreckage trail, Martin kicked through the debris, saw a foot and thought, "Oh, there's a foot. What a *bloody great* foot!" and moved on. But "the smell, the frightful smell that is always the same" was in his nostrils again.

The smell was there, too, in the decaying Chapel of

St. Pierre in Senlis, where the mutilated flesh was being brought in plastic bags. The town nearest the crash, Senlis had been thrust suddenly into violent activity. The team had gone directly to Senlis after their tour of the site. They looked into, but did not enter, the humble church that had become a temporary repository for the dead.

By Wednesday, Martin felt he'd done everything he could in France. During the first crucial days, he'd supported the airline in maintaining its sense of responsibility and its concern for the surviving families. At a delicate time, when no one yet knew who was to blame for the crash, he'd provided a discreet and cautious legal voice for the airline and its insurers. And with the passenger list almost complete, the result of matching flight coupons against the names on the manifest, he had accomplished his mission. It was time to return to London.

There in the quaint old quarters of Beaumont and Son, it would be his job to orchestrate the airline's response to the crash for as long as it would take—perhaps years. After every crash there was a trickle, sometimes a flood, of solicitors and widows who'd find their way up his creaking old elevator. This was always the hardest part. It was then that he was touched by the cold facts of loss that the maudlin stories in the press never really let you understand. By the time their solicitors came to him, widows had forced their eyes open on their bleak new status. They had lost their anchor, would not have enough money to get along. They came to him for money, for a settlement, though it was inherently un-British to be paid for someone's death. He felt for them and for his own position, which was to give them what he could within the rather inadequate settlement standards payable within the bounds of English law, and by the Warsaw Convention, which limited airline obligations on international flights. It was the limit spelled out in the small print on passengers' tickets, though few ever read it. In this crash, it would pay a maximum of $20,000, the Hague Protocol limits. He knew that with England's inflation rate of over 20 percent a year—Europe's highest—it wasn't enough. A simple calculation made the facts inescapable. And yet he would have to defend the Warsaw Convention even though it paid families a pittance, for it was all that stood between the world's airlines and the staggering death settlements being awarded in U.S. courts. He knew that many would turn to lawsuits to try to get more.

At times like these, he could only fall back on the pathetically inadequate tag *"Dura lex, sed lex,"* "the law is hard, but it is the law." Martin was tired of being cast as villain, as insurers' representatives always were, depriving mothers and children of relief to which they were entitled. And he was growing cynical at the speed with which so many grief-stricken people turned so energetically to legal action, to money, when they had suffered no financial loss. This litigious trend was spreading all over the world; it was a moral disease, in his view, a symptom of degraded values. He despised the delays litigation caused, putting emotional and financial burdens on the families—litigation prolonged intolerably by plaintiff lawyers holding out for extravagant awards of damages, or by defendants determined to hold out on *principle* against what they saw as blackmail. And why were the facts on which liability hinged delayed so often by nations whose investigative reports, if issued at all, were biased, incompetent, and incomplete? The French were among the most advanced in investigative and post-crash procedures. But even their reports took *two years,* or more! In this crash, at least, there was physical accessibility. What if this DC-10 had come down in the Arctic en route to Japan . . . or in the Ethiopian highlands? It could happen some day. And how woefully unprepared the world still was to handle it swiftly and efficiently.

He wished the French well.

And he braced himself for what he already sensed would be the biggest, most complex, most stubbornly fought piece of litigation in aviation history. The test Lloyd's had been waiting for.

Chapter Fifteen

The Lawyers

As SOON AS IT became known that a Turkish Airlines' plane, built in California, carrying citizens of more than twenty countries, and brought down on French soil, possibly by a defectively designed and locked door, lawyers knew it would be a textbook piece of international aviation litigation. Perhaps *the* textbook case. In Washington, California, New York, London, Tokyo . . . Istanbul, they prepared with varying degrees of readiness to deal with it.

By a quirk of fate, Bernard Engler, a Manchester solicitor, had seen a Turkish Airlines' DC-10 at Heathrow just a few weeks before the crash and had taken a picture of it for his son, an airplane buff. Four days after the crash, two widows had come to his firm for advice. A curly-haired enthusiast fueled by boundless, compulsive energies and an eclectic mind, Engler had risen to the challenge.

Like all the lawyers tapped for participation in this most special case, he felt a special urgency, for with the filing of the Mary Hope lawsuit, all were suddenly aware that they had been cast into something very big, for which few were prepared. What path to take? Warsaw? England's Lord Campbell's Act? Or an American lawsuit? Warsaw was macabre! It would limit the English to $20,000. And its vagaries could be appalling. There could be wild fluctuation between the value, in death, of two passengers sitting side by side. A passenger might be worth $10,000, $20,000, or $75,000, depending on where he bought his ticket, what his point of departure and destination were, whether he was going round trip or one way, and whether his trip touched the United States. Since Warsaw had been created in 1929, a series of subsequent amendments, protocols and agreements—the Hague, Montreal, Guatemala—had tried to move its limits up to more realistic levels, but they had only made the treaty more capricious. A carrier might even adhere to Montreal, the American wildcat effort to raise limits, but a passenger might claim its $75,000 limits only if the crashed flight had touched the U.S. Warsaw made death by air a lottery.

The Fatal Accidents Act of 1846—Lord Campbell's Act, as it was called, and the act that governed the size of awards that could be paid in wrongful death cases in England—was at least predictable, but too low to keep families going for long. Enacted at the height of the Industrial Revolution, its words "such damages as they may think proportioned to the injury resulting from such death . . ." seemed loose and liberal enough. But growing from a climate of protection for the emerging industrial system, the words had been interpreted with the spirit of Scrooge. Damages had been effectively limited to the replacement of the breadwinner's income and allowed no damages for human and emotional loss. In America, essentially the same words had been interpreted to allow recovery for a whole range of human factors—loss of love, society, nurturing, affection, and so on. Lord Campbell's Act offered cold comfort to widows and orphans facing England's burgeoning inflation and high cost of living.

The Hope suit, with its $125 million class action, offered an interesting but thoroughly confusing alternative. What was a class action? And was it the only way of gaining access to the American courts, as some of the newspaper stories seemed to suggest?

Engler searched for alternatives.

When the Mary Hope suit burst on England, it confirmed what had already been germinating in Engler's

181

mind: that this was a product liability suit, a case in which the building of a defective airplane might be proved against the manufacturers; a case that could be brought only in the United States. And California, the home of the manufacturer, was the obvious venue for litigation. But Engler needed to know more about it. There was a meeting he could attend, where it would all be explained. Mary Hope's American lawyers were conducting a series of meetings for solicitors in London. Engler was eager to go.

The meetings were welcomed by many of the solicitors as an exciting educational opportunity, a chance to ally themselves and their clients with U.S. Aviation attorneys of the first rank. Others feared the Hope action might be exploitive of Mary Hope. For a letter, immediately labeled "the Mary Hope letter," went out on April under her signature to all the families whose names she had acquired by the publicity, alerting them of her decision to sue in the United States and of the meetings, and suggesting they "Instruct your solicitors to ask for information regarding the legal situation from my American lawyers," whose names and addresses she listed. The letter had been inspired by her concern, Mrs. Hope explained, that English solicitors accustomed to England's three-year statute of limitations might let the one-year California statute of limitations go by; and that some English families, unaware of the possibility of much higher damage awards in the United States, might settle their cases in England for a pittance. For her the meetings were a convenient way of answering all the questions about U.S. lawsuits that had been flooding in to her from solicitors of other families. But there were solicitors who spontaneously resisted the entire action as tastelessly early, aggressive, and . . . un-English, a criticism rebuffed by Mary Hope's New York lawyer Stuart Speiser with, "We didn't go over to be English. We went over there to serve our clients!" Most of all, there was resistance to being swept up, willy-nilly, into something about which most solicitors and their clients knew nothing—the class action. But

182

all were intrigued by the meetings. In the chintz-curtained, antique-furnished offices of international law consultant Robert Gurland, Stuart Speiser sat at a long table with an insurance expert and one of his partners, Donald Madole, who specialized in the technical and liability aspects of the case. Speiser, a smoothly groomed man of abstemious habits, highly disciplined mind, and taut nerves, had created one of the most successful aviation law practices in the United States. The author of his own three-foot shelf of books on aviation law, and a former Liberator pilot and crop duster in Florida, he had built a high-powered team of pilot-lawyers. From offices in the Pan Am Building straddling Grand Central Station, he ran a well-oiled machine that moved cases through an efficient legal assembly line in which the various aspects of a lawsuit —overall strategy, liability, damages—were individually handled by specialists. It was a technique that enabled them to handle routinely the big transport cases that would swamp and bankrupt a small firm.

Speiser came to England with a high reputation for consumer advocacy gained when his firm had represented Ralph Nader in his historic invasion-of-privacy suit against General Motors, fighting and winning the case that tested privacy as a constitutional right. In 1970, they had won a settlement of $425,000 for Nader in the case that would help to finance his consumer activities. Speiser's hand would be further strengthened in *Paris* by Jim Butler, the Los Angeles lawyer who had brought Speiser's firm into the Hope case and who would work with them on *Paris*. Another champion of consumerism, Butler had won a $2.75 million verdict in 1971 in the only thalidomide drug deformity case tried in the United States, a case that had been later settled for an undisclosed amount.

In Don Madole, Speiser had perhaps the most broadly trained of any of the specialists being drawn to the case. Born into the dustbowl despair of a small Kansas town, he had driven himself through a training program that was a "how-to-" for any ambitious young

183

aviation lawyer—he had studied engineering as well as law, had a commercial pilot's license, had worked for American Airlines, the FAA, and the Civil Aeronautics Board handling crash investigation hearings and accident reports, before joining the plaintiff's bar.

In a two-and-a-half-hour presentation by two of the most skillful and successful men in the business, Speiser and Madole introduced the English to all the basic issues: Warsaw, choice of law, punitive and moral damages, contingency fees, class actions. Engler listened attentively.

The Hope action, they explained, would be brought in California because McDonnell Douglas had their factory there, and because California juries were sympathetic to large accident claims. In wrongful death actions there, damage could range from $100,000 to well over $1 million. Speiser's estimate was, in fact, conservative, for within nine months of the London meeting, Chicago-based aviation lawyer John J. Kennelly would achieve a record $5 million jury award for a single death in the Hodgson v. Air Iowa case tried in the Circuit Court of Cook County. The total claim of $125 million was well within McDonnell Douglas's liability insurance coverage of $150 million. In any country other than the United States, these were figures as wild and unlikely as the Irish Sweepstakes. He had their ear.

But California's law of damages would not, in Speiser's view, bring the highest settlements. He would argue for French law, which had an exquisite provision for grief and suffering—the *dommage moral*—that would give nondependents like parents, common-law wives, and siblings a chance to sue. Very important to the large number of English nondependency cases. And it was consistent with the tradition of applying the law of the place where the crash had occurred—*lex loci delicti*.

He did not recommend punitive damages, damages that were slapped on as a punishment, because they were not strictly allowed in California; when awarded by outraged juries, they were often overturned by higher courts, and were, he claimed, subject to income taxation under American law.

He explained the class action that was causing such confusion. Hope had been filed as a single action, with a request for a class that would give families easy access to U. S. courts. The class action he had requested would be voluntary, not mandatory, and if denied would not be vital to strategy. A product of consumerism, it allowed any group of similarly damaged persons to sue. It was a far more civilized way of hitting back at institutional injustice than beheading kings.

But how long would it all take? Speiser told the solicitors about Everglades, in which his firm, Speiser & Krause, had handled many cases. Settlement had been prompt, with defendants accepting liability and agreeing to start settling on the eve of trial, less than a year after the crash. The DC-10 case, he felt; could go on for a year or two of litigation.

English ethics bristled when the question of fees was discussed. Speiser would be paid on a contingency fee basis and fees would be the same with or without the class. In the entire world, only the United States, the Philippines, French Canada, and very few other countries allowed them. Because of the large numbers of cases in the Paris litigation, the usual 33⅓ percent would not be charged. It would probably be half that. And if the lawyers lost the case, there would be no fee. But to the English, the system was still gross, greedy, and illegal. A feisty letter to the BBC expressed the general British view of the system: "Do you want to see British lawyers descending to the low levels of their American counterparts? Have you not heard of American ambulance-chasing lawyers? They batten on the grief of survivors and relatives, work up a maximum of mental anguish. They don't ask a fee but do require a 50 percent—rarely less, sometimes more of the award. They play on the sympathies of juries, display horrific photos, and even limbs of victims. Is this what you want?"

British lawyers worked for fees prohibitively expensive for many people. This would be an expensive case to run, and they knew that without American contingency fees as offered by Speiser, few of their clients could afford to bring suit at all.

But the heart of the matter was still "What kind of a case do we have?" How likely was it that liability could be proved against McDonnell Douglas? It was a delicate moment. For if it were *not* a strong case against Douglas, many solicitors would go home and recommend that their clients settle for Warsaw's $20,000. Families might fall away from Mary Hope's banner. Speiser left the nuts and bolts of the case to Don Madole. Madole had developed a reputation for building such a strong technical case during the liability phase that he had forced every defendant he'd faced to the settlement table before trial. He left solicitors with the distinct impression that this *was* an open-and-shut product liability case, and that the scandal of the cargo door involved falsified records and, somehow, was even mixed up with the Watergate affair. A compelling presentation.

But Engler listened, unsatisfied that the Hope initiative and the class action was right for his clients. He rushed off to the Law Society, the English solicitors' professional body, to find out what other firms were involved in the case, and was given a small list of seven or eight firms. One of them was Stephen Mitchell's firm in London. He remembered Mitchell. He had fought a case against him. Mitchell was a Lloyd's man. What on earth was he doing on the plaintiff's side in this one? Engler called him and learned about Prudence.

It had been Prudence's death that had forced Mitchell to cross the line to the plaintiff's side, taking the biggest aviation case of all against Lloyd's. While most of the English rushing into litigation behind Hope's banner thought they were attacking Douglas and believed that a lawsuit would "make them pay," Stephen Mitchell knew that ultimately it was Lloyd's who would pay. No matter how far the risk was spread out over the world, the decisions on claims would be made by the lead insurers on Lime Street. He also knew that crossing the line was a delicate business. You established your reputation as a lawyer either for or against the insurers. But not both. It was rumored that Lloyd's did not easily forget if you crossed over.

But there was no choice. He was more than a shattered man who had suddenly lost "a girl who was very dear to me." He was her family's solicitor. And the family of one of the other models had turned to him for help. But he had not been able to rouse himself to feel any great rage against McDonnell Douglas as so many others had. He was still numb, using work as a drug to knock out pain and memories. He was still assaulted by the song that had been playing on the car radio as he'd driven to Heathrow to meet Prudence. The American pop song. Its popularity never seemed to diminish. Its words seemed almost to hunt him down. "Hey, if you happen to see the most beautiful girl that walked out on me . . . Oh, won't you tell her that I love her . . . I stood alone in the cold, gray dawn and knew I'd lost my morning sun. . . ." An Oxford dropout who reached easily for literary allusions, he kept remembering a poem by Martin Bell that had described lives as continuous "medleys of old pop numbers." "Three whistled bars are all it takes to catch us, defenseless on a District Line platform . . ." He was a man who always controlled his moves. But the song could catch him defenseless in the tube, in a taxi, in a hotel. Anywhere.

The litigation had not really touched him until he had read of the class action in the *Evening Standard*. as he understood it, a class action had been started on behalf of *all* the families as the only means of access to the American courts. His solicitor's blood began to boil. Foreigners had had access to U. S. courts since the early 1800s, and product liability suits in California were by no means novel. He had never given anyone authority to involve his clients in a class action. With the class action thrown down like a gauntlet, there was suddenly something very real and positive he could do about Prudence's death. His own clients and everyone else rushing helter-skelter into an American lawsuit needed guidance. He had worked with New York lawyers, knew how they negotiated and thought. Like Engler, he searched vigorously for alternatives.

With Engler's call, he knew he was not alone. There were others. Between them, they had the core of a rump group. Spontaneously, Engler and Mitchell whipped up a meeting in London to deal with their predicament. They could take the safe route of English damages or Warsaw, or they could risk litigation in American courts, which could take years, and fail. They could fall in behind Mary Hope and American lawyers who would seem a guarantee of success. Or they could find their own lawyer.

But they must move fast. In little more than a week, there was an important hearing coming up in Washington—the multidistrict litigation hearing—when the forum for the case would be decided. It would be the first skirmish for control of the case: whose jurisdiction, what judge, which lawyers. They hammered out their conclusions. It *was* an American lawsuit. And they must find the man to represent them. But why must he be a New York lawyer if the case was going to be in California? No one could think of a good answer.

Engler called his friend Sidney Golman in San Francisco to ask him about West Coast lawyers. Sid recommended a San Francisco aviation specialist, Jerry Sterns. He would call him.

Golman called Sterns and said, "Would you be interested in handling a lot of the English cases in the Paris crash? It might not pay very much."

Sterns was stunned. He had a toehold with the Wright case, which had come to him through his partner Bruce Walkup's old friendship with Fay Wright's father. But no prospects of any others. He placed the call Engler was waiting for.

Engler and Sterns had little time for pleasantries. With history moving away from them at a quick march, they would have to race to catch up. The Judicial Panel on Multidistrict Litigation would sit in Washington on April 26 to decide the jurisdiction of the case and to appoint a judge. It could consolidate into one court the dozens and even hundreds of cases that might be filed all over the country, streamlining complex litigation. And whether or not the English solicitors instructed him to represent them, Sterns said, they must get a brief filed before the panel. He wrote up a brief arguing for California as forum, or home, for the case, and Telexed it to Engler.

Before Engler could get the brief filed with the panel in Washington, he was hit by a crisis in England. A week before the panel was to meet, McDonnell Douglas made the move that had been feared and half expected by the lawyers carrying the case to America. Solicitors for McDonnell Douglas's insurers announced an offer to settle with English families. Turkish Airlines had already invited families to claim $20,000—the limit set by the Hague Protocol that had amended the Warsaw limit upward from the basic $10,000, and the amount most European airlines now paid. Now McDonnell Douglas offered "to proceed to prompt settlement in England of all claims by dependents and relatives of English passengers *according to English law* for the excess of the amount payable by the Airline. . . ." If, under English law, a case was worth $30,000, and Turkish Airlines paid $20,000 of that, McDonnell Douglas would pay the remaining $10,000. Compared to the potential level of settlements in California, it could be an inexpensive way of settling the English cases. It may have been a move made with sincerity in the hope that years of litigation could be avoided.

But to Engler, it was the move that could pull the claws of the entire American litigation effort on the eve of the multidistrict hearings. It could loose a flood of settlements with families who felt guilty about going to America. It called forth Engler's greatest hour. Addicted to the telephone and cavalierly unconcerned with an eight-hour time difference, he rang Jerry Sterns immediately. He tracked Sterns down at the Disneyland Hotel. In transatlantic calls plagued by noisy interruptions from their children, Engler and Sterns hammered out a response to the McDonnell Douglas offer.

In what may historically become known as the Disneyland Decision, he and Sterns agreed that the British should be urged *not* to accept the offer, for they believed the liability of McDonnell Douglas might ultimately far exceed what they were offering.

It came out in the press more like "This is aimed at a quick, cheap settlement. Only a full trial in California will bring the truth out." But Engler's statement was broadcast all over England, on radio and television; it was picked up by all the major London newspapers, echoed in the *East Anglia Daily Times* read by Bury St. Edmunds. For a weekend, his backyard and home became a madhouse of television cables, lights and microphones. On Monday, McDonnell Douglas tried to counter press criticism of the offer by reaffirming the offer to settle "on a generous basis . . . assessed according to English law." But the dike held. There was no flood of settlements. Not even a trickle. Had there been, there might never have been a major DC-10 case in California.

Much later, looking back, almost every faction in the lawsuit would agree that if McDonnell Douglas had publicly accepted responsibility, and made more generous offers, *this was the point where the case could have ended*.

As Engler's statement firmed up wavering families, the die was cast. The insurers knew there would now be no easy settlements.

Chapter Sixteen

Tooling Up for War

THE BATTLE WOULD be fought in America.

The great turgid ceremonial taking shape in Washington with the Judicial Panel on Multidistrict Litigation was the first formal step toward trial. Though both sides knew that there would probably never be a trial on liability, the protracted and incredibly expensive charade must be begun.

With resignation, the lawyers packed their bags for the hearing. Their systems chronically disturbed by jet lag, listing under the weight of their huge black leather legal satchels, the lawyers on both sides knew that they would seldom have their bags unpacked for the next two years. Victims of the MDL that had begun to consolidate and transfer cases at the beginning of the jumbo jet age, in 1968, they had become "a species of twentieth-century aeronautical nomads nesting in one district or another, as the will of the panel dictates," as one of the leading members of the plaintiffs' bar, Lee Kreindler, ruefully put it. They would miss birthdays, graduations, Little League games, long-planned dinner parties, their children. There would be stormy family fights, compensatory affairs, threats of separation. A marriage might break before the case was through. In this special case pressures would build, and test them all to their limits.

But nothing could keep them away. Not from the DC-10.

By Thursday, April 25, the small group of men who run the world's aviation litigation were checking into the Mayflower and the Madison hotels. Had they marched in together, they would have looked like the chorus line for *How to Succeed in Aviation Law by Trying Very Hard*. Well-cut conservative suits. Black satchels bulging with the papers they would wield the next day. Tanned with the tennis they play compulsively to try to overcome a sedentary life of sitting in jets and studying briefs. $100,000-a-year-plus men in their forties with families they saw too seldom. Glasses. Hair beginning to thin. Jewish. Irish. A few Anglo-Protestants.

Sterns was not yet a member of the club. And he did not yet have the English cases. He came to represent the Wright family and to present the English position before the MDL.

Engler had not been able to come. But Mitchell went, representing a group that had swelled to some two dozen solicitors representing between thirty and forty cases. Officially, Mitchell represented only his own four cases. But with the others in his pocket, he carried considerable bargaining power. He had come to choose a lawyer. He would meet Sterns and the others at the MDL, or wherever he had to go to find the best. Having resisted the initial rush to the class action, his group would not now make a precipitous choice.

In Washington, he would be joined by Neville Whittle, a solicitor from Leeds who had got the Sorkin case just five days before the MDL hearings and had grabbed the coattails of the rump group just in time to join forces with it in Washington.

The conflict between staying in the British courts, settling for *Warsaw,* or racing off to California had been very real to Whittle. The Sorkin case was what Americans call a "big" case. Dead were Malcolm Sorkin, one of Leed's most successful criminal litigators, and his wife Ruth. Two daughters, ten and fourteen, had been left orphaned. Sorkin's income had skyrocketed during the past few years as he had established his reputation firmly, and he had clearly not yet reached his peak earning years. In America, it was a case that might have brought a million dollars in damages to each of the two girls. But English law conspired against them. Under English law, Malcolm and Ruth might together be worth less than $4,000. The girls could be penalized for the profits from the sale of the fashionable big house, for falling heir to their parents' assets; they could have these *subtracted* from whatever damages they might be awarded for loss of support. And they had lost their parents. Their close Jewish family, rooted in the strong Jewish community that had grown up around the early immigrant workers who had come to the textile mills and tailoring trade, had been torn apart. Affection so deep that it had endured seven years of courtship while both finished their education, and had inspired Malcolm Sorkin to write, on their tenth wedding anniversary, a letter to Ruth that could only be described as a passionate love letter, had been spilled into the forest. The girls had been split up, one going to her grandmother, Ruth Sorkin's mother, the other to an aunt. They would never have the opportunities their father and mother had worked so hard to guarantee them—the travel, the education, the circle of friends, the elegant home. It pained Whittle to see Debbie, the elder, holding it all inside, unable to cry, remote . . . and the grandmother, thrust into a treadmill of activity as she tried to mother the energetic younger child, while Elizabeth looked restlessly toward the younger household where her sister lived. Irreparable harm had been done, love could not be replaced, but at least the girls need not be victimized by an archaic sense of justice. Whittle made contact with Engler, and flew to America to meet Stephen Mitchell.

The Englishmen watched as the American adversary system tooled up for war. As they gathered like armies on opposite hillsides, the two were given a superb view of the men and the issues at stake.

Stuart Speiser had fired the first shot on March 18, with the filing of Mary Hope's complaint in California, naming McDonnell Douglas as defendant and requesting limited class action treatment. On March 28, Lee Kreindler had thrown down the glove before both Douglas and the U.S. government, naming them as co-defendants in his Flanagan case. Filed as a class action in both California and New York, he had taken the class action route in self-defense, convinced that his firm's own broad experience with securities class actions could ensure that the class was handled properly. Turkish Airlines had been hauled into the fray by the Kalinsky case, filed in New York by the office of flamboyant trial lawyer F. Lee Bailey, who had been trying to break into the aviation cases. Hope. Flanagan. Kalinsky. The early flag-bearers of the case, giving the men who waved them early visibility.

Sterns had filed the Wright cases quietly in San Francisco on April 16, the fourth to file, but the first to name General Dynamics as a defendant, with Douglas; it was a move that was to prove critical to strategy later on.

Mitchell could feel desire for the English cases flowing out from the plaintiff lawyers in palpable waves.

Speiser's firm had already signed up cases in England, France, Turkey, and the United States. But the majority of the cases were still uncommitted. They hovered seductively in Morocco, South Vietnam, Brazil, Israel, Senegal, Switzerland, Denmark—in countries all over the globe. The English rump group, the Japanese with their forty-eight dead, and twenty-two Turkish families stood in the wings, waiting like small armies to commit their strength to the general who appeared most likely to win the war.

For Mitchell and the plaintiff lawyers, there was mutual eagerness to meet. Mitchell was already worn by jet lag, by a meeting in New York with Speiser, and a series of crisis calls from his London office in the middle of the night. But he and Whittle rushed off to Lee Kreindler's hotel room. Jerry Sterns, the lanky San Franciscan Engler had made contact with was there too; but in Kreindler's presence, he had very little to say. It was Kreindler's party that night. Of average height and build, dark hair brushed back in thinning wisps, his glasses giving him an eager, academic look, Kreindler had commanding stature in international aviation law.

Over drinks and dinner, Kreindler told them of his career. Educated at Dartmouth and Harvard, there were few major crash cases of the last two decades in which he had not played a leading role.

He had achieved a record settlement on his very first case twenty years earlier and had never eased the pace. He talked a language of crashes that evoked memories of every crash Mitchell and Whittle had ever heard of, and many they had not: the BOAC that came apart over Mt. Fuji; the 1961 Sabena-Brussels crash that had wiped out the U.S. figure-skating team; Air France-Orly where the Atlanta Art Association died, and Kreindler had settled for the families of sixty-two decedents; the horrifying United-TWA midair collision over Staten Island that had brought the TWA Constellation crashing down into the streets of Brooklyn. His detective work on the famous "reversed propeller" accident in Elizabeth, New Jersey, had made him a folk hero among aviation specialists. But it was his pioneering work in *conflicts of law,* and his landmark Kilberg case, that had him a major figure in American law. *Kilberg* had broken the hold of *lex loci delicti,* where the location of an accident, a random happenstance, determined the laws that would govern the rights of the dead and the surviving families. The Kilberg case had "kicked open the door" to the more sophisticated concept of "paramount interest" in which the courts could apply the law of whatever state or nation involved in the accident had the greatest interest in having its law applied.

Now, Kreindler was caught in an embarrassing situation. In 1972 he had become the first American lawyer ever to participate in an English court proceeding, in the *Staines* Trident case. He had been praised by the judge, lionized by the press, and this, plus a reputation that had just made him president of the International

195

Academy of Trial Lawyers, should have assured him a prominent place in *Paris,* the most international of cases. But he had not one English case. He had two American families and had filed one as a class action, hoping to be named class counsel. It was a "personal frustration" to be clinging with a mere handful of plaintiffs to the world's largest, perhaps most challenging case.

Sterns had said hardly a word all evening, Kreindler had been most impressive, and Sterns doubted that Mitchell had ever heard of Sterns's Pankow case, or Rosendin-Regan.

Until Engler's call, Jerry Sterns's involvement in *Paris* had been typical of West Coast lawyers' involvement in the big transport cases. They always picked up the stragglers in the provinces, while the bulk of the cases flowed like rivers to the sea to a very small handful of East Coast firms. It was they who forged precedents, made legal history, then wrote it all up in law journals and in the multi-volume textbooks that were on every aviation lawyer's shelf. Speiser. Kreindler. Kennelly in Chicago.

Sterns and his partners had been too busy taking money from Lloyd's of London and putting it in the pockets of widows and orphans to write books or set precedents; too busy settling, trying, and winning cases of people killed in the light planes—the Cessnas, Pipers, Bonanzas, Aero Commanders—that darted like insects through the western skies. He fought for the victims of "Indian country," the glutted low-altitude air spaces named for Piper's Comanche, Aztec, and Cherokee; and for the threat these bands of small prop planes posed to the large interloper. Commercial pilots feared descending into Indian country, their fat white planes as vulnerable to ambush as a covered wagon.

As a member of the plaintiff's bar and a specialist in negligence cases, Sterns had become an advocate for the dead, the scarred and crippled; for the limbless, the quadriplegic, the families of fathers who had gone fishing with their buddies in Baja California and ended up incinerated inside their four-place planes; for the bright people who had been turned into vegetables by failed equipment. Privy to a special kind of knowledge about the hazards of everyday life, he drove with his shoulder harness securely buckled, studied the caution signs at railway crossings, took his wife off the Pill, and became a connoisseur of the emergency procedures of every airline he flew.

Heroes to their clients, terrors to doctors who were losing massive malpractice suits to them and to manufacturers skewered by their relentless probing, he and his colleagues were the pariahs of the legal profession. Called "blood lawyers" and "ambulance chasers" by the corporate and securities lawyers who sedately collected $100 an hour, and more, in fees, plus retainers, they were motivated by the contingency fee system that paid them only if they won.

They were always under attack. Restrained by stern ethical codes from advertising or soliciting of any kind, they could be subjected to inquisition by the bar if accused of transgression. They could be hounded by state bar associations closing on them like a baying pack and punished with a swift and heavy hand. The threat of disbarment was always there.

Yet there was no way to reach out to the people who were suddenly, desperately, in need of their specialized services. "I can look out my window and see a Beech Baron come down; and yet, ethically, there is nothing I can do about it until somebody calls me. Yet, if I'm representing Beech, or the pilot's insurers, it's perfectly ethical to be on that widow's doorstep tomorrow saying, 'Aw, dear lady, we're sorry as hell your husband got killed. Of course, it's his fault because he's a dumb pilot, but we do want to pay the funeral bills. . . .'" A widow could call her family lawyer, of course, and have *him* find an aviation specialist; but with legal directories listing lawyers only by firm name—not by specialists like the *Yellow Pages*—that could be difficult, too. Yet referrals from other lawyers were the only ethical way.

The firm of Walkup, Downing and Sterns was in the enviable position of having a 100 percent referral practice.

But they all admitted that gross ambulance chasing did go on. "Blood lawyers" themselves talked of flagrant bribery of policemen and ambulance drivers at the scenes of car crashes; of airline and hospital personnel who sometimes sneaked a plaintiff lawyer—with gown, surgical mask, and retainer agreement ready to sign—to the bedside of a critically injured crash victim. They condemned the excesses in their own profession, but were frustrated by the fact that the airline's or manufacturer's insurers had access to the bedside with *their* contracts, giving the defense an early opportunity to settle; and putting the stunned patient, bereaved family, and the protectors of their rights—the plaintiff's bar—at an intolerable disadvantage. And it wasn't just the bedside. Plaintiffs couldn't get at the wreckage, either. It angered Sterns that "we very often do not get near these cases until the airplane is gone; and without the airplane, you're in big trouble to prove what happened." This was aggravated in the small-plane crashes by the fact that the "carcass" could be hauled off by a junk dealer within a week or so, that the cause of the crash might be locked up in the trunk of some insurance agent's car.

There was attack, too, on the contingency fee system by doctors who claimed that extortionary malpractice suits, and the rising cost of malpractice insurance were forcing them out of practice; and by lobbyists for automobile insurers urging no-fault automobile legislation that would largely eliminate the role of the contingency fee lawyer.

It was the high fees that seemed to catch in the craw, for contingency fees were commonly as high as 33⅓ percent. The plaintiff lawyers snarled back with a rationale for their fee scale. Without the contingency fee system, those unable to pay lawyers' fees would go unrepresented. Yes, workmen's compensation covered workers for minor injuries. But who except a viable plaintiff's bar could afford to mount a case for catastrophic injury or death that might run to $100,000 or more in expenses, expenses that would be water down the drain if the case were lost? That was the chance contingency fee lawyers took. And without these cases, would dangerous defects and practices ever be corrected or punished? Sterns believed that, too often, the government did not play its regulatory role with real vigor until forced to by a lawsuit or a major disaster.

As the contingency fee issue—now becoming a national movement—built to a crisis for the plaintiff's bar in California, Sterns found himself fighting not only for his clients, but also for his profession. Already on a frantic schedule of depositions, trials, and settlement meetings in cities all over the West, he was increasingly leaping into his car and speeding to Sacramento to stick his finger in the dike; to tell his side of the story to legislators drafting bills.

Beleaguered, laying out hundreds of thousands of dollars in expenses for cases they might never win, the plaintiff lawyers came into the adversary system with a chip on their shoulders and fought like tigers for the reputation and survival of their profession, and for the victims of progress who were their clients. They often won. Nagged perhaps by the collective guilt, judges and juries were eager to be generous to technology's victims. They paid society's debt with dollars. Great outpourings of dollars.

Unlike the English, Americans have no moral difficulties in translating death, injury, and grief into dollars. Dollars have traditionally been the clearest measure of value and the most direct means of punishment in a profit-seeking society. It was believed that hitting a corporation in the pocketbook was "hitting them where it hurts."

Belligerent and tough, Stern's kind of law was alien to his California and Iowa upbringing, his Irish/English background, and to his own gentle instincts.

After law school, he had joined Bruce Walkup, a trial lawyer already setting records in the new field of negligence law, and quickly built a busy practice in light-plane litigation. In the courtroom, he discovered that he could respond to the unexpected, think fast on his feet, and articulate his case effectively. Juries responded easily to Stern's humanness. As he would begin to unravel his 6-feet 7-inch body from a hard courtroom chair, loose-jointed and friendly, chemistry was already working in his behalf. He had a good, craggy, believable face, and wore horn-rimmed glasses that made him look sincere and . . . interesting. His suits, even expensive charcoal-gray pinstripes, always looked as if he'd caught them on the run and slung them on his rangy frame. Sometimes a seam was split, making woman jurors want to reach out for a needle and thread. Though forty, there was a boyish ingenuousness about him that made you feel that his arms would outgrow his sleeves before the case was over.

His courtroom style combined the most appealing traits of the corn-belt lawyer and the gentle academic. He moved his body with an ease and openness that was expressive of the West; East Coast lawyers hated it. Delivering his arguments, he was at his most effective. With jacket flung open and left hand on his hip, he leaned toward the judge or jury. Fingers straight and emphatic, he slashed the air with his right arm to make his points. He would give the jury a basic education in the physics of flight and the structure of airplanes. Simply, patiently. They would be fascinated, grateful, drawn in as participants in the case. Handling plane models and specially made mock-ups of the vital parts of the plane in question, he would move them into the specific mechanical defect, letting his own amazement at discovery of bad design and negligence come through. You could feel shock and resentment take hold of the jury as he carried them through the detective job of searching files and probing reluctant witnesses for clues to the gut causes of the crash—causes that he was convinced would often go undetected if there were no plaintiff's bar. He was still a midwestern boy who had not yet lost the capacity to feel and show righteous indignation. You could hear his own excitement at knowing he was on to something that would win his case, improve the plane, save the life of the next guy.

Moved by his presentation, full of compassion and public spirit, juries would find for the plaintiff. And children who had lost a father would be able to stay in a decent home and get through college.

Shrewd, intelligent application of the law always underlay his homey presentation. But to the defense, Sterns's style was "apple pie and motherhood," an indecent appeal to gross emotion that was beneath contempt. They would scowl about it all the way to the maintenance hangars where killer parts on airplanes would be replaced.

Wichita, where Beech and Cessna were headquartered, was his beat. But he argued now in Washington for a California forum for the DC-10 case.

The defense—all but the airline—argued against California, as they took up their early positions. Stephen Mitchell knew that the defense lawyers here were simply spokesmen for the powerful syndicate leaders in London who would ultimately pay the bills and who would control strategy. The deep struggle, invisible to all but insiders, had been going on in London since the afternoon of the crash. Since then, Lloyd's and the London insurance market had been going through a Byzantine shuffling of insurance policies among the syndicates, divesting themselves of conflicting interests. For the moment a major crash occurs, the same small group of men find themselves involved in the same risks to a greater or lesser degree.

In the Paris crash, there had been four different insurances involved: hull and passenger liability on the airlines, and product liability for both McDonnell Douglas and General Dynamics Corporation, the subcontractor that had built the cargo doors. And everybody was involved.

As the dust settled, J. M. T. Hewitt, underwriter of the Ariel Syndicate, found himself leading the McDonnell Douglas risk; C. R. Jeffs of the Aviation and General Insurance Company would handle the airline's hull and liability policies. Once the responsibilities had been sorted out, the two devoted themselves with remarkable single-mindedness to their particular interest in the Paris case, closing their minds to other conflicts their syndicates still carried.

Jeffs continued Peter Martin's assignment to represent the passenger liability risk and Martin in turn had instructed George Tompkins of Condon and Forsythe in New York to work with him in America. The two would be in almost daily contact with each other by phone and Telex from London to New York.

Tompkins, in dark-blue city suit that could still not hide the musculature of a Canadian ice hockey youth, had a reputation as an intelligent and reasonable lawyer with no love of the Warsaw Convention. Though he respected its usefulness outside the United States, and to a lesser extent within it, he shared the general American distaste for its inequities and unrealistically low awards. But, like Martin, he was bound to uphold it. Most of the world still accepted it without question. New York courts upheld it. If the walls were breached here, with a mass of foreign cases, the whole structure could collapse. It could make it impossible for him, and for Martin, to try to invoke it successfully in future crashes. His best defense would be to avoid the jurisdiction of American courts altogether. Turkish Airlines did not fly to the United States, and there was a very real question under Warsaw as to whether they could be touched by U.S. courts. With McDonnell Douglas and the Kalinsky case trying to yank the airline into the case, it was going to be extremely difficult to stay aloof.

Philip Bostwick, a member of the Washington firm of Shaw, Pittman, Potts, and Towbridge would represent the insurers of the hull.

Ariel's Hewitt, and his claims manager David Dann, would carry the burden of responsibility for the insurers of McDonnell Douglas in aviation's most formidable product liability suit. They had little difficulty choosing an American lawyer. It would be James FitzSimons of the New York firm of Mendes and Mount. The Mendes and Mount connection with Lloyd's went back nearly a century, and now the firm often represented the Ariel Syndicate in American actions. The firm's ties to Lloyd's and to the Ariel Syndicate were the envy and frustration of other aviation defense specialists in the United States.

Jim FitzSimons, a close-shaven, sharp-featured, straight-arrow Irish-Catholic from New York, would be lead counsel. A consummate defense lawyer, he identified fully with his corporate clients and took attacks on them personally. If encumbered with doubts, he never let them show. Powered by a clear view of right and wrong, black and white, he drove through the nuances and subtleties of complex litigation with an almost pious determination. Although his affability outside the courtroom had given him the nickname "Sunny Jim," his courtroom mode was one of thin, tight lips and earnest jotting of notes on his yellow legal pad. Under the lawyerly style, one always sensed a scrappy Irishman who hated to lose.

FitzSimons, in turn, would hire the firm of Kirtland and Packard of Los Angeles to aid in the defense. Robert Packard, an experienced California trial lawyer, would share the defense table with FitzSimons throughout the case.

FitzSimons would fight to keep the case in New York, where some of the earliest cases had been filed. A manufacturer facing a major product liability suit wants to be anywhere in the universe but California, at the mercy of a lay jury who must make decisions on engineering judgment made after many millions of man-hours of study by professionals and subject to the state's strict liability law, a law under which you no longer had to prove that a defect in a product was the result of negligence. You simply had to prove that a defect existed and that it caused the death or injury. Increasingly, the manufacturers stood bared to the bullets, victims, they felt, of the "deep pockets theory"—the one with the deepest pockets pays. Part of McDonnell

Douglas's strategy would be to try to implicate the air-line in responsibility and pull it from behind its Warsaw shield to share the cost.

They would fight, too, to avoid the court of Judge Peirson M. Hall. Hall, the eighty-year-old grand vizier of the aviation judiciary, had already been assigned to the early cases filed in California. He had held his first hearing in the federal courthouse in Los Angeles. Even before the MDL, *Paris* was falling into his lap, and with his prestige and seniority, it was clear that the case would be transferred by the multidistrict litigation panel to his court. With a childhood of poverty and institutions, and five of his own six marriages broken by death or divorce, Hall had been left acutely tuned to the tragedy of shattered families. He was known to protect the rights of widows and orphans with all his judicial powers.

The moment the cargo door had been implicated in the crash, the insurers knew that there was another potential defendant—General Dynamics Corporation. General Dynamics' Convair Division had built sections of the fuselage and the aft cargo door in its San Diego plant. And though the lead was in New York, the General Dynamics' liability policy had been reinsured in London, pulling it, too, into the maneuvering on Lime Street.

U.S. Government lawyers defending the FAA and counsel for General Dynamics would try to keep a very low profile, hoping, through invisibility, to avoid the spotlight now blazing down on McDonnell Douglas.

The men from London would seldom be seen. Pulling the strings from London, they would remain aloof and enigmatic to the Americans. Martin and Dann would surface from time to time at court hearings, shedding an aura of British respectability that made the American lawyers buff their shoes and straighten their ties. Jeffs and Hewitt would work discreetly in London, trying to resolve between themselves the share of liability the airlines and manufacturers should pay. Their in-house negotiations would fume on, like a smoldering peat fire, invisible, but keeping heat on the action in America.

Mitchell watched the lawyers closely as they argued before the panel. The lawyers watched each other, trying to get a feel for the shape the case would take as this pretrial ritual breathed life into it.

For several hours, the panel listened to arguments, and announced that it would make its decision within the next few weeks. No one waited with baited breath. It was a forgone conclusion that it would be California. And Hall. From now on, the words *In Re: Paris Air Crash* would stand as symbols for the tattered horror of Ermenonville Forest. Names like Hope, Kalinsky, Flanagan, Wright, Backhouse, typed up on complaints, would become legal vehicles stripped of the flesh and personalities that had been attached to the names until March 3. *In Re: Paris Air Crash,* removed from the site, the wreckage, the families, would develop its own momentum, free of the drag of grief or personal entanglement with the crash. To the lawyers, the crash was the event that had put their world into motion.

Although he had enjoyed the show in Washington, Mitchell had not been won over by the wooing he and Whittle had received. Alone among all the solicitors involved in the case, he had been touched personally by the reality of the crash; he still felt its stab in his heart whenever he let his mind drift to it. It gave an extra thrust to his determination to find the best man.

He doubted he would ever instruct Speiser or Madole. It was not only resistance to the way in which they had rushed into England with what Mitchell considered inappropriate haste after the crash. It was also a matter of style, very different styles. He had been very taken by Kreindler. But he could see no point in paying for two law firms: one in New York and another in California hired to assist the first. He still hardly knew Sterns.

He and Whittle would go to California to talk to

Judge Hall. As they left Washington and flew off to Palm Desert, Sterns sighed to himself, "Well, there goes the DC-10."

Tanned and an active golfer at eighty, Judge Hall had the look of an aging cherub. Jowls softening a face that must have been exceedingly handsome, thick tufts of gray eyebrows arcing over twinkling eyes like puffs of cloud over a lake, his face was the Hollywood ideal of the gentle man of justice popularized by Lionel Barrymore. Hall, though, was the original. He reminisced over cases and cautioned the two Englishmen to be wary of the figures quoted by the lawyers as to how much their cases might be worth. Though known for his concern for families, it was when damages were discussed that he showed the balance that made him a great judge; he did not approve wildly excessive damages, reining back on abuses in what was already the world's most liberal forum for death and personal injury lawsuits.

At the time, Mitchell did not know that the charming man sipping Scotch in his shorts and flowered shirt was the judiciary's most powerful advocate of aviation law reform. He was having legislation drafted for a federal aviation law—something that did not exist. Always innovating, daring the court of appeals to turn back decisions that raced ahead of their time, he drove cases through the courts like a cowboy driving stubborn cattle through a creek bed. But Mitchell did observe that "he was a literate frontiersman. A westerner. A Californian." Mitchell guessed that he dispensed his justice in a rough, honest, individualistic way.

In California, Mitchell found himself thinking about Jerry Sterns. He was coming to the conclusion that a California lawyer was critical, and he liked Sterns's low-key style. His lack of visible eagerness for the cases. He looked honest. He decided to see Sterns the next day in San Francisco.

As Mitchell negotiated with Sterns and his senior partner Bruce Walkup, he knew he didn't hold all the aces: American lawyers were trading access to their

206

courts. But with the block of cases growing daily, he held enough. He tentatively negotiated a sliding scale of contingency fees, in which Walkup, Downing and Sterns would get a maximum of 15 percent and a minimum of 10 percent of damages, depending on the total sum. With the high potential awards, the rate was almost certain to be 10 percent, a considerable saving for the English clients over the previous best offer. Mitchell was pleased.

In the north of England, nearly forty lawyers waited for a report from Mitchell. Engler had set up a meeting with all of them for 2 P.M. on May 1, in Manchester.

Mitchell had another, personal reason for having to return. Prudence's remains had finally been identified, nearly two months after the crash. There had been rumors that Dérobert had been having great success with the use of fingerprints; a spate of new identifications had been made. But Mitchell didn't like to think about it too closely, for he could not imagine how the *professeur* could have acquired a set of Prudence's fingerprints. He suspected that, under pressure from the English, the Institut had in desperation begun to throw a few bits and pieces into coffins and nail down the lids. He and Mrs. Pratt were grateful to have her coming home and asked no questions. He must be in Tunbridge Wells for her cremation the day after the meeting with Engler and the other lawyers.

Drained, stimulated, pumped full of sales pitches, Mitchell and Whittle flew home through eight time zones, raced from London by plane, bus, and car to Manchester for the meeting. They recommended that the firm of Walkup, Downing and Sterns be instructed. If the group agreed, each solicitor would have to instruct Sterns individually. The English don't hire lawyers; they *instruct them*. They called Sterns from the meeting and invited him to come to England immediately. Already a large and powerful force, about to swell to more than eighty cases following an unprece-

207

dented announcement in the *Law Society Journal* that month, the rump group had made its choice.

Next day, Mitchell took Mrs. Pratt to Prudence's cremation. Though he hated cremations, it gave him the finality he needed. An earlier memorial service for the dead models had helped, too. All the fashion photographers had closed for the day and every model in London had come to the posh and beautiful service. After the cremation, he and Mrs. Pratt had tea together at the Pratt home. At least that anxious phase was finished for both of them. And he had, he prayed, put Prudence's case and all the others' into honorable hands. Driving home to London, he fell asleep at the wheel and drove off the road. He turned off the engine and slept.

Chapter Seventeen

"Extremely Improbable"

JERRY STERNS LEANED back against his seat on the flight to London, astounded by what had transpired. For him, for any western lawyer, a major role in *Paris* was a quantum leap forward. He had been slowly moving into the transport cases. But the tools he'd need for Paris had been honed in Wichita.

The flavor of Wichita got into the blood of any lawyer who spent time there—its good steaks, bad motels, the flatlands that stretched away like a lonely ocean when you viewed them from the bar on top of the Holiday Inn Plaza downtown. Wichita was where you had to go to depose witnesses from Beech and Cessna, or to get at the files and documents subpoenaed by the court for the discovery, or fact-finding, process that always precedes trial. You could get at FAA files there, too. The FAA had just opened an office in Wichita, though the regional office was still in Kansas City. The two cities had initiated Sterns into the mysteries of governmental regulation of the aviation industry.

Just a month ago, he had been in Wichita deposing witnesses on a Beech case. It was March 26, 1974. And the possibility of being involved in the Paris crash had seemed as remote as his being asked to play the Brandenburg Concerto with the San Francisco Symphony. It was the day that the DC-10 Senate hearings were being televised. By symbolic coincidence, the crash that would propel him into the international arena was spilled out to him in his hotel room in Wichita, the city where he had learned the skills and the facts of life he would bring to bear on the DC-10.

Back in his hotel room after the depositions, he'd poured a drink. As he started working on his papers, he had switched on the television to watch the news and caught the highlights of the hearings. Bob Ginther, counsel for the Senate's subcommittee on aviation, had written his scenario well. Suddenly, Sterns was riveted to the TV set. He couldn't believe what was pouring out. As he listened to the parade of NTSB, FAA, and Douglas people, he began to realize that he was watching "the biggest goddamn product liability case in history" take shape before his eyes. If he worked his butt off, the Beech case might be worth $700,000. The DC-10 could soar past $100 million.

But it wasn't the size that was compelling. It was something else. As the story spilled out, an eerie sense of *déjà vu* came over him. HE HAD HEARD IT ALL BEFORE. In Wichita. With the Beech Baron. The DC-10 was just the Baron writ large.

The Beech case had walked in the door like any other case, referred by the lawyers representing the San Francisco-based construction company that had leased the crashed plane. Their thirty-seven-year-old executive vice-president had been killed flying the company's Beech Baron. The Baron was Beech's Cadillac, with high-powered twin-engines and a $125,000-plus price tag, which paid for itself in the time saved getting key executives fast from one branch or construction site to another. The accident had happened on October 13, 1965, near Salinas, in California's flat agricultural heartland. Bill Pankow, who had just had the plane in at the Salinas Engine Works for a one-hundred-hour inspection and minor maintenance, was checking it out before a business flight to Seattle. He went up with an aircraft mechanic, Vernon Laird, who would monitor propeller alignments and fuel mixture controls for him as he flew.

No one would ever know precisely what happened to

Bill Pankow on his fatal flight. But test flights flown later by other pilots can let us speculate. He and Laird walked out to the plane through a light drizzle. They took off into a darkening, overcast California sky, flying on instruments. Pankow had logged 185 hours of night flying. He followed a radio beam that led him through the air like a thread, his invisible lifeline. He flew out into an element that, perhaps even more than the ocean at night, is awesome and alien to man. It breeds apprehension. In a ship, there is always the sea supporting you, keeping you in rough equilibrium with the sky and horizon, telling you which way is up. But as you take off at night, the bottom falls away and is replaced by a dimension of uncertainty. Terror of the dark and fear of falling are suppressed by intense concentration in the cockpit. But the lodestars, the visual cues diurnal animals like man depend on, are gone. You can no longer rely on your senses. With no horizon or land, the inner gyro gets confused. You can feel as if you are flying level when you are steeply banked. Your sink rate can be dropping you down toward a jagged peak when you believe you are climbing to safety. Where the commercial or military pilot is trained to use instruments as his sixth sense, a less-experienced private pilot has to fight his instincts to rely on them. He desperately wants to look out the window for help; but if the airplane gets ahead of him, if he becomes confused, gets vertigo, he can be lost in a bottomless black ocean. He cannot throw out the anchor. He will fall when he runs out of fuel.

At 600 feet, Bill Pankow climbed through the ragged ceiling into thick cloud. He broke out on top at 2,200 feet, and for nearly 15 minutes he and the young mechanic performed the functional checks normally done after a one-hundred-hour inspection. He then descended back through the low cloud and drizzle for his approach to Salinas airport. Bill Pankow may have been using rudder to make minor flight-path corrections. At low altitude, in the final stages of an instrument approach, you must not stray far from your lifeline. He

211

had taken off with fuel sloshing in his main wing tanks; the main tanks for his two engines were only partially full. He wouldn't be up for long.

In kicking the nose of the plane around, or perhaps in sliding into a turn, his plane had temporarily gone into an uncoordinated maneuver—a condition passengers on commercial airlines rarely experience, the feeling of going around a corner too fast in a car. Commercial pilots pride themselves on smooth coordinated flight, where gravity and centrifugal force are in such perfect balance that, in theory, they could stand the plane on its wingtip and passengers wouldn't even have their coffee tip in its cup; and the fuel would stay level in its tank. Children practice coordinated turns by swinging a bucket of water around to see if they can keep it from sloshing out. In a light plane, coordinated turns are more difficult to make, particularly by an inexperienced pilot. Fuel seldom stays serenely level in its tanks.

During the period of uncoordinated flight, the fuel in the long rubber bladder in his left wing sloshed toward the outer tip of the wing, exposing the small fuel intake hole near the root of the wing. It is through that hole that fuel is sucked into the engine. Air was sucked in instead, and it moved toward the engine like a bubble of air moving toward the heart. Within seconds, it entered the engine, killing it. The propeller lost its power, but continued to "windmill," acting like a massive brake. He now had asymmetric thrust working against him. The right engine, still under power, threw the plane into a violent yaw to the left. Pankow didn't know what had happened. Flying on instruments, it took a little longer to diagnose a lost engine. The left engine must be gone. But WHY? He had fuel. What was happening? He frantically worked on the dead engine, trying to get it back running and get the plane under control again. But another crisis was moving toward him. When the plane had yawed to the left, it had thrown the fuel in the right wing tank sloshing toward the tip of the right wing, exposing the fuel intake in *that* tank, letting in a lethal shot of air to the right engine. Pankow's fate now hung on a small stream of air moving inexorably toward the right engine. He managed to get the left engine running again and fought to get the airplane back on course. If he got too far off course, he'd be devoured by darkness. But, before he could get back, the right engine cut out, yanking the plane into a tortuous yaw to the right.

In a plane that had gone inexplicably berserk, bucking him like a maddened bull, Pankow fought for his life. And for the life of Vernon Laird, sitting beside him. But he was a construction executive, an experienced pilot, but not a test pilot, and without much time on instruments. As he grappled with controls and instruments, the final blow hit him. With the left engine now generating power and the right propeller acting as a brake, the Baron yawed hard right and rolled over into a death spin. It was more than Bill Pankow could handle. More than most pilots could handle.

Ten miles from Salinas airport, Edward Reeder heard a low plane and the sound of engines cutting out, and he rushed from his house. There was just enough light to see "the plane losing altitude and trying to turn, then it seemed to go straight and stalled and began to spin downward. Then spun into wires. It was three or four spins above the wires before it hit them. Then it burst into flames."

Two miles away, the lights in Manuel Freitas's garage went out, one minute after Freitas had heard the "fluttering" engines of a plane in distress. Pankow's right wing had snapped high-voltage lines. As it came into an artichoke field, the plane was in a "flat, wings level attitude with little or no forward speed." Both men were using safety belts and might have been saved. But the right wing had dragged a live 12,000-volt wire with it. With a ball of flame, the fuel ignited, feeding Pankow's funeral pyre.

The crash was baffling. It was the first of a series of similar Beech Baron crashes that would occur over the next three years, pulling planes from the sky as mysteriously as the Bermuda Triangle. An investigation was conducted by the FAA and the CAB, the Civil Aeronautics Board, which continued to take responsibility for crash investigation until the creation of the NTSB in 1967. In doing their investigation, it would have been easy for the investigators to write it off as pilot error. Perhaps the pilot had done something stupid up there in the sky at night, or had mismanaged his fuel. But Willard H. Hart, the CAB investigator assigned to the case by the Oakland office, was disturbed by the wreckage. The terrible fires that had consumed the plane and its occupants indicated unburned fuel. Hart calculated that each main tank would still have had eleven gallons of fuel. On examination, the engines showed no evidence of "operational distress"; no evidence of in-flight fire. Engine ignition switches were on. Why, then, had the engines died?

He was going to find out. He would test-fly a Baron, trying to duplicate what the wreckage had told him of Pankow's flight, and see if he could solve the mystery. On February 2, 1966, he took off with only fifteen gallons in each of his forty-gallon main tanks; he had already sniffed out an explanation. He was going to see if uncoordinated maneuvers with minimum fuel in the main tanks could disrupt the flow. If he was right, and if the engines died, he might crash as Pankow had. But he was a dedicated man, and he was not flying at night, on instruments, having no idea what to expect. In the kind of flight you don't tell your wife about until it's over, he skidded and slipped the plane while climbing, cruising, and descending. Nothing happened in the skidding turns. But during slipping turns, in each phase of flight, a disruption of fuel flow to the lower engine occurred. At climb power settings, the engine sputtered "within three to five seconds," and at low-power settings it took ten. Anticipating it, he was able to get back on course and his engines running normally in five seconds using the electric boost pumps that increase fuel pressure and flow. But when he resisted using the boost pumps, it took forty-five seconds for the engines to run normally again. Forty-five seconds, or even five, had been too long for Bill Pankow, as it would be for any nonprofessional pilot trying, at the same time, to recover from a violent yaw.

The report of the test flight went to CAB headquarters in Washington on March 14, 1966, five months after the crash; but it wasn't until January 1967, fifteen months after the crash, that the board sent a recommendation up to FAA that the Baron's fuel system be reevaluated. Then, as if batting feather balls to each other, a series of letters began to drift back and forth among the CAB's successor, the NTSB, the FAA and Beech. Meanwhile, more Barons were being built and sold. More than a year after NTSB's first letter, the FAA wrote back rejecting it, stating that "we do not propose to require any corrective measures for the Beech 95-B55 airplane." And they made the implication that was to become Beech's classic defense—that the "unporting" of the fuel outlet occurred only during maneuvers the plane was never intended to perform. Though Hart had engine trouble doing normal turns with a bank angle of no more than 15 degrees and moderate slip, the FAA discarded his flight test as having been "apparently more severe than that required by the current regulations." There had been no violation of the sacred touchstones, the Federal Air Regulations, the FARs.

Sterns had started his digging in Wichita and Kansas City, where "they treated me like hoof-and-mouth disease." There wasn't much product liability law yet; and the Freedom of Information Act, which would force corporate skeletons out of closets, had not yet been passed. "What records the FAA gave you were what they *chose* to give you." To Sterns, their position was very simple: "If we let any uppity lawyers or other muckrakers and undesirables come in here and look at these files, Beech will not be candid with us. They will be reluctant to make full disclosure." Many manufacturers and safety professionals did genuinely believe that aggressive litigation could harm rather than help

215

air safety by throwing the industry into an evasive, overly protective posture that might prevent disclosure.

But to Sterns, "That is just bullshit . . . because once we got into those files, we saw that they had all this disclosure and weren't doing anything about it." He was becoming, like many after him, a Baron fanatic.

He had found a letter from Tom Mitchell, Beech's manager for the western states at the time, to Dell Spillman in Beech's customer service department in Wichita. Written in January 1961, over four years before the Pankow crash, it dealt with the unporting of the fuel outlets in the Bonanza, a single-engine Beech plane with *the same long rubber fuel tank and same wing as the Baron.* In the "Spillman memo" he wrote:

A condition which is extremely dangerous and corrective action should be taken immediately exists. When making a rolling takeoff [a takeoff initiated while turning onto the runway] when the tanks register half full, the centrifugal force throws the gas to the outside of the tanks and the engine quits dead after the airplane is airborne. . . It looks to me like our Quality Control and/or our Flight Department, when testing and checking these airplanes, are letting a lot of things through that certainly should not be.

As welcome as an undertaker, Sterns kept digging and found a response to Mitchell's worried letter. It had been issued *four years later,* in April 1965, as an innocuous Service Letter, the general aviation equivalent of the Service Bulletin. Within the West Coast aviation legal fraternity that handled most of the Baron cases, the letter would become famous for what Sterns described as "the artful use of the language to try to describe this problem lightly without scaring too many people off." The letter stated that "it's possible" that air will be allowed into the fuel system just after a rolling takeoff, and that in such a case "the air will reach the engine *at about the same time the airplane be-*

comes airborne and could cause momentary power in-
terruption. *This does not create a hazard but can be
disconcerting.*" Sterns started "foaming at the mouth"
when he read it. Power failure at the most critical phase
of flight—at *takeoff*—not hazardous! "This has to be
the understatement of the decade!" It could be even
more critical in the Baron. The Bonanza might lose its
single engine but would at least hold its heading while
you regained power. But the Baron had a significant
difference—the asymmetric power situation caused by
first one engine cutting out, creating yaw in one direction, then the other engine cutting out, throwing you
into a yaw in the opposite direction. Where normally
two engines meant safety, here they could mean crisis,
particularly to someone who did not make flying his
profession.

Sterns fed the letter into the files he was painstakingly building against Beech. He was learning the facts
of life. The regulatory relationship between Beech and
the FAA appalled him most. He had discovered that
"by and large the making of light aircraft has been left
almost entirely to the manufacturer." Beech designed
and built its Barons under a *delegation option authority*
in which, as the FAA itself described it, "the manufacturer makes a finding of compliance with the applicable regulations without full participation of the Federal Aviation Agency." *Planes were built on the honor
system, with the job of inspecting the plane delegated
to Beech personnel who, with their Beech hats on, designed and built the plane; then, with their FAA hats
on, inspected it on behalf of the FAA.*

By the summer of 1968, Sterns was "really cranked
up" and taking depositions in Wichita, where his evidence against Beech was piling up. In testimony, it
came out that the unporting problems of the Bonanza
had never even been taken across the hall to the
Baron's designers. A Beech engineer explained the
lack of communication away with "an incredible statement like 'does Macy's tell Gimbels?' "

Finally goaded into action, the FAA had sent test-pilot Stewart Present to test the Baron's fuel system, in July of 1968. And Sterns couldn't wait to get him on the stand. His report was dynamite. He had recommended grounding the entire Baron fleet. The FAA had allowed Sterns to take a quick look at, though not to copy, Present's original report in their files. There it was. Ground the Barons. Present had confirmed his recommendation to Sterns in informal conversation. But when he went on the stand, he wouldn't answer questions about the grounding. His official report, the one that went on the record, made no mention of grounding the planes, though it did caution that "it is felt that this condition is one that could be encountered by an inexperienced pilot. It is recommended that action be taken to improve the fuel system in this model. . . ."

Sterns was one of the few people who knew that Present's tough report had ended up "on the cutting room floor." And Present would never be able to clear the air himself; never be able to explain and identify the pressures that weighed on him as he took the stand. He was dead, killed in the crash of a moon-landing vehicle.

Sterns, an even-tempered man, was growing angry. He had uncovered a Bonanza crash in Tacoma, Washington, and a nonfatal accident in Philadelphia, both fuel starvation crashes that had occurred even before Pankow's. By the end of 1968, there had been *five* reported Baron crashes. Families were being killed. Nagged by the NTSB, who were beginning to see a deadly pattern in the crashes, the FAA had finally issued an Airworthiness Directive on January 1, 1969; but all it had required was a *warning placard* in the cockpit. Like Windsor. Like Air Canada. It did nothing to physically prevent the sloshing of the fuel or warn the pilot of the insidious nature of the phenomenon. In ads showing hard-matted young executives at construction sites, Beech made it clear that they built the plane for businessmen. Not for Wiley Post. They had given layman pilots a sophisticated piece of equipment they could not always handle. But Beech would not admit it.

Nor would they correct the fuel cell by installing baffles, or some other device, that would prevent the sloshing when the tanks were not full. And yet, Sterns had found in the "Beech archives" plans from a rubber company for a baffling system as far back as 1956. Sterns wanted to go to trial.

He was determined to prove, publicly, that unporting could occur in the kind of ordinary takeoff turn pilots made all the time and, even more deadly, in flight. Sterns had an idea. They would make a movie of the unporting and show it to the jury, making the impact Hart and Present had not been able to make with their test flights. He had a plastic model fuel tank built, partially filled with green fluid, and set on rollers so that it could be rocked back and forth, sloshing the liquid inside.

But he talked to Dave Holladay, an aviation consultant and test pilot in Los Angeles, and they came up with a better idea. Holladay would take a Baron up and take movies of the unporting during actual flight. He would get a camera and light source inside a forty-gallon fuel tank partially filled with volatile fuel. He would slip and turn the plane until an engine died, keep the cameras going, and pray that the heat of the light source didn't ignite the fuel, causing an explosion that would end the test rather decisively. It sounded complex and dangerous, but Holladay was confident that he could do it.

Sterns got his money's worth. The movies were too good to be true. There it was—the unporting of the fuel intake Beech had implied only a stunt pilot was likely to experience. Holladay did not do aerobatics. But as he slid into an uncoordinated turn, the fuel flowed away, baring a small finger guard over the fuel intake, sucking in air.

Sterns showed the movies to the Beech lawyer a week before trial was to begin. Though he was eager to get into court with the films, trial was always the last resort. And as Sterns and his client, Pankow's widow, walked toward the courtroom for the beginning of the trial several days later, the lawyer caught him in the hall and made a settlement offer—$300,000, a high sum at that time. Torn between his passion to get the Baron story out before a jury and the best interests of his client, Sterns hesitated. Marie Pankow needed the money now to raise her two teen-agers. The "loss of society" portion of the damages had had the "bottom shot out of it" by the fact that the Pankows were separated and already had an interlocutory decree. There was no telling what a jury might do. Marie Pankow urged him to accept the offer. Sterns told her to shake her head vigorously, as if saying no. The defense lawyer saw her and came back with $325,000 . . ." They settled.

But the movies went to court. In a gesture of cooperation that would become the norm for lawyers involved in Baron litigation, Sterns gave them, with his files, to Dan Cathcart of Los Angeles for the landmark Santa Ana case in which a jury awarded $21 million for four deaths in a Beech Baron. When they had seen the movies and heard the story, the jury had "gone bananas," awarding $17 million of the award as punitive damages—disciplinary damages not strictly allowed in California but allowed here through a legal gimmick. The punitive award was subsequently appealed and reversed. But the jury had spoken and given Beech and its insurers a shock they would not forget.

But there had been no Senate hearings on that crash, or on the other Baron crashes. One death did not titillate the public or attract the press. Nor did four or five. Hidden away in Wichita, the Baron problem had been allowed to slumber on for years. As late as 1970, there was still no AD requiring correction of the existing fuel tanks; though from that time on, all new Barons were built with an improved tank. Sterns felt satisfied that his tenacious crusade had started the snowballing pressure on Beech and the FAA that had ultimately led to correction of the fuel cell. For the Barons already flying, the FAA had allowed Beech to go the *voluntary* route. A kit containing antislosh devices was offered to Baron owners, which they could buy and install at their own expense, if they wished. The voluntary kit lacked urgency, as had the Service Bulletins issued after *Windsor* on the DC-10.

But there was no way the DC-10 was going to be hidden. It would be scrutinized and fixed. For the DC-10, "Mickey Mouse" fixes were over. Two days of televised Senate hearings in Washington would do more, he knew, for air safety than all his own exhausting, frustrating years in Wichita.

He focused on the highlights of the hearings, drawn by a story being told by C. O. Miller of the NTSB about the Windsor Incident, an event Sterns only dimly remembered. Miller was talking about some vital piece missing from the cargo door in Paris and about placards on the cargo door that hadn't solved the problem. They never did.

The placards on the DC-10 door, telling you not to force the handle, had been written in English. But it was revealed in testimony that perhaps the baggage handler who had closed the cargo door in Paris could not read English. Transcripts of the testimony at the Senate's public hearings suggested that the man was "possibly illiterate." Though it was quickly learned that the man was not in fact "illiterate"—he could speak and read three languages but could not read English— the word from the testimony was grabbed by the press and used by the president of McDonnell Douglas at the company's annual meeting. It would sweep through a nervous industry as a rationale for what happened in Paris. DC-10 pilots, wanting to believe in the plane they had to fly, would blame the baggage handler confidentially to anyone who asked. The baggage handler would give hundreds of Douglas engineers who had genuinely tried to build a failsafe locking system someone to accuse.

Miller was testifying for the last time as head of the NTSB's Bureau of Aviation Safety. He knew that his bureau would be blamed for not having followed up more vigorously after Windsor, for having evaluated the

FAA's responses to the board's recommendations as "marginally acceptable," when, in fact, only the peephole and placards had been achieved. But he knew that without the personnel, his hands had been tied. He would go out fighting for improvement of the bureau.

When Senator Howard Cannon, the aviation subcommittee chairman, asked him what priority had been given to the follow-up system, he snapped, "As such, it is anything but a top priority in view of the manpower we have." He was perplexed and frustrated, and he let it show. "I have been director of the bureau for almost six years. In the last three years, I have made recommendations for the numbers of people we need to do the job." He had never been given the men he needed, and it had been like sparring with shadows to find out *why.* Cannon cut into Miller's plea with some heartening news. "We are holding oversight hearings on the ninth and tenth of next month, of April, for the very purpose of . . . the possible reorganization of the National Transportation Safety Board; and . . . we will certainly go into getting those answers at that time."

Miller would not be there to see an independent board. The pressures of fighting for personnel, fighting to keep the quality of NTSB reports high were finding a weak spot, and he would soon have to get away from the pressure cooker environment of the bureau until he could find out how serious his symptoms were. Miller's heart condition did not make headlines in the *Sunday Times.* But the tall, athletic man who walked away from the hearings after saying his piece would be one of the quiet casualties of a battle that would never be completely won as long as men built planes.

For a public with a growing appetite for information on the world's worst plane crash, Miller was only the hors d'oeuvre. As the real scandal of the case, the Gentlemen's Agreement, was revealed, Sterns felt his plaintiff instincts come alive.

Arvin Basnight took the stand. As head of the FAA's western regional office in Los Angeles, he had midwifed the birth of all three American wide-body planes: the

747, the L-1011, and the DC-10. He and his staff had monitored the growth of the big new breed, using the Federal Air Regulations as their standard. The FARs defined the minimum standards planes must meet before certification, and no new plane can fly without compliance.

Although FARs set the standards for airworthiness, Sterns knew they could be ten years behind the state-of-the-art. FARs could be exploited by manufacturers who, as Sterns complained, "filed application for type certification as early as they possibly can because that freezes the date of the applicable regulations."

When a new breed of plane could not be squeezed within the limits of the FARs, an attempt was made by the FAA to bend with the state-of-the-art by issuing a series of new requirements for the new planes—the so-called Special Conditions that were a piecemeal attempt to patch up the gaps in the FARs and provide regulations that would contain adequate safety standards for the "novel and unusual features" of a new plane. Sometimes, but not always, the Special Conditions became FARs, providing a gradual, sluggish regeneration of the regulations. The FAA's first biennial Airworthiness Review, scheduled for December, 1974, would be an attempt, at last, to establish a systematic method of keeping airworthiness standards up to the state-of-the-art. In the thirty pages of Special Conditions for the DC-10, there were sections devoted to the unique three-main landing gear, to emergency exit facilities, to fireproof materials, to the control and propulsion systems. But there was no reference to the size effect. Basnight's men had not seen the implications early enough to write them into the DC-10's Special Conditions. No matter how dedicated, they did not sit at the threshold of change. How could you keep civil servants, removed form the firing line in industry, up to speed technologically?

Delegation of authority to the industry had been one answer. Let the men who knew the most do it themselves. The FAA had heaped responsibility on the senior engineers of Douglas, Boeing, and Lockheed who designed and built the planes; and who, as Designated Engineering Representatives of the FAA, changed hats and inspected their own work. Begun in 1933, it was the same system Sterns had seen at Beech.

In the same spirit, the FAA had, in recent years, been encouraging the correction of safety hazards by the *voluntary Service Bulletins issued by the manufacturer*. The FAA would shake its fingers at worrisome problems with cautionary letters and telegrams; it would rattle ADs menacingly at serious safety hazards. But fewer and fewer ADs were issued as manufacturers increasingly took the in-house route to self-correction. To work, a system of self-regulation demanded a high level of honesty and trust. And the FAA did trust industry.

From its formation in 1958 as part of the Department of Transport, the FAA had been assigned a double mandate, a conflicting one: it was to be an advocate of both *public safety* and of *industry*. Founded at a time when young airlines and manufacturers needed protection and encouragement, the FAA and its predecessors had always stayed close to industry. In regional environments, trust and friendship grew. The FAA and industry worked out problems together. With trust, there was openness and, ideally, a free flow of information to the FAA that would bring safety problems out in the open.

As Arvin Basnight told his story, it was clear that the system of trust could fail. He bared the Gentlemen's Agreement. Senator Cannon opened the can of worms with the question, "After the incident over Windsor, Ontario, in 1972, did you prepare an Airworthiness Directive with respect to modification on the DC-10?" Basnight answered, "The staff of the region did, yes sir." The staff had reeled with shock at the Windsor Incident. They had certificated the door as being failsafe. To qualify the door as failsafe, Douglas had apparently satisfied the FAA that the possibility of door failure was "extremely improbable" even though exhaustive fault analysis tests on the doors had not been required. But what did *extremely improbable* mean? The Federal Air Regulations were rampant with subjective probability terms like *extremely improbable, extremely remote, negligible, improbable, foreseeable, likely*—loosely worded probability terms that had never been quantified. In the case of the DC-10 doors, extremely improbable was found to have been interpreted as meaning anything from "one failure in 10,000 flight hours" to "one in a billion."

The door had blown within the first 5,000 hours of service, falling catastrophically short of most interpretations of the failsafe criteria. Failure had *not* been "*extremely improbable.*"

Windsor clearly called for an AD; and Basnight's Airworthiness Directive Board had started drafting one immediately after the incident. But the AD *was never issued.* Room 318 of the Russell Senate Office Building went silent as Basnight dropped his bombshell.

Chapter Eighteen

The Gentlemen's Agreement

BASNIGHT'S BOMBSHELL was contained in a memo
which he read now to the senators:

On Friday, June 16, 1972, at 8:50 A.M., I received a phone call from Mr. Jack McGowan,
president, Douglas Aircraft Co., who indicated
that late on Thursday, June 15, he had received a
call from Mr. Shaffer, FAA Administrator, asking
what the company had found out about the problem about the carge door that caused American
Airlines to have an explosive decompression . . .
Mr. McGowan said he had reviewed with the Administrator the facts developed, which included
the need to beef up the electrical wiring and related factors that had been developed by the Douglas Co. working with the FAA. He indicated that
Mr. Shaffer had expressed pleasure in finding reasonable corrective actions and had told Mr. Mc-
Gowan that the corrective measures could be
undertaken as a product of a *gentlemen's agreement* thereby not requiring the issuance of an FAA
Airworthiness Directive.

When he received the call, the board was already in
session drafting the AD. Basnight had called to consult
with Dick Sliff of his engineering division and got more
disturbing news. Sliff told him that when FAA engineers
had tried earlier in the week to get data from Douglas,

Douglas would not give them the reports on operational difficulties on the cargo doors. When Sliff "raised a fuss" they *produced data showing that approximately 100 complaints had been received by the company indicating that the airlines using the DC-10 had noted and reported to the company mechanical problems in locking the cargo doors.* The FAA had apparently not known of the cargo door difficulties.

The Airworthiness Directive Board was still in session, working over the AD. Should he continue? Basnight wondered. More convinced than ever that an AD should go through, he set the phone lines buzzing between Los Angeles and Washington. He called Jim Rudolph, head of the Flight Standards Service, to consult with him on whether or not to go on with it. Rudolph told him to continue. Shaffer could not be found. But the deputy director, Ken Smith, called Basnight and confirmed that he should proceed with the AD. But confirmation would have to come from Shaffer. Basnight waited all day, while the board continued to sweat out the refinements on the draft AD. Hearing nothing, he called Rudolph again later in the day and was told that Rudolph and Smith were planning a telephone conference with Douglas and the three airlines flying the DC-10 to start getting the proposals that would be in the AD accomplished in the field. It was Friday night, and Basnight's contact with Washington closed up for the weekend.

On Monday morning he learned that an alert bulletin, a General Notice, had been sent to the three airlines, outlining the fixes that were to be made, including the placards. The notice did not say "You must"; it just said "I understand that your company will . . ." This was followed by an Alert Service Bulletin on blue paper, SB 52-35, from Douglas, outlining the fixes, including the peephole aimed at visually determining whether the lockpins were in place.

Basnight had never been told not to issue the AD. But he had never been told to issue it. Douglas and the airlines, it appeared, would fix it themselves, via the voluntary SB route. As if sensing what was going to happen and wanting his own actions on record, Basnight wrote and filed a long memorandum on the Gentlemen's Agreement.

The memo had been buried so deeply that the hearing's staff had had a hard time retrieving it from the files. Why hadn't Basnight spoken out? Perhaps more deeply revealing was the discouraged testimony of FAA engineer Everett Pittman during House hearings held simultaneously with the Senate hearings. He was the man who had drafted the AD that was never sent. "When we found out that in fact the AD had been stopped, we were, I guess you could say, charged up. We were ready to go with getting this door fixed. To have it stopped at that time produced a natural reaction of something like *'if that is the way it is, let them take care of it.'* Unfortunately, that carried on and we were not even inclined to try, later on, to issue an AD." No AD had ever been canceled like this before in anyone's memory. The western region, which knew the plane more intimately than anyone in Washington, had been overruled, undermined. Disheartened, they had given up. Pittman gave perhaps the clearest look anyone at any of the hearings would give of what may have been the real villains in the DC-10 case—the many minor, apparently insignificant abdications of personal responsibility that, cumulatively, could lead—*had led!*—to catastrophe.

The senators grabbed the Gentlemen's Agreement and ran, throwing the FAA and Douglas onto the defensive. McGowan and Shaffer were grilled. The senators attacked the choice of a voluntary Service Bulletin over the AD. Wasn't it true that an AD was mandatory? That it would be seen by foreign governments and embassies, where an SB could be slipped in quietly to the airlines? How could you be sure an SB would get the job done, when it had no more urgency than the changing of a light bulb? Wasn't it true that the AD is published in the Federal Register, giving the public general notice? Had an SB been used to protect the *industry* rather than the *public?*

With the finesse of a Mack truck, jut-jawed Shaffer

228

defended the SB, claiming that World War II had been won by them. Then, suddenly, with a thrust by Senator Cannon, the pall of Watergate was cast over the hearings. Had Shaffer been involved in the solicitation of funds for President Nixon's reelection campaign from McDonnell Douglas at that time? The question was inspired by some information that had been dug out in preparation for the Senate and House hearings. Testimony in the House hearings reported that Common Cause, the General Accounting Office, and other sources had released information on donations from McDonnell Douglas officers and the corporation itself of nearly $75,000 to the reelection fund and to the Republican National Committee in the months immediately before and after the Windsor Incident. The Gentlemen's Agreement had reportedly been followed by contributions of over $40,000 of that amount. The implication of the question was clear: Had McDonnell Douglas bought its immunity from the threatened AD— an AD that might have hurt the plane's image just at a time when Douglas was fighting the L-1011 for sales, and about to send a DC-10 on a round-the-world public relations' trip, replete with Danny Kaye as a come-on? The question cast a sinister shadow, in hindsight, over then-Vice-President Spiro Agnew's participation in the delivery ceremonies for the first two DC-10s.

The question was asked in a Washington agonizing through the death throes of a disgraced administration. The specter of Watergate loomed over the FAA, for the administrator who had replaced Shaffer was Alexander Butterfield, the presidential assistant who had broken the news that the infamous White House tapes existed. He, like Shaffer, was a retired military man and was criticized by many in aviation as an inappropriate choice.

With Senator Adlai E. Stevenson III pressing the question, Shaffer blustered denials. One of the President's men had visited him, yes, and had asked for a list of people to "pluck." "I told him he could buy for thirteen dollars and fifty cents the *World Aviation Directory*." Shaffer had made a donation "but they did not get any help from me on shaking down or plucking anybody else."

The day after the election, Shaffer had been asked for his resignation.

"Mr. Shaffer, how do you make your living now?"

"I own and operate Pioneer Van Lines, a moving and storage company, and I am also a director of the Beech Aircraft Co., and director of . . ."

"Beech!" Sterns hooted when he heard it. "Beech!" It was too much to believe. Now he'd be deposing Shaffer on his Beech cases.

Shaffer had come off badly. Next, McDonnell Douglas's president John Brizendine would testify. Program manager of Douglas's three jet transports, the DC-8, the -9, and the -10, John Brizendine had the delicate task of trying to hold the good reputation and public image of Douglas together through the most severe turbulence in forty years of building planes. Though he had a sophisticated corporate style, he was still a Douglas engineer who instinctively explained things with quick engineer's sketches. Now he was a man attempting to integrate two severe shocks. First, the attack on the company had been "absolute shock! . . . It was inconceivable to us that we would ever find *our company* being accused of flagrant misconduct." Then, he'd flown to Washington for the hearings, and in his hotel room just the night before "I found out we were going to be accused of Watergate-type deals with the FAA—contributing to the fund to reelect the President, being favorably treated by an AD of the FAA. It was the most farfetched thing I could imagine. But the thing that really got me—I didn't sleep all night—was to realize that this kind of thing could happen in the United States of America, where I had naïvely believed that a man has rights, a company has rights, where you expect to be protected from almost despotic treatment in your personal rights. I just couldn't believe this was happening in our country."

He had already alluded to the missing torque tube plate in a press conference, but now it was his humiliating duty to put it on congressional record. He did not

230

look forward to it. He believed that, with the shock of Watergate, "people, and in large part the media, are looking for villains." And he recognized the impact of it on "our *reputation* . . . our customers have to have absolute confidence in the integrity of our product. That's part of what's made this transportation system what it is—innate confidence people have in our transportation system, and Douglas is part of that. The reason I came to work for Douglas was simply that I thought they work on a little higher plane than, maybe, other companies." Now, a tiny, inexpensive piece of metal was bringing this "integrity of product" and the entire system of inspection and delegation under fire. He made his statement to the senators.

"It has been reported from Paris that a key part of one of the modifications of the aft cargo door . . . was found missing upon inspection of the aft cargo door located at the accident site. According to our manufacturing records, all Service Bulletins that had been issued to improve the cargo door latching mechanisms had been incorporated in the Turkish Airlines [plane] prior to its delivery. At this time we are unable to satisfactorily explain this discrepancy, but we are continuing to investigate this matter."

Douglas had discovered that the inspector who should have checked to make sure the plate had been attached—the support plate that should have made it physically impossible to close the door by force—had put his stamp on the inspection sheet, guaranteeing that the modification had been done, *when, in fact, the plate had never been attached*. Nor had it been attached to a DC-10 owned by Laker Airways in England, which had gone through the predelivery modifications at the same time. The inspector had been subsequently identified, reprimanded, and removed from inspection duties. But his error could never be withdrawn. When the two planes had been delivered in December of 1972, the inspection sheets had gone along as part of the planes' pedigree of airworthiness. Airlines relied on those sheets. The only other way the defect could have been spotted would have been to take the door apart, strip off the fiber glass panel covering the locking mechanisms, and look.

News of the missing plate had stunning impact. It was one of those screaming admissions for which there could be no answer, no excuse, no escape. To lawyers, this was gross negligence—the stuff of massive lawsuits. Letting revelation build on revelation, the senators picked up the scenario and probed in to the more basic problem—the integrity of the floors. The vents and floor strengths that had nagged the Dutch since the late sixties. Brizendine reported that venting studies had been done as early as 1970 at the request of the Netherlands. They had done additional studies after *Windsor* and had continued to work at a "modest low level of intense activity" ever since. Now, under pressure from the FAA, the press, Congress, the level of activity had increased.

No one—not the industry, the FAA, or NASA, which could have done basic research on the volumes and pressures in the new generation of jets—had fully recognized the serious implications of the size effect. When the FAA had asked Douglas to reassess the jumbo jet design with regard to fuselage holes, Douglas had replied, just a week before the Paris crash, that they felt it was a burden that should be shared by the entire industry. The FAA, they suggested, should fund the study. It was clear that, even after Paris, the aviation industry would have to be pried, like an abalone from a rock, from what had become a compulsive attachment to failsafe doors as the *only* solution to the size effect. "Douglas's primary efforts," Brizendine confirmed, "have been to insure the integrity of the pressure vessel."

That they had finally achieved, to the infinite relief of all those who had read about the door and who flew DC-10s.

Within months of the Paris crash, the door would be as safe as it was possible for Douglas engineers to make it and, by general consensus, failsafe at last. Two weeks after the crash, the FAA had issued an AD forcing airlines to incorporate the "closed-loop" system, which had been phase four of Douglas's door improvement program, the subject of a generally neglected Service Bulletin SB 52-49. It was a locking system in which the closing of the vent door could *only* be achieved by proper movement of the locktube—a system in which the closing of the vent door *did mean* that the lockpins were properly engaged. July 1, 1974, was the date set for completion of the closed-loop system for every DC-10, with foreign airlines eagerly and voluntarily complying.

At last they had fixed the door, but they still hadn't fixed the plane. Floors had not been strengthened; more venting had not been installed. Yet floors had collapsed twice in flight. And now 346 had died.

Watching the hearings from his Wichita hotel room, Sterns had sensed a burgeoning scandal, sure now that this would be the biggest product liability case in history. And what had been revealed in the hearings—the Gentlemen's Agreement, the Windsor Incident, the missing plate, the vulnerable floors—was only the tip of the iceberg, he knew, compared to what discovery would bring out. The public case had been made. But the legal case was still hidden in California, in documents. He could taste it.

That was a month ago. Then the Wright case had come in. And the call from Engler. Now he was on his way to England to receive his instructions.

Sterns met the English solicitors in Mitchell's offices on the Thames. Below them, in full view, Denmark's Queen Margrethe's visit was coming to an end; royalty were saying good-bye with full ceremonial pomp. Flags waved. Plumed guards saluted. And as the whistle of the Danish royal yacht blew, Sterns felt powerfully moved by this persistence of tradition. The Tower Bridge loomed in the background, adding its weight of history to the scene. He was a western boy who never felt completely comfortable in New York. But here, strangely, he felt very much at home.

233

Chapter Nineteen

The Great
Birthday Card Debate

LIKE A HOUSEWIFE who's just heard twenty unexpected guests are coming for dinner, Thelma Alden, Judge Hall's court clerk, was scurrying around getting the house in order. The federal courthouse in Los Angeles. On June 6, the Judicial Panel on Multidistrict Litigation had transferred the case to California and assigned it to her boss, Judge Peirson M. Hall, senior judge in the U.S. District Court for the Central District of California. By mid-June, twenty or thirty lawyers would be jetting into town for hearings on the class action and the start of depositions on *In Re: Paris Air Crash MDL No. 172*. But unlike dinner guests, they'd be hanging around the house for at least a year. And the place was still bustling from previous crashes. There were still three hundred deaths pending in Hall's other crash cases. *Air Canada, General Dynamics,* and *Air Alaska* were still hanging on, clogging the calendar with court hearings. *Pago Pago,* already being referred to as "Pango" by the insiders on the case, had just arrived. The Pan Am 707 had crashed in western Samoa just a month before the Paris crash and had been MDLd to Judge Hall's court, too. She would now have to find space for both *Pago Pago* and *Paris* without overtaxing the judge.

With the major aviation cases flowing into Hall's hands, it was hard for Thelma to give him enough time

234

between hearings to relax at his Palm Desert home. And there was, increasingly, the pressure of time. Of mortality. The judge was turning eighty this month. He had a pacemaker buried in his chest. He could have retired at full salary. But there was so much more he was determined to do. There might never be another chance for him to apply the finest minds in the field to the issue that had challenged his intellect for years—Warsaw . . . choice of law . . . or another crash that would more vividly display the need for a standardized body of aviation law. Through *Paris,* he might bring this dream a little closer to reality. Thelma was dedicated to preserving his still-formidable energies.

She hated housework in her own home. But as a housekeeper of the courts, she was a jewel. It would take three or four months to work the kinks out of *Paris.* It always did. Each case was an organic thing, with its own rhythms and rites of passage. Still in its infancy, full of complexity and competition among all the lawyers, *Paris* was having a wobbly start. But she had tried to smooth things by sending off a two-page list of procedures to all the lawyers' offices, Thelma Alden's HELPFUL HOUSEHOLD HINTS TO COUNSEL OF COMPLEX LITIGATION IN JUDGE HALL'S COURT. It would tell them what the judge's procedural requirements were, even how to have their secretaries type up a properly titled document.

The lawyers were setting up housekeeping, too. During the day, the plaintiff attorneys hung their hats, and left files and briefcases, at Jim Butler's office in downtown Los Angeles. Butler was the Los Angeles lawyer who had brought Speiser into the Hope case and who now shared the case load with Speiser's firm. It was near Bob Packard's offices where the depositions were being held on a schedule of two weeks on, one week off. At night, they pursued their consuming diversion— the search for the perfect hotel. It was an intense, competitive search, for not only was going "first class" one of the few compensations for being away from home but status was at stake in one's life-style. The search

235

for the perfect restaurant was another serious mission. Le Restaurant. The Pavilion atop the new Music Center. Chasen's, the Hollywood status eatery where you could always see a star or two. Perino's on Wilshire. And the little restaurants that Marshall Morgan knew about. Morgan, a top trial lawyer in California, had been asked by Kreindler to help him handle his cases. He, Butler, and Sterns were the most experienced trial lawyers on the plaintiff's side, and if it came to trial on liability or damages, Morgan would be very busy in court. Though not an aviation specialist, Morgan was a pilot and had handled the crew cases in the Disneyland to Los Angeles airport helicopter crash. A quick study, he had become skilled in helicopter terminology. With the same ease, he would now master the language of torque tubes and lockpins of *Paris*. Stylishly dressed, with a diamond-bright wit and wordly panache that San Franciscans like to pretend Los Angeles is incapable of, he became *Paris*'s resident *bon vivant*. With a flourishing practice handling both defense and plaintiff cases, he socialized easily in both camps. He lived in a splendid Tudor mansion in Pasadena that he loaned out to symphony fund-raising galas and television series. He came to depositions one morning and told his colleagues, "Janet Leigh climbed out of my bathroom window this morning." For an episode of *Columbo*. Over steaks at the Pacific Dining Car, Morgan's droll wit would lighten many dreary evenings for the *Paris* lawyers.

The position of the plaintiff lawyers was still very tense and unsettled. Kreindler wanted to be made class counsel, knowing that, as counsel, he would be put on the plaintiff's committee, the only way to effectively represent his eleven clients. The lawyers with large blocks of cases resented his attempt to parlay his cases into a controlling position. He waited, hopefully, for Hall's ruling on the class action. For in spite of the fact that the English press had made the class action seem a *fait accompli*, until certified by the judge it did not exist. Kreindler was now carrying the class action banner, which had been dropped by Speiser immediately after the MDL hearings. In his regular newsletter to the English solicitors instructing him, Speiser told his English clients that "since the panel has taken jurisdiction, we have decided that it is unnecessary to proceed with the class action. . . ." He cited opposition and possible delaying appeals by McDonnell Douglas's attorneys as the principal reasons for discontinuing the action and expressed satisfaction "that the procedures available through the Judicial Panel on Multidistrict Litigation contain all the desirable features of a class action. . . ." Both did include consolidation for discovery and liability, a time-saving device. And he had been concerned that even if the class was granted by Hall, the 9th Circuit Court of Appeals might reverse it in response to a writ of prohibition by the defense. But his argument made little sense to lawyers who could not see that the MDLing of the case replaced in any way the two prime advantages the class action might have offered; protecting the as-yet unrepresented from the running out of California's one-year statute of limitations and the right to send a notice to all the families informing them of the lawsuit, something the judge wanted, but had no clear authority to do under the MDL. Lawyers on both sides saw considerable irony in the fact that the class action, the dramatic and much-publicized device that had captivated the English and left many with the impression that it was the only way to gain access to the California courts, had been abandoned so precipitously. And discussion of Speiser's motives would be one of the litigation's liveliest parlor games.

The Speiser-Butler camp had been dramatically strengthened in July by the Bury St. Edmunds cases. Bury solicitor John Sheerin, who had considered affiliation with the Mitchell-Enger rump group, would head the English committee of solicitors instructing Speiser. But there were still dozens of uncommitted cases. The Japanese were holding back. As they debated their moves, an aggressive system that had evolved to process multi-death transport crashes was put into effect by plaintiff lawyers. They had initiated discovery immediately, putting pressure on the defense by shooting off lengthy interrogatories and demands for production of documents, and deposing witnesses. Denied access to the wreckage or to the investigation, they activated whatever network of contacts they had for collecting facts. They called their French connections; assigned para-legals and law clerks to research and write briefs; flew out to all of Hall's hearings, maintaining the highest possible profile in the hope of being assigned to the plaintiff's committee. The committee was the small group of lawyers who would run discovery, control strategy, and who were usually paid for their extra services by all the lawyers not on the committee. Once a lawyer was on the committee, cases often came to him, as there were other lawyers in the provinces who had stumbled on a case or two and who knew it would be too expensive to try to run a single case themselves. Intimidated by the barrage of activity, they would hand over the running of their cases to members of the plaintiff's committee for a fee. Though the system smoothly put the control of complex cases into the hands of the specialists who knew aviation law best, the men who would handle the cases skillfully and work hard, and who could afford to run up the tens or even hundreds of thousands of dollars it cost to run a big case, there was smoldering resentment of the system among lawyers cut out of the plaintiff's committee. It flared early in Paris.

It exploded with the choosing of the plaintiff's committee. Sterns, the new man from San Francisco, was making waves. He was still uninitiated and had listened, incredulous, as lawyers who had learned the hard way in *Air Alaska* and *Duarte,* two transport cases that had been MDLd to Judge Hall's court, argued that it was vital to grab a commanding position on the plaintiff's committee. But in early June, even before he could think through his strategy. Sterns had been thrust into the power seat. Suddenly heavy with the infusion of the English cases, he had been appointed by Hall as chairman of the plaintiff's committee. That left Madole, Butler, F. Lee Bailey's man Seymour Madow, and Seattle lawyer Richard Krutch, the latter two with only one case each, as members of Stern's committee. That, of course, would never do. Long, unhappy letters had been written to the judge and to each other, trying to dethrone Sterns, and a furor was raised at hearings on June 17. The argument became so heated that at one point one of Kreindler's partners, steaming with anger, had snapped at Sterns, "You'll need Lee Kreindler in this case and you'll have to pay for him." Sterns had countered with, "We recognize Mr. Kreindler's talent, but we can get along very well without him!" The judge had expelled the public and press and, in closed session, let the lawyers thrash it out. At the end of the donnybrook, Sterns knew that he *must* hold a seat in the cockpit but that no one person could be chairman and accomplish anything. The pressures were too great, and the case would suffer. The only solution was a compromise—a *troika,* which would consist of Sterns and Butler representing the two major blocks of clients, and Kreindler, as a favor to the judge who wanted both his scholarly ability and his class action, the vehicle for the notice the judge was determined to send to the families. But they would all have to wait for weeks for the final ruling from the judge on both the plaintiff's committee and the class action. The issues would hang in limbo until early August, with stress and tension building.

The lawyers took some of it out on the tennis court. Kreindler and Madole had arranged for guest privileges at the Los Angeles Racket Club in West Los Angeles, and Kreindler, his young aide Marc Moller, Madole, and Sterns smashed balls at each other through late spring and early summer. Waiting. Sterns had never learned to play tennis, but he had just bought a home with a tennis court and his wife had outfitted him with white shorts and shirt and a wooden racket. He did not hesitate to challenge his more experienced colleagues. At 6 feet 7, he could almost envelop the court with a single leap. He hit "home runs" regularly, lobbing balls into adjoining courts. Kreindler, he felt, delighted in smashing drives past him. Balls ponged in aggression as the case moved into summer.

Tensions eased a little at the Hyatt Regency bar in the evenings. Even FitzSimons, who rarely smiled in court, developed an amusing takeoff on Sterns's apple-pie-and-motherhood courtroom style, leaning on the bar the way Sterns lounged over the lectern, saying, "Gosh, Your Honor, I'd just love to stay here and argue with these fine gentlemen for the rest of the afternoon, but my daughter's graduating from high school tonight, and. . . ." Coming from FitzSimons, a lawyer who had fought and won many of the big transport cases for Boeing as well as for Douglas, it was a high form of flattery. Passing through San Francisco, FitzSimons relaxed with Sterns over drinks and dinner at Sterns's home in the east bay before catching a night plane to Seattle for meetings with Boeing's senior counsel. At ease, the men felt considerable affection and respect for each other. They talked about the case, told jokes, tried out new restaurants, drank each other's expensive wines. Later in the winter, when *Paris* appeared to be choking on its own paper, Sterns would tell a roomful of English solicitors that "FitzSimons and I have settled this case six times over a drink at the Hyatt Regency bar," the early favorite.

But, like enemy officers who toast each other's gallantry before strapping on their swords, they were at war. And the constant contact at the Hyatt Regency became too cloying. Part of a new complex of hotel, shops, and offices, its lobby had the hustle of an airport terminal. Yet social activity always narrowed down to the one tiny, dark bar off the lobby. Like a ship at sea, the hotel intensified contact. To Stephen Mitchell, observing the lawyers gliding past each other at elevators, holding secret meetings in one room, and then another, it was "something out of Agatha Christie."

Gradually, the men began to disperse to other hotels. FitzSimons stayed at the Jonathan Club, a dignified wood-paneled private club that exuded the ostentatious pomp of the prestigious New York clubs built by robber barons in the late nineteenth century. Free of the Hyatt's hustle, he, Dann, Packard, and the defense team could hold strategy meetings in the vast, hushed lounge. Here they could invite the plaintiff lawyers over individually for breakfast meetings and gain a distinct negotiating advantage as FitzSimons and his men—a phalanx of dark suits in this traditional milieu of male power—rose to meet a guest.

Kreindler, a very hard worker who valued convenience over splendor, tended to stay on at the Hyatt. He liked their efficient little suites, if he was meeting with clients. And it was close to the depositions. Don Madole, though, had decided that the hotel was full of "Kleenex and light bulb salesmen," and had moved a mile or two up Wilshire Boulevard to the Ambassador. Home of the Coconut Grove, symbol of Hollywood's night life in the thirties and forties, the Ambassador sat among its palm and bougainvillaea, all pink stucco and rococo Spanish glamour, like an aging, overpowdered movie queen. There, Madole rented a cottage set back in the gardens, a tropical setting that was worlds removed from the glass and steel of downtown Los Angeles, from FitzSimon's staid club, and from the Kansas dust bowl of his childhood. Gold-carved cherubs blessed the bed, which was separated from the living room by swags of yellow and flame-colored drapery. The sofa was circular, the telephones were undulating pieces of white plastic with the dial on the bottom, and the small private garden had a tiny free-form turquoise pool that Madole crossed in two strokes.

The government lawyers defending the FAA could be seen at the Ambassador, too, but sitting in a blue-suited circle in the patio bar, they lacked that fine edge of flamboyance needed to look fully at home there.

Sterns settled, more or less, into the Century Plaza, but still ranged restlessly between it, the Beverly Hilton across the road, and the Hyatt Regency. The Century Plaza's amenities met most of the stiff first-class criteria set by Sterns over the years: every room had windows that opened to air, balconies, and the sound of fountains; each had a refrigerator and ice maker, queen-size beds, twenty-four-hour room service, clothesline. . . . Turkish Airlines' defense George Tompkins and Desmond Barry, Jr., settled in there, too. Aviation lawyers would forgo quaint decor and dripping regional ambience any day, anywhere in the world, for these amenities. Its lobby lounge was very large, a genteel sunken pit, as open and bright as the Hyatt bar was dark and conspiratorial, and this may have been part of the appeal. It was thirty minutes removed from the tense atmosphere of the deposition room, and for Tompkins and Barry, closer to the golf course. And it was a nice place to take your wife. Dianne Sterns could fly down from San Francisco in an hour, an advantage over the wives in New York. Family tensions were hard to keep at bay, with the consuming demands of time the case placed on the men. Sterns brought his children down for weekends occasionally. Having failed to see any celebrities at Schwab's drugstore, his daughter Janet waited disconsolately to fly back to San Francisco after a weekend in Los Angeles. But in the airport washroom, his son John found himself standing next to Bob Hope at the urinal. As Hope left the washroom, both children dashed after him, and he graciously posed for a picture with them, while Janet grinned triumphantly.

But on Monday morning, the tensions were there again. Even the Birthday Card Debate had not cleared the air. The debate had started as twenty lawyers gathered around the long deposition table in Packard's office to interrogate one of the Douglas witnesses. Unrecorded, it is difficult to reconstruct. But it appears to have been initiated by Jim Butler. His straggling hair and graying beard had inspired Hall to refer to him as "Moses," but his well-fed Lucullan style suggested, more, a hip Henry VIII. Butler, like Sterns, had received a notice from Hall's friends suggesting that he send a card to the judge to help celebrate his eightieth birthday on July 30.

Sterns had wanted to send one, but had held back, thinking that, with the delicacy of his position right then, the card might be misconstrued. But Butler was eager to send a card. In fact, he had gone out and bought one, a big Snoopy card that carried the general theme "Who says a committee can't get things done?" He showed it around the table. The plaintiff lawyers, delighted at the reference to the current brouhaha over the plaintiff's committee, thought it "charming, whimsical, just perfect," and agreed that they should *all* sign and send it. But Sterns saw FitzSimons looking "very sour" at the end of the table and knew that it would not be that simple. There would be debate. Hold on! What were the implications? Could not the plaintiffs, sending a Snoopy card alone, be accused of currying favor at the expense of the defense? And could not the defense *abstaining* from a card be interpreted as a personal slight to the judge . . . or as a criticism of his court? Bostwick, of the hull suit, took an academic view, earnestly weighing the pros and cons. Herb Lyons, representing the government, took a distinctly dour view. He had been keeping a profile so low as to be almost invisible. At that point, he was devoted to disassociating the government from the case and sat at a small table at the back of the room, as detached as it was possible to be without actually sitting in the hall. He was reluctant to commit himself to *anything*—even a birthday card—that might be seen as an admission of government involvement in the case.

For forty-five minutes, twenty of the world's highest paid aviation lawyers debated the merits of the Snoopy card, swinging from stalemate to consensus and back again. Completely forgotten in the rhetoric was the innocuous mission of sending a dear old man greetings on his eightieth birthday. The westerners and the plaintiffs tended toward sympathy for a card, and fought to keep a consortium of defense and eastern-seaboard lawyers from polarizing around a stiff anticard stance. From the spectrum of opinion, Bostwick was at last able to identify what he saw as the only two proper

243

courses of action: either the plaintiffs and defense could each send their own group card, or all could join in sending the *same* card. There were murmurs of approval and a sense of hope that men of reason were within arm's reach of agreement. It was the moment that, grasped, might have settled the lawsuit, for, as Sterns observed, "We would have *had to work* together to pick the right birthday card." But it was not to be.

Hostility bristled at the defense's end of the table. Hall had just denied FitzSimon's *forum non conveniens* motion, a final attempt to escape California jurisdiction, and the failure of this had sent dozens of the English who had been holding back, pens poised over retainer forms, surging into the Speiser camp. FitzSimons announced that he would not be party to sending a "groupie" birthday card. He would not be a party to sending any birthday card. It was not the way things were done in New York.

In the finest tradition of party pooping, he killed the card and brought the Birthday Card Debate to a crashing halt. Now, with the plaintiff lawyers in disarray, the anticard faction wrapped it up with the warning that anyone sending his own individual card did so at his own peril.

They went on, sullenly, to depositions. And if anyone ever sent a card to Judge Hall on his eightieth birthday, they never told. But the regional conflicts, the personal characteristics, the stubborn intransigence that would make the case a "microcosm of war" had been laid bare on the deposition table.

Chapter Twenty

The Birth of the Plane

IT WAS THEIR BABY. A baby that is the synthesis of 10,000 minds, that weighs more than twenty elephants, but flies.

Every one of the millions of decisions that had furthered this "birth of committee" had been recorded on hundreds of thousands of pieces of paper that had been kept and filed as part of the genetic data that would help build the next baby. The DC-11.

This paper—boxes of it, cartons of it, files of it—would now be produced by *discovery,* the legal process that would largely determine the critical outlines of the case for liability. Discovery would bring forth the memos which, skillfully used, could make the front page of *The New York Times* and force the defense to squirm toward the settlement table.

The story of birth would arrive in Los Angeles in file cabinets, boxes, and wooden crates from McDonnell Douglas, the FAA, Turkish Airlines, and General Dynamics. It was there, and in the hundreds of hours of deposition testimony that was also part of discovery, that evidence of genetic defects, if any, would be found.

Plaintiff lawyers took little interest in the miracle of birth. They were more prone to see a jet plane as simply "a conglomerate of low bids." They were after the dynamite. And in the witch-hunt environment that now surrounded the DC-10, even the most innocent note, taken out of context and years removed from the atmosphere in which it was written, could be dangerous to the defense. McDonnell Douglas faced discovery with distaste. Since the crash, few days had gone by when Douglas executives did not smart from another assault. It would soon be hard to find anyone in America or England who did not know of the Paris crash as, "Oh, the one where the door came off." Ghosts of the Comet and the Electra hovered, for the press campaign was equaling the Electra's in intensity. The press, too, had made the sprawling Long Beach plant that bustled with short-sleeved engineers seem a sinister fortress.

Mendes and Mount assigned a lawyer full-time to McDonnell Douglas to coach engineers on how to handle themselves under this unprecedented pressure: how to deal with press questions, how to recognize and deal with lawyers' manipulative questions when they were in the deposition chair. These were things not taught in engineering school, but essential since the advent of the product liability lawsuit.

Even John Brizendine, a cool and articulate man, would get tripped up by questions shrewdly phrased to draw out testimony that would sound good later in court.

In a classic trap that infuriates engineers because of its apparent theatricalism rather than relevancy, Sterns would prod him with questions about the man who had falsely stamped the inspection sheets saying the vital support plate had been installed. "Did you ever have a discussion with him, a personal discussion?" "Did you ever see any statement or statements given by him?" "Did you look at anything else, say his personnel file?" Sterns was fishing for something, somehting he wanted to come out, and he took many minutes to help Brizendine paint the incriminating picture he had in mind. Brizendine's responses were vague, laced with "I might have . . ." "Maybe . . ." "In due course, I probably looked at it." Gradually, Sterns's questions began to focus on the target. "Nothing struck you in there as unusual?" "Do you remember reading about him being off work for a substantial period of time a few years ago?"

"No . . . I don't think so." "You don't remember *anything* about his file that was unusual in that respect?" "No, I can't recall the details. . . ."

Sterns let Brizendine build his own trap, denying any knowledge of anything unusual about the disgraced inspector. Then, suddenly, he got to the point: "*Do you know as you sit there this very day that he was out of work for a year with a brain tumor operation back in the sixties?*" It was out, another knife in the jugular. Crucial inspection, inspection on which the safety of the plane and the survival of 346 people might well have depended, had been in the hands of a man who had been operated on for a brain tumor! Brizendine backed off, admitting, "Now that you mention it, I guess there was something about that. . . ." But Sterns knew better than to "beat a dead horse." He had no medical facts. He had no proof that there was any connection at all between the operation and the man's capacity to do his job. But he had what he wanted, and the court reporter had it down on the record. It would be beautiful in court. He dropped the issue cold and went on to question about floor vents. It was the kind of verbal trap Douglas's senior engineers would face daily as Sterns, Morgan, Madole, Kreindler, Butler, Bostwick, and others came at them.

The lawyers went into depositions on July 18, 1974, with a new language honed around the tiny tables at the Hyatt Regency bar, the language of *torque tubes, actuators, shims,* and *psis* that would be the special vocabulary of the Paris case. They went at the first McDonnell Douglas witness with glib expertise. Chasing shadows, plaintiff lawyers tried to pin down individual responsibility. Who had designed the DC-10? In fact, the father of the DC-10 had been a conglomerate of engineering minds. But with a stroke of luck, DC-10 Program Manager William Gross named Harold Adams as "the daddy of design." As assistant chief designer and then chief designer, Harold Adams had authored the memos that set down design policy. He or his assistant Gene Dubil had chaired the weekly and daily design meetings that had kept the design evolving at a tumultuous pace during 1968 and 1969. He had been a crucial link in the chain of command, for it was to his desk that the lead engineers' design recommendations were brought for approval before they were sent up to the program manager, who was then John Brizendine. It was the perpetual revisions and refinements of design coming from Adam's office that had channeled the growth of the DC-10.

Though he never appeared and had retired before *Windsor* and *Paris,* Adams quickly became known to the Paris case as the "father of the DC-10," all the more legendary because he now lived on a beach on a Pacific island. He was the man who believed that great airplanes were designed not by paper pushers, but by men who found time each day to put their feet up on the desk to think and dream. Yet, as chief designer, he had been in the hot seat, barraged continually by crucial decisions . . . by resolving problems, providing top-level design guidance, setting policy. A man who had to live with the knowledge that "the buck stops here." He was the man whose safety statements in the late fifties had become Douglas's creed; who had been asked, in retirement, to write down his design philosophy before it turned into myth; the maintainability, reliability, dispatchability man who, in his forty years at Douglas, had helped put the world into the air. His passionate belief that the safe design was the simple design had come to fruition in the DC-9, the plane he was most proud of.

Because the -9 had not been the sexy, prestige, transoceanic transport for the airlines, Adams had been free of *some* of the terrible pressures of time, weight, and cost imposed by the customer airlines who had to be pleased—the pressures that more relentlessly drove the design of the big glamour planes like the DC-10.

On the -10, the pressure to accommodate the airlines had been extreme. Engineers had been able to talk them out of a below-deck cocktail lounge as uneconomic. But when sales to Alitalia, a member of the ATLAS consortium, had hinged on increasing the passenger payload, Adams had leaped onto a plane to Rome and had redesigned the interior configuration of the plane on the back of an envelope on the way over, moving lavatories around and taking out an aisle. In Rome, he had worked all night with his design team to do the drawing. The next morning, he had presented Alitalia with a configuration that would give them not the eight more seats they wanted but twelve, without sacrifice of comfort or safety. They had bought the plane. He had no illusions about the competitive pressures on the DC-10. But, he would tell his friends after the Paris crash, he had never been forced to do anything that compromised safety in his forty years at Douglas, had never been turned down on anything he considered essential. "Of course, you learn not to ask for things you know can't happen."

Dug up in discovery, his original design policy memo of September 1967 seemed to breathe these practical realities. In it, Adams the dreamer did not come through. It inspired lawyers to ask, *"Had* he really been the 'daddy of design'?" Or had the DC-10 design, in fact, been sired by the profit motive? The memo was nailed to the wall as a doctrine of greed. In depositions, it was read out to the company's president, John Brizendine. *"For the DC-10 aircraft to be profitable for McDonnell Douglas Corporation, it must be successful so that it will be sold in sufficient quantity to more than recover the initial investment. . . ."* Research and development would cost well over one and a half billion. *"For a successful airplane to make a profit for the McDonnell Douglas Corporation, it must be low in cost."* In earlier times, before *Paris* and consumerism, the emphasis on profitability would have seemed a valid corporate mission. To Brizendine, and indeed to any businessman, Adams's statements were still "fundamentally axiomatic" for anyone undertaking a commercial venture. But a door had come off, killing 346 people, and the profit motive took on an evil aura.

Lawyers learned that the DC-10 program had come explosively alive with the awarding to Douglas of contracts by American and United Airlines in early 1968. Written into American's contract was a delivery date of October 1971. FAA certification by that date was an imperative. And from the signing of the contract, "CERTIFICATION" strode like a galley master over the thousands of engineers gathering up into disciplined design groups. Airlines could sue for late delivery. October 1971 was the "drop dead" date, and it must be met. Or beaten.

There had been other pressures forcing the -10 ahead. Douglas needed a new plane for the seventies. The DC-8 was still being produced through the mid-sixties, but its time was running out. The DC-9 was just coming into production, with first deliveries in 1965, but was a smaller, short-haul plane. Though stretched three times, it would never replace the -8 as their major intercontinental craft. To stay in business, they had to have a big new plane. Before the competition.

General ideas on the DC-10 had been on drawing boards since 1964/65, inspired by high bypass ratio engines that made a new generation of jets possible. Activity on the design of the -10 had accelerated after the merger of McDonnell and Douglas in April 1967, a corporate marriage consummated to give Douglas working capital. And with the contracts from American and United, the DC-10 program went into high gear. Three thousand engineers were assigned to the DC-10 at Douglas, and hundreds more were sent out to work with the subcontractors being signed up to help build the DC-10. Twenty-five hundred subcontractors would be drawn into the program. At drawing boards, engineers worked feverishly on the engineering layouts. Computer rooms clattered and hummed, digesting data, spitting back specifications. Two hundred different possible configurations were run through the computers, saving man-years in calculations. At this stage, no data was sacred. It was discarded daily for new. The ship was taking shape out of concepts, and life was a series of deadlines, increasingly ruthless deadlines for getting the layouts "off board," locking up the specifications.

The efforts of thousands of men, all working on different elements of the design, came together in Harold Adams's design meetings, held, now, every day. It was here, over engineering drawings, that Adams earned the commanding respect of his engineers with his ability to scan complex designs from any department, to send engineers back to their drawing boards with a simpler solution, and have then return an hour later muttering, "By God, he's right. It'll work that way." Discarding, adding, changing, the form of the plane was rapidly coming together into a body of numbers that defined the new airplane. Weights. Speeds. The dimensions of wings, fuselage, tail, doors. Center of gravity limits. Altitudes and cabin pressures. Fuel capacity. Tires, wheels, and brakes. Engines. The number and placement of passenger seats, galleys, and lavatories to suit the customer airline's needs. Some of the numbers defined years earlier, some changing daily. Documents revealed a story of decisions. Three or four engines? Three . . . But where was the third engine to go? It was decided to hoist it up onto the vertical tail, moving the air straight through rather than into an S duct that "bent" the air twice, with a loss of energy. The design would give them 3 percent greater efficiency than the L-1011 and provide "a better environment for the engine." Though it was a purely functional decision, that mighty sheathed power plant, apparently speared by the tail fin high above the ground would become the most distinctive visual characteristic of the DC-10. Clean, male, massive, the aesthetic of engine number 2 had evolved, like any well-engineered product, out of the job it had to do. By the mid-1970s, Douglas's great silver cigar would be clearly visible above the sprawling terminal buildings of many of the world's airports. Some of the numbers that would cast the fate of 346 people had been established by July of 1968. Pressures. And doors. The plane would fly at a maximum altitude of 42,000 feet, with the cabin altitude kept to a maximum of 7,610 feet—like sitting in Aspen, Colorado. The cabin pressure, in normal operation, would be 8.6

psi higher than the air pressure outside with pressure-relief valves preventing pressures in excess of 9.1, though the fuselage could withstand still higher pressures. The bulk cargo compartment door would be on the left-hand side of the plane, at station 1811. It would close over an opening 44 inches wide and 48 inches high, and would be the smallest of the lower cargo doors in the plane—18.5 square feet, much larger than the .9 square foot fuselage hole that the plane must be able to sustain to satisfy the FAA.

The choice of a potential hole size in the shell was one of the most significant in the development of the plane. It was the number that allowed engineers to proceed with designing the venting that would protect the floor. They already knew the other vital numbers. The normal operating pressure would be 8.6 psi and, in flight, would be the same in all pressurized compartments. The same pressure that pressed down on the cabin floor would press up on it from the cargo holds beneath. But the floor was designed to withstand a pressure differential of only 3 psi, which meant that it would be safe as long as pressures were roughly equal on both sides of the floor, pressing on it like two hands pushing with equal force on either side of a piece of plywood. But if a compartment on either side of the floor—a cargo hold or the cabin—lost pressure, it would be like one hand suddenly being pulled away. When the pressure differential rose to 3 psi, the floor would collapse into the vacuum on the other side. It was venting that would allow the air to flow from one compartment to another, to prevent an excessive pressure buildup on either side of the floor. And the amount of venting depended on the size of the hole through which air would evacuate.

But what size hole? There were meetings. Discussions. What might cause decompression? Bombs. Volatile cargoes exploding, or being thrown around in turbulence. A turbine blade flung from an engine. A bird through the cockpit windshield. Migration season sent over four million ten-pound Canada Geese flying in close formation at altitudes of up to 20,000 feet. And one hundred million ducks! There were lightning strikes. A door coming off. How big was the hole likely to be? Who knew?

John Brizendine, the -10's program manager at that time, knew that "the experience with jet aircraft and pressurized aircraft was quite good with regard to the puncturing of the pressure vessel, so there was nothing in the experience that said that the probability of puncturing this pressure vessel was anything to worry about." The FAA had established an industry standard for hole size that seemed to make sense—the area between two frames and two longerons, which was just under one square foot. The size of a writing tablet. The frames and longerons were the aluminum skeleton that gridded the plane. Skin was laid over the skeleton and riveted on, creating thousands of small rectangular areas, or panels, defined by the crisscrossing members. If the fuselage were pierced, or if it cracked from fatigue, the skin might fly back in the rush of decompression; but the rivets would contain the ripping of the skin.

It was a Douglas design tradition to design enough venting to handle the loss of *two* panels, doubling the roughly one square foot industry standard. And there were other factors that helped them determine the hole size. The air outflow valve, if it failed, would open up a hole significantly larger than one square foot. And they had to cover "all loading and rigidity conditions." The hole size they came up with was between 3 and 8 square feet, depending on location. The front of the plane could withstand an 8 square foot hole; the rear of the plane where the bulk cargo door was located could withstand a hole of only 3 square feet—much larger than the minimum criterion. But it was still far smaller than the smallest door. "Doors," said Brizendine, "were not considered. *Doors are supposed to stay closed!*" Even the Dutch agreed. The numbers were locked up with the rest of the design load criteria in November 1967, and subsequently certificated by the FAA.

And what kind of cargo doors would they design?

Would they be outward opening latch type? Or inward opening plug type? Would they open and close hydraulically . . . or electrically? Significant choices, in hindsight, but in the overall scheme of things, these were not global decisions. They were just *doors*. Douglas had been designing doors for pressure vessels for thirty years and, as John Brizendine had said, they had never been much of a problem. Doors were a small element in the total complexity of a big jet. The DC-10 was about five times as complex as the DC-9. It was the *innovations* in a new plane that you worried about. The Electra's powerful new turbo props had torn her wings off. The Comet's skin, not fully designed and tested for the pressures of high altitudes, had cracked with fatigue. The DC-10 must not have an Achilles heel. To Harold Adams, its longitudinal controls, fully powered for the first time in a Douglas aircraft, seemed far more critical than the cargo doors.

And underlying the design was always the broader philosophical worry, too, over the fixed "set" of engineers' minds. They measured systems by their strengths, not their weaknesses, and reveled in the perfection of a design on paper. Adams always pushed his engineers to take the human factor into account. But it was distasteful for them to let human frailty "torque" their designs. Murphy compromised mathematical purity. It was Adams's last chance to crack minds open before he retired.

But a small cargo door with a fatal susceptibility to human error had slipped through. In spite of an admirable pedigree, a door had been bred that was a bad seed. Lawyers grabbed memos on the doors, hoping to find answers or at least hard questions to ask witnesses. As they read the documents, they began to grasp General Dynamics' role in the DC-10 saga—a connection the Senate hearings and the press had not even touched, and only Sterns of the plaintiff lawyers had considered it seriously enough to name in his complaints. He had learned from his Air Force T-29 case against General Dynamics that the company was involved in the DC-10, but he could only guess at the depth of their involvement.

The Convair Aerospace Division of General Dynamics Corporation had been awarded a contract in early August 1968 to design and build four sections of the fuselage, including floors and doors, to Douglas's general specifications. The section that attached to the wings had been designed by Douglas, though built by Convair. Douglas had decided such things as type and placement of control cables, cabin pressures, and the type of door.

The design of the cargo doors was still in flux when the contract was signed. There was a tug-of-war over the tradeoffs in the plug- versus latch-type door. A compelling argument for latch-type doors was the airline's requirement for a containerized cargo system. It gave you more cubic feet in the cargo hold for payload and allowed the uninhibited movement in and out of containers. To an engineer, the outward-opening latch-type door was structurally superior. For large doors, it gave you a better seal. And when it was properly closed, it was integrated into the surrounding structure, behaving as if there was no door there; it became part of the shell, sharing the load. Beautiful. If you could forget the human factor. It *had* to be closed right. That was the tradeoff. The latch type would *open* under pressure, if not quite closed. The plug door would close tighter, like a bathtub plug. Inherently safer. And the plug door weighed less—another vital factor in its favor. And yet outward-opening latch-type doors, hydraulically operated, had been used successfully on the DC-8 and -9 cargo doors.

In the atmosphere of growth and change, of reviews, revisions, meetings, no one seemed to remember precisely when or why the tradeoffs tipped the decision in favor of the outward-opening latch-type door. Or who tipped the scales. But once chosen for the two large cargo doors, it was selected for the small bulk cargo door mainly for *consistency*—an important operational factor.

As with the entire Convair relationship, the exchange of data, ideas, and design responsibilities between the two firms was so constant and so complex, the communications with direct phones, shuttle planes, and exchanged personnel so close that it was impossible to trace all the millions of threads of thought back to their points of origin. For the lawyers, the tiny fragments of decision and responsibility tended to tangle into a great gummy ball.

The moment of decision to operate the doors *electrically* was equally elusive, but was one of the most significant decisions in the design of the doors. The doors were originally to have been powered hydraulically like the cargo doors on the DC-8 and DC-9. That had been the early understanding between Douglas and General Dynamics. Hydraulics had some inherent safety advantages. If improperly latched and under pressure, a hydraulic door oozed open, bleeding air gently, preventing the plane from being fully pressurized inside, thus keeping the buildup of pressure to less than a normal level. On the other hand, an electrically powered door, if only partially latched, would *not* ooze open. Once closed, it would grip the fuselage tightly, allowing the pressure inside the plane to build up to the point where it could hold on no longer—until a failure occurred. But looming above these considerations was one vital factor. Weight. There would be a 28-pound weight-saving per door using electrical actuators, an 84-pound saving per plane. In the DC-10, as in any commercial transport, "Every pound's worth its weight in gold." For the DC-10 a $100 a pound weight tradeoff was established, which meant that if you could make a technically sound change that would save a pound at an extra cost of less than $100, you were to do it. The decision was made to go with the electrical system, a decision that may have been one of the major steps toward *Paris*.

As they plunged toward the "off-board" design deadlines, weight began to hover over the drawing boards as tyrannically as certification. On December 5, 1968, the chiefs of structural engineering, weights, and structural mechanics put out a memo instituting a major weight-reduction program. ". . . The guaranteed weights for the DC-10 must be met and a greater effort than has heretofore been expended must be made to achieve this goal." The customers' profitability was at stake; the lighter the plane, the greater the payload. Airplane weights were *guaranteed* to the customer. The memo provided a lengthy weight-saving checklist: "Can any parts be eliminated?" "Can two or more pieces be combined into one part?" "Consider chemical milling for cheaper, lighter, and thinner parts." "Titanium alloy in place of steel?" "Can more lightening holes be added?" "Can more lightening area be obtained from other than round holes?" "Can grooves be cut in fittings to remove material not required?" Like a grade-school contest, weight savings by each group were to be posted up on display.

But this was still not enough. On April 10, Harold Adams issued a memo to all his section chiefs, giving insights the lawyers largely overlooked into just how difficult the decisions were that Adams, and the handful of men who shared with him the design responsibility, had to make "to guarantee the DC-10 is of minimum weight." Here, they began to see *design factors*—those extra margins of safety always added by engineers to ensure that a plane gets built a little stronger than is believed necessary—being reduced. The list of immediate go-ahead items in the memo reads like a thesaurus for weight watchers. Of twenty-five items, nineteen are directions to *"reduce, eliminate, remove, decrease, use minimum, delete."* "Reduce the factor for the vertical stabilizer banjo fitting of the lower section from 10 percent to 5 percent." "Eliminate the 1.2 factor on rudder torque." "Reduce skin thickness on the basic wing box." "Delete emergency ram air system." In reducing margins, Harold Adams was being called upon to decide how much is enough. Should a component be able to carry twice the load that it was ever predicted to carry? One and one half times the load? Who could really say? And with the tendency of engineers to cascade safety factors one upon the other well above minimum requirements, clearly many could be reduced or eliminated without compromising safety. Because of the unknowns, the early jets had been overdesigned, but with experience, and with advances in design techniques—with computers appraising stresses and strains with high precision—the DC-10 could be more efficiently designed. Design margins could be safely reduced. How to cut weight and keep the plane safe—this was where Adams's forty years of engineering judgment and a passionate concern for the sound, safe plane were priceless.

Planes never came in lighter than designed. Chipping away at weight had always been a consuming challenge to designers of heavier-than-air craft. If you looked under the skin, planes were riddled like Swiss cheese with lightening holes of varying sizes, drilled wherever they could be without compromising strength. It is efficient design. But as Sterns read the documents, he sensed that Douglas was "going bananas" on weight. He and his colleagues focused on the hunt for compromises that might have been forced by the pressures of weight, deadlines, and cost.

As weight grew into a preoccupation, the deadlines pressed irresistibly. Layouts were being reviewed, approved, and released from the board. As they came off board, they were transferred to San Diego with batches of Convair engineers who would return to their home plant to do the detail design.

When the General Dynamics' documents arrived in the discovery room, they set off whistles and whispers among the plaintiff lawyers. It was "devastating stuff." They could hardly wait their turns at interrogation. In the spring of 1969, a year before the fateful blowout in the pressure vessel test, *General Dynamics had known that something could go wrong with the door and had written it down.* Reference to potential catastrophic failure had been in one of a series of hazard analyses that were being done as part of the required precertification hunt for any possible failure modes. The report had been written in the midst of a dramatic time in the life of the DC-10, when Douglas and General Dynamics were making the rite of passage from designing to building the plane, and Convair was tooling up. Fabrication of the plane had already begun at Douglas in January with the milling of the cockpit window frames. The number of machined parts that would be made by Convair kept growing, moving into the thousands. "Make or buy" meetings defined items that would be bought from outside. New tracer and control mills to precision-carve the metal were bought and moved into the San Diego plant. Shiny aluminum skin arrived from Alcoa. It was only one eighth of an inch thick. But with an extra layer of pure aluminum to resist corrosion and with the design loads distributed correctly, it was a tough and durable protector of the pressure vessel. The extra layer was one of the "costly things that make it cheaper for the airlines" for the DC-10's wings and fuselage would not have to be reskinned for the life of the plane. Preparations were being made to build the first mock-up of the door.

In the context of the entire plane, the cargo doors did not appear to be one of the hard-core problems. Yet at least one engineer had been worried. In a sheaf of papers that Convair sent to Douglas reporting on the potential failure modes—the Failure Mode and Effect Analyses, or FMEAs—the potential failure of the latching system was classified as a fourth-degree hazard, a *catastrophic* hazard. A hazard that held the potential for a crash. The FMEA reported that under a number of conditions the "door will open in flight resulting in sudden depressurization and possible structural failure of the floor." Dated August 12, 1969, the FMEA was a forecast for *Windsor* and *Paris*. This would be great material for court, for it showed that *Convair had identified, and told Douglas about, the catastrophic potential of the cargo door*. When it reached Douglas, *someone there deleted the alarming reference to the potential for catastrophe.*

259

Lee Kreindler went after Ray Bates, vice-president for engineering at Douglas and the man who had co-signed most of the design memos with Adams. Why had they changed the FMEA? Bates, one of the small number of men who had had an "overall cognizance" of the DC-10 as it had evolved, explained that Douglas had disagreed with findings of the initial FMEA prepared by Convair, that the door referred to in that FMEA was actually an early design in an evolving process of door design; that Douglas did not consider the failure of the floor to be the result of a single failure or even a dual failure, but rather a result of three or four successive failures. In other words, *remote,* and not requiring mention in the FMEA. Kreindler read a definition of secondary failure to Bates: *"Secondary failure occurs when failure of one system or structure overloads another system causing its failure."* By that definition, "clearly, failure of the floor was a secondary failure!"

Had Douglas ever sent the FMEA, or a fault analysis including the FMEA's reference to the catastrophic failure mode, on to the FAA? Kreindler asked. No, it had not, Bates said. The FAA certificating office in Los Angeles had not required extensive systems safety analyses for the DC-10's cargo door latching, locking, and warning systems. Kreindler flipped his notebook open and produced a letter proving that the FAA had set up a working policy requiring Douglas to provide them with fault analyses. *And Douglas had not done it on the door mechanism.* The FMEA contained the first hints of *Windsor* and *Paris,* and it had sat on Douglas desks as early as 1969. Kreindler would get mileage out of this.

The FMEA had defined theoretical hazards. The pressure vessel would be physically put to the test on May 29, 1970.

The DC-10 program had gained irresistible momentum by this time. The Guppy air freighter had delivered the first fuselage section to Long Beach on January 9; and on the assembly line, 270,00 parts were being fastened with two and a half million fasteners; they were being riveted and bolted together. Engineers were bandying about the old joke about a plane being "a million small parts flying in close formation" as the excitement built.

On March 30, the wings and all fuselage sections of the first DC-10 had been mated, readying for the first test flight. After three intensive years, the marvel of creation was becoming dramatically apparent. On the assembly line, the parts were fitting together like a three-dimensional jigsaw puzzle. Wings from Canada. Fuselage sections from San Diego. Vertical stabilizer and rudders from Italy. They fit. They worked. Wires, cables, hydraulic and pneumatic lines were all mated, connected together in a multicolored network of veins and arteries that would bring the plane to life by flicking a series of switches in the cockpit. A product of management techniques that were virtually born in the aerospace industry, the mission was being accomplished, as a Douglas engineer explained it with uncharacteristic flippancy, "the same way you eat an elephant—a bite at a time."

As the plane came together on the assembly line, a new weekly deadline was putting pressure on the program, giving a new rhythm to life at Douglas. At 2:30, every Tuesday afternoon, the whole assembly line moved forward one step. Each immense aircraft section was physically moved, from station to station, from the periphery toward the center of the hangar, coming closer to completion with each step. Finally they would be mated to other sections that had been moved through the same relentless series of Tuesday deadlines.

Through the spring, memos reflected the countdown atmosphere. "As of this date, there are 130 days to first flight." By May 29, the day of the pressure vessel test, there were only ninety-three days.

The pressure vessel test of fuselage number 2—a standard functional test of the air conditioning and pressurization ssytems conducted by the structural engineering group—was held outside hangar number 54.

Because there was no electrical power yet on the plane, a door—the forward cargo door—was cranked closed by mechanics unfamiliar with the nuances of the closing mechanism. They did not crank long enough to move the latches all the way around the spools, however, and did not make the proper visual check. Between 3 and 4 psi the forward cargo compartment door blew out with a violence that tore the door off its hinges and buckled the floor adjacent to the door.

It was a shock to both Douglas and Convair. They reacted with a flurry of meetings and extra engineers working overtime, searching for ways to solve the problem. A basic decision had to be made: whether to make the consequences of losing a door less catastrophic, *or* to make the probability of losing the door less likely. To change the airplane? Or the door.

They considered the plane. They believed they had a "safe and sturdy" floor.

Rerouting the control cables that went through the floor had been considered, but rejected as impractical and as a possible compromise of the control system that had been integrated into the plane from the initial design phase. They did contemplate more venting between the cabin and cargo holds, but because of the placement of the lavatories and other factors, more venting to the aft cargo compartment, where the most critical problem existed, was considered impractical.

The flight-test program was pressing. Structures and environmental control brainstormed at design meetings. By September, a vent door had risen above all other possibilities as the most probable solution. A tiny door cut into the cargo doors. Boeing had used it. A door within a door that would stay open if the door was improperly latched, preventing pressurization.

In retrospect, the DC-10 cargo door problem might have ended right there. Had they returned then to the originally specified hydraulic actuators, the whole problem of pressure buildup behind an improperly locked door might have been eliminated. Instead, they added a new element—a little vent door—to the problem they already had.

In the air, the DC-10 was amassing hours in its test flights. It had made its maiden flight on schedule on August 29, 1970, taking off from Long Beach Airport and landing at Edwards Air Force Base three hours and twenty-six minutes later.

On the ground, with the failure of the pressure vessel test and the decision on the vent door, the mood of the General Dynamics-Douglas relationship changed as abruptly as if clouds had suddenly covered the sun.

Vent doors would have to be put in fuselage number 1, now flying; in fuselage number 2, being prepared for tests; and in all subsequent cargo doors. The job of building and installing the vent doors on the first three hundred planes would cost, by early "guesstimate," $2.6 million—a figure later moved up to over $4 million. *Who was going to pay?* By November 1970, the two companies had taken the defensive positions which they would hold so staunchly that they would become part of the baggage of intransigence and rancor that would be carried into the Paris case.

The dispute hinged on interpretation of the contract between them. Douglas maintained that the vent door was a design change that should be considered "normal and anticipated" as part of Convair's responsibility; that the failure of the door and the floor collapse had been the result of a design flaw Convair should have recognized; and that the FAA would probably require the change before certification. The contract obligated Convair to provide a satisfactory and safe design, under Douglas's direction, or to specifically advise Douglas if the direction was unsafe or unsatisfactory. To avoid paying, Convair would have to prove that the vent door was a "significant" change; that the original design was sound; that it had complied with FAA requirements; and that the vent doors were a voluntary product improvement by Douglas.

To protect themselves, Convair's stance would be that the door was just fine, and that Douglas's obsession

263

with vent doors was simply "overkill." And if a fix *were* needed, there were other, better ways to accomplish it.

Meetings, letters, phone calls tried to solve the dilemma. But the disagreement only grew deeper. Through the winter of 1970–1971, it gradually emerged on paper as a battle between two men. For Douglas, it was Steve Dillon, director of special procurement programs; and for Convair, J. B. Hurt, Convair's DC-10 program support manager. Convair continued to insist that the vent doors were an "out-of-scope" product improvement, *not* a correction; that there was no way that they could *reasonably* have known the design would be deficient—and they denied that it *was* deficient—with the successful history of the DC-8 and -9, and Douglas's clear design authority. They wanted *proof* that the FAA required the change. They were sure that that was just a verbal threat Douglas had dreamed up to add weight to the argument that there had been a design flaw. Convair smoldered that, as subcontractors, they were denied direct contact with the FAA. They had not been allowed to discuss the damning FMEAs directly with the FAA but had had to hope that Douglas would transmit the worrisome message to the FAA. And they were restrained now from discussing the need for a vent door with the FAA. They were caught in the dilemma of doubting the door, but having to defend it.

Douglas tossed out a veiled threat that they would return all cargo doors to Convair as unacceptable. They claimed that Convair owed them a new floor to replace the one that had collapsed.

The fight over who would pay for the vent doors went on even as vent doors were designed, incorporated into the cargo doors, and submitted to the FAA for certification. The plane was ahead of schedule and might beat the original October 1971 deadline by two months. As they pressed toward a new certification and first delivery date of July 29, the vent door issue reached an angry stalemate, in which Dillon told Hurt that "I suppose we will be seeing you in court. . . ."

On July 29, 1971, the DC-10 was certificated and delivered to American and United Airlines in a joint ceremony. It had met all of its criteria, with more payload than promised. Vying to be first in the air, American scooped United a week later by sneaking a DC-10 onto a morning flight from Los Angeles to Chicago. As it landed in Chicago, a mission begun in the mid-sixties was completed. The DC-10 had entered scheduled airline service.

That same week, the Guppy freighter flew in section E and the main landing gear of fuselage number 29, the hull that would eventually be sold to Turkish Airlines. It had already been sold to Mitsui, a giant Japanese holding company that was speculating on DC-10s. They had contracted to buy six, which would be sold at a profit to All-Nippon Airlines.

The dispute over the vent doors was no closer to settlement by May 1972 and was now being referred to in Convair's in-house memos as the "Cargo Door Vent Door Issue." Neither firm had budged. And then, within a month, *Windsor.*

F. D. Applegate, Convair's director of product engineering, sat down and poured out his frustrations over the cargo door and his concerns for Convair's position. In a memo titled "DC-10 Future Accident Liability," he gave the lawyers precisely what they had been looking for. The Applegate memo would become to the litigation what the Gentlemen's Agreement had been to the Senate hearings. Lawyers stroked through the key phrases with yellow felt-tip pens. *"The fundamental safety of the cargo door latching system has been progressively degraded since the program began in 1968. . . . The airplane demonstrated an inherent susceptibility to catastrophic failure when exposed to explosive decompression of the cargo compartment in 1970 ground tests."* Applegate regretted the change from hydraulic to electric actuation, which he believed was "fundamentally less positive." *Fundamentally less positive*—a superb new weapon in the legal battle. Though Douglas and Convair had jointly pursued a suitable "fix" following the pressure vessel blowout, Applegate was convinced that "since 'Murphy's law' being what it is, cargo doors will come open sometime during the twenty-plus years of use ahead for the DC-10. . . . *I would expect this to usually result in the loss of the airplane.*" And, to Applegate, the vent doors had been "a 'Band-Aid fix' " that had "not only failed to correct the inherent DC-10 catastrophic failure mode of cabin floor collapse, but the detail design of the vent door change further degraded the safety of the original latch system by replacing the direct, short-coupled and stiff latch 'lock' indicator system with a complex and relatively flexible linkage." It was the flexible linkage that had been overpowered by the baggage handler's knee on the handle at Detroit. Applegate criticized the peepholes then being designed as "more Band-Aids." Even if the door were finally made "foolproof," it would not "solve the fundamental deficiency in the airplane"—the vulnerability of the floor to catastrophic collapse. Why then, he posed, had Convair "not originally detail designed a cabin floor to withstand the loads of cargo compartment explosive decompression"? Or designed adequate venting? Because Douglas had supplied *the pressure loads and criteria* to which floors, vents, and doors had been designed. He believed that nothing in the "experience history" of either Convair or Douglas would have led either to suspect the catastrophic failure mode of the cabin floor in explosive decompression. *"My only criticism, therefore, of Douglas in this regard is that once this inherent weakness was demonstrated by the July 1970 test failure, they did not take immediate steps to correct it."*

He wrote with the disciplined style of the engineer. But his words gave a sense of the intercorporate conflict that, even after *Windsor,* was preventing a satisfactory fix. "This fundamental failure mode has been discussed in the past and is being discussed again in the bowels of both the Douglas and Convair organizations. It appears however that Douglas is waiting and hoping for government direction or regulations in the hope of passing costs on to us or their customers. . . . If you can judge from Douglas's position during ongoing contract change negotiations, they may feel that any liability incurred in the meantime for loss of life, property, and equipment may be legally passed on to us." Applegate recommended "that overtures be made at the highest management level to persuade Douglas to immediately make a decision to incorporate changes in the DC-10 which will correct the fundamental cabin floor catastrophic failure mode," changes that were "more expensive every day as production continues." *It might still be less expensive,* he believed, *"than the cost of damages resulting from the loss of one plane load of people."*

J. B. Hurt read Applegate's memo and on July 3, 1972, wrote his own memo to Convair's DC-10 general manager, M. C. Curtis. In it he said, "I do not take issue with the facts or the concern expressed in the referenced memo. However we should look at the 'other side of the coin.' " He had considered recommending more floor venting as a better fix, he said, but had not done it because *"I am sure that Douglas would immediately interpret such recommendations as a tacit admission on Convair's part that the original concurrence by Convair of the design philosophy was in error and that therefore Convair was liable for all problems and corrections that have subsequently occurred. . . . We have an interesting legal and moral problem, and I feel that any direct conversation on this subject with Douglas should be based on the assumption that, as a result, Convair may subsequently find itself in a position where it must assume all or a significant portion of the costs that are involved."*

Laid out on a table, removed by time and distance from the corporate environment in which it is written, the letter was perhaps the most incriminating document to emerge from discovery. To the lawyers, it was the kind that shines out from the others like the first nugget found in a gold rush.

Hurt would claim much later in depositions that his

memo had not expressed his personal opinion but had been an attempt to air both sides of the issue. No rational man consciously conspires to kill 346 people. But Convair was boxed in, apparently convinced that they were trapped by a contract that could force them to pay if they admitted the DC-10 had flaws in the door/floor/vent design.

When Hurt sent his memo recommending inaction on the Applegate memo to his general manager, Curtis, the letter apparently stopped there. Hurt would later tell lawyers of a meeting at Convair called to discuss Applegate's memo, but he would not be able to remember that any conclusive actions were taken. The issue was not taken to the "highest management level" at Douglas. Disclosure of the memo had been "a surprise" to Brizendine. And questioned by Sterns in depositions, he claimed, in fact, that he would have expected Convair to come to him with a serious safety problem. Convair did not. Why? With the two memos before them—one warning of lost dollars, the other posing the chilling alternative to corrective action—Convair would seem to have had no choice. Clearly, it was the time to sit down and work out a compromise that both companies could live with, technically and financially. It might have been a painful swallowing of pride. But it might have saved an airplane.

What held them back? What are the dynamics that let common sense get lost in rationales; that permit loyal company men to make decisions that ultimately undermine the corporate mission? For the mission, most basically, had to be to build safe airplanes. Was it a misplaced obligation to stockholders; a belief that capitulation on the vent doors would look bad on the balance sheet? Perhaps the three events—Applegate's memo, Hurt's memo, and the corporate silence—are a rare view of the dynamics of the "company line," the remarkable forging of disparate opinion into one view. It is what lets two groups of engineers with the same training and background examine the same data for different companies and arrive at totally different conclusions. Approaching it with even a gentle company bias, the engineers can find themselves extending the bias into a genuine *belief*—one that conforms to the corporate position—*with no conscious compromise of ideals*. It let three Dutchmen and the American aviation industry see size effect differently. It lets men fight wars with conviction.

It is when ego is intruded into the company line that morality can go disastrously askew, and the corporate mission can be undermined. Judgment suffers when ego-driven rationales are pushed in the hope of giving moral substance to them. It is the astronauts degrading the space program by taking homemade sandwiches into space.

This dynamic does not move men only when millions of dollars are at stake. It drives them to unhealthy pride in petty matters, too. Just four days after the Windsor Incident, Hurt wrote another memo to Curtis. Convair had negotiated to buy some surplus cargo door parts from Douglas at a price of $6,000. On reinspection at Convair, after their purchase, their value was reappraised at $18,000—a profit of $12,000 for Convair. "Thought you would be interested in this bargain." Written by the man who helped to bury the Applegate memo, it seemed to exhibit the same small-boy competitivenes psychologists call the "mine-is-bigger-than-yours" syndrome.

Memos do not show a man's private personality—his family, his good works, his kindness to animals. They show only his corporate behavior, baring it mercilessly. But memos produced by discovery in the Paris case have given insight into a syndrome that, writ large and applied universally, may be one of the dilemmas of man.

Chapter Twenty-One

In Court

KREINDLER FLEW BACK to New York, his fourth flight
across the country in a week, in time for his twenty-fifth
reunion at Harvard. A few days later, he reported to his
firm's weekly luncheon meeting at the 60 East Club on
Forty-second Street that he had had "a lot of fun with
Bates" during depositions in what was becoming "one
hell of a case." "We caught their hands in the cookie
jar." He felt optimistic, as did the other plaintiff lawyers, that the evidence was giving them a strong case
against the defendants. With each damaging disclosure,
the defendants seemed to sink more deeply into their
own entrenched positions, baring their teeth at each
other, trying to shift blame. And like predators waiting
to move in on the carcasses, the plaintiff lawyers sat
back and watched as the defense attacked and weak-
ened each other.

Though Herb Lyons still sat at the back of the deposition room trying to detach the government from the
case, discovery was putting the FAA on the defensive,
showing their surveillance of the cargo door to have
been less than complete.

Comparing FAA and Douglas documents, lawyers
found just the kind of incriminating penciled note they
are always looking for. In Douglas's copy of an FAA
letter of February 5, 1971, and in the certification
board minutes, the FAA had stated that "it is our
understanding that the vent door is designed in such a

way that, if the cargo door is improperly locked, the vent door *will open* to relieve the cargo compartment pressure and to forestall subsequent blowing open of the cargo door."

Clearly, the FAA had believed that the vent door was an active pressure-relief mechanism that would *open* to relieve pressure. But, with Sterns pressing the point hard in depositions, it was confirmed that that was precisely what it was not. *Once closed, it became a plug-type door, tightening its seal as pressure differential built up.* It was not a relief valve. In a copy of the same documents produced from the FAA's files, the word *remain* had been penciled in, so that the line read "the vent door will *remain* open. . . ." Under questioning, an FAA man, Richard Sliff, who was chief of the western region's aircraft engineering division, admitted that he had penciled the word in at some later date. The guess was that he had penciled it in immediately after *Windsor,* or *Paris,* in an inept attempt to cover evidence that the FAA had certificated a vent door it did not understand. Douglas had seen the letter and had not enlightened the FAA. Kreindler and Sterns went wild, for this smacked of fraudulent certification!

Plaintiff lawyers watched with satisfaction as McDonnell Douglas offered Turkish Airlines' head on a plate. FitzSimons had suggested privately to several plaintiff lawyers that they should put Marchall Caldwell, member of Douglas's investigative team in Paris, and Robert LaCombe, who had been part of the support team assigned to THY before the crash, in the deposition chair to give evidence that seemed to shift the blame to the airline. The plaintiffs were delighted. It was part of tactics to keep the pressure on as many defendants as possible. And without physical evidence—the door or any of the wreckage—the testimony of a Douglas expert who had been on the scene might be as authoritative as any evidence they would get. They might never see the cargo door—they didn't even know where it was—and Caldwell's testimony could be vital in court. They questioned him and drew out the "misrigging" theory that was to become the basis of McDonnell Douglas's counterattack.

On the shattered door that had fallen in St. Pathus with the six bodies, there was evidence that adjustments to the lockpin mechanisms had been done—but done wrong. On examination, almost imperceptible scoring, or scuff marks, had been detected on the tiny lockpins, telling them that, as the handle was stowed, the lockpins *had not moved as far as they should have,* making it possible to close the handle with very little force and to turn off the warning light *too soon,* before the door was properly locked. In an effort to make it impossible for a baggage handler to close the handle on an improperly locked door, as had been done in Detroit, Douglas had issued SB 52-37 recommending the infamous missing support plate, and rigging changes (adjustments) that, even without the support plate, would have required approximately 250 pounds of force on the handle to overpower it.

But Caldwell reported that Douglas tests after the crash confirmed what the scoring on the lockpins had suggested—that the mechanism could be overpowered with very little force, perhaps as little as *thirteen pounds*—the amount of force a child could easily exert. Even if there had been a support plate, it would only have taken 33 pounds to overpower the handle, he said, well within the capability of a baggage handler and so close to the normal 15 to 35 pound force required to close a properly latched door that it would not have been noticed.

There was a stir of surprise, pencils scratched, and lawyers listened, absorbed, as he led the case into a whole new dimension, describing the minute but vital factors that may have actually *let* the baggage handler close the door improperly. Caldwell explained that the force required to close the handle of an improperly latched door could be altered by adjusting the lockpins —by turning an adjusting rod on its threads. In the crashed plane, the adjustment had been made in the wrong direction. The rod had been turned 3 revolutions

272

the wrong way, shortening the distance of lockpin travel .407 inches from where SB 52-37 had said it should have been, and reducing the force required on the handle to the perilously light 13 pounds. The implication was that the Turks had made the negative lockpin adjustment. And that they had added shims, tiny metal washers, to the striker on the lockpin tube that turned off the cockpit warning light. The shims contacted the switch too soon, turning off the warning light before the door was locked. Another shim—a crumpled, paper-thin shim not of Douglas stock or of aeronautical quality—was also found, defective installation. LaCombe testified that it was common practice for the Turks to put on their own shims to turn off the warning light in the cockpit. The Turks were accused, too, of ignoring the peephole and with removing the factory-installed actuator and installing their own.

Implying that through inept maintenance the Turks had brought the crash on themselves, McDonnell Douglas was hanging its case—and millions and millions of dollars—on fractions of an inch and a paper-thin metal shim. But it was to be a wildly controversial theory. *Had* the Turks misrigged the plane? Sterns speculated that if Douglas could make one mistake in the factory on SB 52-37, why not two. More important, in Kreindler's view, was why Douglas had produced a door that could be misrigged, especially since rigging of the door in the field was a regular procedure.

Others were ready to believe the Turks had done it, rightly or wrongly, in response to operational problems with the plane. DC-10 program manager William T. Gross confirmed in depositions that from the beginning of operations, airlines had reported difficulties with the cargo door. Actuators working too slowly . . . hooks binding on spools . . . troubles that had inspired Douglas's Field Service Representative in Turkey and Germany, D. Y. Krug, to write just two months before the crash, "If there was need to Murphy-proof the cargo doors on DC-10-10s, there is also a need to Murphy-proof the doors on the -30s." And the Turks had been *told* to use shims by SB 52-55, which said, "The operators have reported numerous instances of false cargo door warning indications. These *nuisance indications* are attributed to the flexing of the fuselage. . . . Shimming the light switches . . . will alleviate this condition . . . *If not corrected, flight delays and cancellations may result.*" Was the bastard shim that Douglas had disowned a Turkish response to this economic pressure?

There was controversy, too, over the force on the handle. How many pounds of force had Mahmoudi used to close the door? Thirteen pounds? The NTSB had written it up as *31 pounds.* The French investigators would finally say *50 pounds,* finding the lockpin travel in error by .312 of an inch, not the .407 of an inch reported by both Douglas and the NTSB. Exasperated, lawyers tried to pin down the numbers, for it was on just this kind of technical minutiae that aviation cases were won or lost.

It had all come out by late autumn. The altered FMEA. The Applegate and Hurt memos. The misrigging theory. The FAA's lack of vigor and understanding. And more, much more. The elite group of lawyers carrying the world's largest crash case had had a rich banquet of incriminating facts laid before them. Corporate fingerprints seemed to be everywhere. The story seemed to be one of staggering engineering achievement brought down by human failure. A story without real criminals but of decent men whose personal destinies had become so merged with the corporate goal that they had not always followed—or perhaps had not even been able to define—the rational path. It was a story of corporate disputes magnified by personality clashes into great stubborn schisms.

To the plaintiffs, it was, more than ever, an open and shut case of product liability. But the defendants were not crawling to the settlement table. The principals had gathered in New York for a preliminary settlement meeting, but it had been futile. The two sides were obviously too many millions of dollars apart to even talk at this early stage. But the sense of stalemate was coming as much from the defendants' in-fighting as from inability to come to terms with the plaintiffs. The problems that had existed before the crash were being dumped into the litigation. It was becoming clear that the defendants were as unwilling to admit liability to each other as to the plaintiffs. Turkish Airlines had sued Douglas for the hull. Douglas had countersued the airline and had sued General Dynamics as well. The issue was going to be as much "What share do we pay?" as "How much?" Contribution and indemnity. The issues at stake between them were becoming tests of strength. For they all knew that whatever happened in *this* crash would set a pattern for all future crashes, all over the world.

It all came down to money. In London, the two powerful underwriters 'at Lloyd's who ultimately controlled the insurance payments—Hewitt for Douglas and Jeffs for the airline—were locking horns like bucks in combat over the same issues.

At a hearing in late October, Kreindler saw an opportunity to blast the case into motion and, perhaps, to improve his own position. Though he now had twenty-two cases, including most of the dead from the American community in London, his position was still frustrating for an attorney of his stature. Though Hall was evidently eager to have someone of Kriendler's reputation and scholarship in the case, and had named him as counsel for the class action, the class was more or less moribund, for Hall now waited for the 9th Circuit Court of Appeals' ruling on the defense's writ of prohibition, an attempt to kill the class. The defense would not produce a passenger list. Without the list and the notice sent to families, the class, if allowed, had little chance of growing.

Sterns and Madole were keeping numbers close to their chests, but it was rumored that Sterns had at least sixty English cases; Madole and Butler, perhaps 120, and getting more all the time from many countries. The group of twenty-two Turkish families had come to the Washington-based firm of international lawyers, Mc-

Grail and Nordlund, through their Istanbul office. Responsibility for the crew cases was being shared by Mark Robinson in Los Angeles and Richard Jones in Alexandria, Virginia. But the forty-eight Japanese families—the largest national group next to the English—were still uncommitted. They had reportedly been offered a settlement of $82,000 for each of the dead young men and were zealously shopping the offer around among the plaintiff lawyers to see what better prospects there might be. They would move as a group. An earnest little delegation of Japanese had come to Los Angeles several times, interviewing lawyers, attending the hearings, and researching the case with characteristic thoroughness. Black-suited and formal, they were in striking contrast to the cosmopolitan style of Stephen Mitchell as he and Whittle had cruised the country looking for the right lawyer. The Japanese had interviewed Kreindler, had been impressed, but were holding back. They would not enter litigation lightly. The adversary system was alien to them. In Japan, the guilty party in a car crash still rushed to the injured party's hospital bed with flowers, candy, and formal apologies—an admission of guilt that would kill your case in the United States. They would rather negotiate than fight. Stephen Mitchell had handled a Japanese tanker crash in which, at the request of the parties involved, he had represented both the ship owner and lessee, and had settled the case by mediating between the two. It was hardly litigation. The Japanese, though, were becoming more litigious, a trend that had recently been disturbing Peter Martin's efforts to settle crash cases within Warsaw limits. They were becoming attracted to American-style settlements. Yet, traditionally, they hated courts as much as they hated death; and tradition was strong in Japan. If the Japanese came into the case at all, it would be more for moral redress than for the money. They would probably want a lawyer to fight for punitive as well as the usual damages, for only punitive damages were applied as a punishment.

The lawyers all met in Judge Hall's courtroom on October 29, 1974, for one of the regular hearings ordered by the judge. Formally, they were there to discuss a trial date. Sitting in the audience was Richard Witkin, transportation editor of *The New York Times,* considered by McDonnell Douglas and others to be the most influential aviation writer in the United States. He had been covering Kreindler since joining *The New York Times* twenty-one years earlier, for Kreindler's office had been a laboratory for aviation law and, therefore, eminently newsworthy. While waiting for the move Kreindler planned to make, he would be treated to an excellent hillside view of the skirmishing that had been screened from public view by the press ban from depositions.

Though lacking the monumental themes of the arguments on Warsaw and choice of law that would come later, the hearing was a classic of its genre. And it would send the case and Kreindler lurching ahead.

The only man who started the afternoon out with a commanding position was Don Madole. His senior partner, Stuart Speiser, had written and filed a beefy 119-page brief on choice of law, the first lawyer to do so. An elegant argument for the application of French law that swept from the Napoleonic code to the rights of a common-law wife, several pounds of it sat as an intimidating presence in each *Paris* lawyer's office. Now everyone would rush to try to get one out, in spite of the sixty days they had been given for filing their briefs. For sheer size, Speiser's would be a hard act to follow.

Madole entered the courtroom with the quiet confidence of a lone soldier who knows he is backed by gunboats. The judge had, of course, read the brief and started right off by ruminating on the relative merits of French and California law. The defense and plaintiff lawyers were thrown into panic. The judge could run his hearings any way he wished, and it suddenly looked as if he was going to argue choice of law—the argument that would have more to do with the eventual size of damages than any other in the case. Suddenly lawyers were popping up in their gray suits saying, "Your Honor, I want to file a brief." "We want to file one, *too*, Your Honor." "*I* would want to file a brief!"

Madole rose to his feet, cool and solicitous, and introduced himself as representing 125 decedents. Then, with knuckles on the table, body pitched forward, and a wisp of a smile on his smooth, round face, he said, "We've done our homework. . . . We are ready to argue it right now. . . ." He turned his head cautiously toward the other lawyers, as if looking for someone over his shoulder, dismissed his slothful colleagues with a shrug, and continued, "But it's unfair to expect *them* to argue it *today*." The judge, eager to have the best minds in the business brought properly to bear on this most crucial question with well-researched briefs, confirmed the original sixty-day time span for filing. With the relief of reprieve, they all sat down.

Before Kreindler could rise to make his planned presentation both sides were back on their feet. The judge's request for a deposition schedule had forced all the hostilities being nurtured among the defendants into full bloom. The judge had asked, as well, for a list of the witnesses both sides wished to depose. The defense had submitted 247 names, which, at the sluggish rate the depositions were going, would take years to complete. It was instantly branded as "harassment," "oppressive," "just another delaying tactic." The frustrations were beginning to focus on Phillip Bostwick, the tall and conscientious young lawyer from the Washington, D.C. law firm of Shaw, Pittman, Potts & Towbridge. Bostwick found himself not only prosecuting the hull suit, but representing the passenger suits as well in depositions. To prevent duplication of effort, THY had consolidated its defense for discovery. Men on both sides blamed Bostwick for the delays that were stalling discovery, complaining that he was questioning the witnesses repetitively, going over the same ground again and again.

FitzSimons now proposed splitting off the hull suit "for the purposes of discovery," removing Bostwick

278

from the depositions. Bostwick's aggravating questions, aimed at proving that the airline had not misused the plane or caused the crash had "simply nothing to do with the Paris air crash or passengers." They were, like the dispute with General Dynamics, a matter of sales agreements, warranties, and contracts. "We are trying to keep contractual battles between McDonnell Douglas and General Dynamics out of this case. They go beyond fuselage 29, this episode . . . they've been going on for several years." He wanted that dispute, as well as the hull suit, severed from the passenger cases. "We put people before property."

Bostwick wanted to stay, and stood to attack "the argument being made before Your Honor that the hull suit is somehow impeding the progress of this matter." He had to defend the airline against "the allegations of those plaintiffs who have sued the airline, and against the cross-claims of McDonnell Douglas that we did something improper with the airplane, that we didn't maintain it properly, that we didn't know how to read the manuals and rig the doors, and so forth." Bostwick had supporters. Des Barry, of THY's passenger suit, argued that the hull suit was not causing delays. Kreindler echoed the thought. Bostwick felt it was FitzSimons who was delaying things. The plaintiffs were ready to come to trial next month or *this week* against McDonnell Douglas, but Douglas was avoiding trial, he said. Madole, on behalf of the plaintiffs, supported FitzSimons in severing the hull suit. Scoring a few more points, he reminded Judge Hall of the Everglades case, "where I also served on the plaintiff's committee," and where "there was severed from discovery the question of the hull suit . . . leaving just the question of the decedents. . . ."

Hall knew that these third-party disputes among the defense could delay passenger cases, and he was, above all, concerned to get the money out to the widows and orphans. Reminiscing over his own big cases, he recalled that in *United* v. *United States Government,* the plaintiffs put their case on in three days; the airline and government had taken *thirteen weeks.* Kreindler agreed that "Your Honor's point is well taken ... I personally would favor it." FitzSimons summed up the good sense of separating off the hull suit with a grand emphatic gesture of his arms, circling them as if holding a huge bundle and setting it, first to the right, the hull suit; and, next, off to the left, the passenger suits.

But Hall put his elbows on his desk, his chin in his hands, and rolled his eyes to the ceiling contemplatively. "What keeps haunting me is, if I do sever the hull suit ... and some question comes up—a critical one—that will involve liability for the hull, what happens then?" What would happen if one defendant were not there to defend himself from inculpation by the other three? And if he severed the hull, would they not have to duplicate discovery, duplicate the entire exhausting, time-consuming process of depositions for the hull? FitzSimons, still placing his imaginary bundles side by side, continued the argument with his arms. Hall cut in, freezing FitzSimons's arms mid-gesture. He removed his glasses with judicial dignity, and asked, "Why can't they be heard now?" The hull issue. "Couldn't they be heard in three days?"

"Oh Lord, no!" said FitzSimons. Madole countered that it "had been done very efficiently in other cases." FitzSimons kept resisting, "They're not just dreaming, they're whistling Dixie in the woods if they think they can get through this in an hour or a day." All the lawyers squirmed, laughed, aroused by the test of wills. For the second time that afternoon, Hall had caught the lawyers off guard. He had cut through the rhetoric, challenging them to air the issues in public argument and get them out of the way. To keep the case moving. The lawyers shook their heads in amazement. At times, he seemed a vague old man, letting his mind wander over old cases like old loves, riffling through his papers, debating with himself as if he were alone in the courtroom. The lawyers would sometimes talk to him slowly, condescendingly, as if lecturing a dull child. Then, with a quiet, ingenuous question like "Why can't they be heard now?" he would crack their heads together and put the pressure on. He would take motions "under advisement," delay his opinions, maintain an air of uncertainty over what he would do. It had taken several months for most to appreciate the subtle pressure he kept on the lawyers and on the case by keeping them guessing. Those who had not had a case before him before only gradually began to understand the ways of the wily old man who, in his seventies, had developed most of the techniques that now moved complex aviation cases through the courts with remarkable speed.

It was not realistic to argue the hull suit that moment, and everyone knew it. But Hall had called their bluff and let them know that he, like Thelma Alden, wanted the messes cleaned up. He did not want the hull suit, or any other dispute, impeding the case. The mothers and children could not wait. And neither could he.

It was time for Kreindler to rise. With the unconcerned air of the scholar, he took over the lectern. Dick Witkin took notes. In a rambling tour through the most sensational documents and testimony, Kreindler claimed that the plaintiffs now had "Knowledge—shocking knowledge!—that catastrophe was in the minds of these people" as early as 1969. He told about the doctored FMEA. He alluded to the Applegate memo. He exposed an FAA letter written after *Windsor* in which the FAA admitted that it was not optimistic that hazards from nonplug doors could be eliminated. He brought up the rerigging evidence, brought home from Paris by Caldwell, that had thrown the question of cause into confusion. The rigging had been changed. But by whom? He said that the evidence went beyond negligence, quite possibly to *fraud*—the grounds for punitive damages.

But Turkish Airlines' documents would not arrive until next week. They might cast more light on the rerigging controversy. "Let's get an overview. Let's put the *shape* of the case on the table so the various interests can take a look at it." It seemed to scuttle premature argument that afternoon on the hull suit.

Kreindler was a master at keeping pressure on the defense, at breaking logjams. But both defense and plaintiff lawyers fumed at his presentation. To Fitz-

Simons, with his clear Irish-Catholic vision of right and wrong, Kreindler had been wrong to put privileged deposition material on the public record, in violation of the partial gag order. It gave the world's press access to material that could only be embarrassing to the defense. The plaintiffs thought Kreindler was grandstanding.

Sterns had been silent. But he was finally fed up with the delays, with what he saw as self-serving rhetoric, with being upstaged by East Coast lawyers. He had been involved, too, in having the Applegate and Hurt memos produced by General Dynamics' attorneys in New York, and now Kreindler was getting all the mileage out of them. The judge kept forgetting his name and had even joked that Sterns had been off in the desert hustling "Ay-rab" cases—a joke that, to him, was neither funny nor true. He represented sixty-five cases, a dominating number in any case. He unwound from his chair and ambled to the lectern. He gripped the edge of the lectern with his right hand, threw his jacket open as he put his left hand on his hip, and let go. "We've heard several long speeches. We all know the evidence, we *all* helped develop it. And, as Mr. Kreindler so eloquently stated in *some detail,* the case is shaping up nicely. But I'm not interested in essays on Warsaw or writing books. Today, the issue is to get a trial date. That's the issue at hand. Your order was for April 7, 1975. We'll be ready, and *I'd like to go to trial.* The way cases come to a head, the way cases get settled is with a *trial date. Set* a trial date, give us a sixty-day pretrial, and *let's go!*" He said it fast and emphatically, coming down on the lectern with a karate chop as he closed. He stretched his body up in a gesture of impatience, let it slump down again, and sat down.

The two western boys were beginning to understand each other. Like cattle drivers, they wanted to keep 'em movin'. The judge said, "I'm going to leave my order stand here for trial on April 7, 1975." The date would now hang before them all as threateningly as certification had for the DC-10. Keeping the pressure on.

But the hull suit would not be severed yet. Bostwick's questioning would go on with the same rigor, inspiring complaints that would continue to sputter and fume through the next half year, climaxing finally in a hearing before Judge Hall in May in which Bostwick would be vindicated of 'bad faith' charges by the Judge.

The story appeared on the front page of *The New York Times* on October 31, two days after the hearing. "DESIGN NEGLIGENCE ALLEGED IN JET CRASH FATAL TO 346." The lead went on: "A Federal district court here was told yesterday that there was new evidence of negligence in aircraft design and development and possibly of fraud, in connection with the crash of a DC-10 airliner near Paris in March. . . . The new statements were made by Lee S. Kreindler, one of a number of plaintiff lawyers who . . ." The story was reprinted overseas. It was seen by the Japanese, translated, and added to a dossier of material on Kreindler that they had been collecting and translating, including his DC-10 article in the *New York Law Journal,* his pleadings in the case, and a photograph they had taken of him in the United States.

At the invitation of the Japanese, Lee Kreindler was on a jet to Tokyo in early December. The meetings between a famous Jewish lawyer and forty-eight Japanese families and their legal representatives, mostly Buddhist, would be the most "extraordinary" of his long career. By the time he returned to New York four days later, he had been retained. As he flew home via Fairbanks—exhausted, stiff from bowing and sitting on the floor, his system permeated with the gin that had been the social lubricant of the visit—he mused on the rare moment of jest when, sitting together on the floor of a Japanese restaurant, one of the Japanese lawyers had told him that the real reason he had been retained was because of the photograph in their file. They had all studied it carefully, observed that he had a very large and balding head, and concluded that anyone with such a large head must have some brains. And, with so little hair, he could not hide the truth!

In Los Angeles, it was clear that the hearing had not cleared the air. The depositions were still going too slowly. Phil Bostwick was still taking hours and days on his interrogations. After six months of depositions, only a handful of witnesses had been deposed. The list filed with the judge stretched on and on. Trial, an abstract threat up to now, was beginning to seem a real possibility. Restless for the Christmas recess, they all wanted to get away from the case and go home. On the second to last day before the break for Christmas, several of the lawyers had railed at Bostwick to hurry up. Bostwick, impatient with the bad memory of the DC-10's project engineer Ray Bates and with obstructions from McDonnell Douglas' lawyer, threatened to adjourn his cross-examination and ask the judge for a ruling to force responsive answers and an end to the obstructive interruptions. In a stormy recess, sufficient accord was reached for the depositions to continue. But it had been a petulant, frustrating session and made the prospects of an early settlement look even more remote.

Next morning, they gathered again around the deposition table, tired and tense. The witness had not yet been brought in for the final round of questioning before recess. A paper airplane skimmed across the table. Another looped up and crashed. There was the sound of paper being ripped from legal notepads and folded. A fleet of darts took off. Madole's had severe handling problems. The court reporter, Walter Holden, thought the left wing needed more dihedral and, perhaps, more wing area. Herb Lyons's flew well, but did wild loop-the-loops. "Ha! The FAA going round in circles again!" They were getting into it, feverishly trying to remember how they'd folded them as boys. A sleek model would soar up, then nose-dive to the floor. Guffaws. Glee. "Oh, oh! There goes another DC-10!"

Briefly, they had unbuckled their sword belts to sit under a tree together. As depositions ended, they hurriedly dumped notes and documents into huge briefcases, eager to get to the airport. They shook hands, joked, and said good-bye with the hearty old clichés that, for them, held special meaning. "Good trip." "Have a good flight." And, of course, "Merry Christmas!"

Chapter Twenty-Two

The First Anniversary

CHRISTMAS PASSED, leaving the first anniversary of the crash before them all, inescapable. For the families, the weeks before March 3, 1975, began to swell with fearful anticipation.

Like many others who had no graves to visit, Shirley Backhouse went to France on March 3. She wrote down her thoughts.

I went to both Thiais and l'Ermenonville Forest. It was a day I was very glad to have behind me. There were many families from many countries there in Paris on March 3, and all, I know, with similar feelings. The common grave in Thiais has now been grassed over and has a simple French marble scroll with the following inscription written in French: "To the memory of the unidentified victims of the air disaster in Ermenonville Forest, 3 March, 1974." The area itself has been planted with conifer trees and is indeed a very quiet corner of the cemetery.

In the forest itself on the Monday were again many families. There were flowers all over from individuals, embassies, and relatives. But the scene is still one of complete devastation. Obviously until Nature covers it once again in foliage it will remain like this. There was no official ceremony either at the cemetery or the forest. People just

*went along and made their own private farewells,
or whatever one likes to call it in these circumstances. It is very difficult to judge other people's
feelings on these sorts of occasions, but faces register all sorts of emotions. The feeling that I felt
very strongly on Monday, March 3, 1975, standing
in Ermenonville, was what a terrible waste of life
for so many hundreds of people.*

At 4 P.M. that afternoon, Shirley Backhouse and the
other members of the International Association formed
to plan the memorial met at the Alboro Hotel, near
Thiais cemetery. The association represented families of
80 percent of the decedents, joined together to share
the cost of the monument and of planting of trees
nearby.

Shirley was moving soon to a house closer to the
office. She felt that she must make a new life for herself
and for Lucy, her baby. Steve's presence was still there.
"I can *see* him walking around in the rose garden. I
can *see* him coming home from gym, picking up his
paper, calling me to say 'meet me in such and such a
pub.' They'll be with me as long as I'm here." She
would have to leave. "But always, no matter what happens to me for the rest of my life, in whatever circumstances, he will be there somewhere."

As Shirley Backhouse arrived at the forest, she saw
a Turkish Airlines' crew leaving and was moved by the
gesture.

For the Turks, it had been a tragic year. In just 370
days, 452 people had been killed in three major crashes,
a devastating reversal of a safety record so good that
they had been boasting of it in their advertisements.
Only fifteen people had been killed in three crashes during the entire 1960s. The 1970s had been so good that
there must have been some holding of breaths in Istanbul. Only one crash, with one death, in 1972. Then
Izmir on January 26, just a month before Paris, when
seventy-three were killed in the crash of a Fokker

Friendship. Paris had come on March 3, with the loss of 346. Then on January 30, 1975, another Fokker had crashed into the bay at Istanbul, killing forty-one.

The Paris crash had been followed by attacks in court and in discovery on the airline's competence, and by the humiliation of a major story in the *Sunday Times,* headlined "Fit to Fly?" The case was casting the airline's crews and maintenance men as aviation Neanderthals, handling supersophisticated machines like crude clubs, and paralyzed by pride from admitting deficiencies. A DC-10 in the hands of a Turk was being made to sound like a gun in the hands of a child. Turks bristled at documents that painted the early period of DC-10 operations as a black comedy of errors, a period in which flight engineers—a new breed created for the DC-10 by converting military pilots to the job—had ignored warning lights and fuel logs, and had reportedly viewed the job disdainfully as merely a stepping-stone to being captain.

Pride in what they had achieved was being undermined. For, though still lacking the broad base of technical proficiency that would rank them with the advanced aviation nations, they had achieved more than had seemed possible half a century earlier when Kemal Atatürk had gathered the disheveled remains of the Ottoman Empire up into a nation, imposed Western suits and airplanes, and told them, "The future is in the air."

Atatürk, rising with "a company of poor men from the stern hills and valleys" of Anatolia, had made them believe they could successfully throw off their medieval trappings in a generation and attain full membership in a technological world. Winston Churchill had fanned their hopes and historic pride: "Loaded with follies, stained with crimes, rotted with misgovernment, shattered by battle, worn down by long disastrous wars, his empire falling to pieces around him, the Turk was still alive. In his breast was beating the heart of a race that had challenged the world and for centuries had contended victoriously against all comers."

Turkey had tried to live up to Atatürk's belief that "the future is in the air." But among the crews making sad visits to the forest on March 3, some must have wondered if he had been right.

The repercussions of grief seemed, for some families, to grow more severe as time went by. Even after a year, Mrs. Wright was still having the terrible dreams. If anything, they were more vivid, the ghostly presences more real. "In the back of my mind, they're there all the time." She would suddenly feel "someone occupying the air space. I could almost reach out and touch them. One day, I said, 'Why Tom's here.' Another time, I was resting, not sleeping, and Fay said, 'Hi, Mom.' And the accident, I keep seeing it over and over. I can hear them going down." Tom, her only son. Fay and the three children, little Jackson taking the Wright bloodline with him. Sherry had not been brought back for burial. What must the child have experienced? She watched an hour-long television documentary on the crash and it had only made it worse. Cameras had ruthlessly panned the crash site. She thought she had seen Tom's body. "There was a close-up of a man that looked so much like Tom. And there was a woman reaching out toward him, on her stomach. I thought it was Fay." She knew it couldn't have been Fay. "Fay was shredded." The American consul had told them as much by letter, when they had asked. But "Tom wasn't so badly mangled." She wanted to see the tape again, to verify. She called Ginny, Mr. Sterns's secretary, to see if they could get the tape for her. She liked to call Ginny from time to time for reassurance and to tell her about the dreams.

Ginny wanted desperately to be able to tell her that there had been no great terror, no pain, no knowledge that death was seconds away. She wanted to go to Berkeley to visit with Mrs. Wright and let her talk out the fears that had put her into a severe nervous condition, and given her heart an alarmingly irregular beat. But she couldn't lie. She didn't know. How could anybody know? And she didn't dare get any more emotionally involved with the clients than she already was. It was difficult enough to work in an office in which catastrophic injury, terminal illness, and violent death were the daily fare. Tragedy filled the files she handled. She welcomed and soothed clients who sat with their crutches in the reception room. And she took the calls from Mrs. Wright and others who looked on Walkup, Downing and Sterns not only as lawyers, but also as a sustaining link. Ginny was hope and someone to talk to.

Mr. Sterns couldn't—and shouldn't—take the calls. She made a note of each call from Mrs. Wright and put it in the file, heartsick at the inadequacy of a note to record what had transpired between a young secretary and an elderly woman trying to adjust to the fact that her only son and his family had been wiped out. Leaning against a doorjamb, Ginny would glance occasionally over the bay to Berkeley and sigh a deep compassionate sigh for all the sorrow she just wasn't able to shoulder.

The litigation was painful . . . endless. But she wondered if, sometimes, it gave people the will to live. Mrs. Wright's attitude toward McDonnell Douglas had not softened with time. It had hardened. She was determined that crashes must *not* be allowed to take bright young Americans like Tom who had to travel doing business for their country's corporations. "I am so bitter. I want them to suffer some way, though it won't bring my family back." She wanted meetings with friends to hurry and be over, so that she could be alone. But she knew she had to get out to survive. She started working as a volunteer at a thrift shop on Saturdays. Gradually, very gradually, there were "longer periods when I can think of something else."

She kept in touch with McCulloch Campbell, Fay's father, who lived a few miles away in the Berkeley hills where both their children had grown up. Everyone worried about him, for he was withdrawing more and more. And he, too, was growing more bitter. He spent increasing amounts of time in the cozy rumpled den with the neatly tied packets of Fay's blue airmail letters and with the cassette tapes that still carried her voice. His son, Barrie, tried to lure him up to Redding to visit with his grandchildren there, but McCulloch Campbell retreated more and more from life, into the house he had been keeping for Fay, the house he had hoped she would come back to with her family. The house she had been raised in. The death of his wife a year before the crash had been the most devastating loss of his life. That death had brought him and his daughter closer together than they had ever been. Fay had sustained him. He had gone to England for Christmas with her, just before the crash. He ran shaking fingers over pictures of the last Christmas tree, the gifts spread out, waiting for three little children. . . .

Within eighteen months of the crash, McCulloch Campbell would be dead. And Barrie would be sorting through the family home as Fay and Tom's friends had done in London after the crash. Friends drove down from Sacramento and Redding to help. They joked and drank beer as they helped him move out nearly forty years' accumulation. Barrie was now alone, with his own young family. He would carry on the lawsuit, as his father would have wanted him to do.

Grappling with the seventh death to strike his family within two years, Barrie would say, "If it is possible to die from a broken heart, my father did."

In Polegate, the Barrows prepared for the anniversary. Weeks before, Harold had ordered Gene's favorite red roses and would take them to her grave at the foot of the downs on March 3. They all felt that, from then on, they would be "home free." For the Barrows, it was the first Christmas without Gene, that had been the big stumbling block.

They had dreaded Christmas. For them, as for all the families, life had become a series of symbolic hurdles: wedding anniversaries and birthdays, traditional family get-togethers—the occasions that stood out in relief from everyday life to celebrate the enduring human bonds.

Harold Barrow and the girls didn't talk much about their feelings as they prepared for Christmas. Each was quietly preoccupied with doing everything exactly as Gene had done it, duplicating each candle and polished fork. They cut holly and mistletoe from the garden and lavished it round the house, remembering how their mother had "really gone to town, just like a kid." It was as if even the slightest violation of tradition might bring their tenuous defenses tumbling down and send them back into sobs and despair. Harold's mother and sister had come to help fill the void, though no one spoke of it. They dreaded sitting down to dinner. But the girls served at four. Roast turkey with onion stuffing. Brussels sprouts and potatoes. Cranberries.

Ritually, they pulled Christmas crackers until they popped and put on the silly hats. Harold Barrow looked around the table. With the tissue-paper hats perched on their heads, and long straight hair, they looked like little girls playing princess. But in each of them, an elegance and maturity was coming through. Sally, whose two-year marriage had failed since Gene's death, working now at a television commercial studio in London. Home for Christmas. Teresa, helping him run the house and working at a hotel in Eastbourne. Helena, only sixteen, but grown so capable since her mother's death. She was already at college studying to be a nurse. The eagerness they had put into Christmas was more than just a cover-up. It was Gene's spirit, and it was still alive.

The girls looked around at their grandmother, their aunt, and at their father with his lean, sad face and ridiculous hat. He still hadn't touched the garden, but he'd learned to make a nice Irish lamb stew. Smiles began to spread around the table like a glowing fuse. They started to laugh. They were going to get through the day.

"Where's the plum pudding?"

Sally had forgotten to steam it. She stuck a piece of

holly in it, doused it with her father's good brandy, and paraded it in, stone cold. They lit it up and roared at the burst of flame. The old glow was gone forever. But they had created their own.

Half a world away, in Bangkok, the patriarch of Thailand's Buddhists and two priests, all in saffron robes, walked up the ramp of Thai International's new DC-10. It was 9 minutes after nine in the morning, a symbolically auspicious hour. Chanting, they sprinkled holy water on the plane's white and silver skin. They moved through the cabin, sprinkling the interior. As they exited at the rear, they scattered drops of holy water on the brilliant Thai silks of the stewardesses, clustered like flowers at the bottom of the ramp.

Watched by a hushed group of government and airline officials and invited guests, all formally dressed in dark suits, the priests had come to bless the craft that would introduce the blazing new colors and symbols of the nation's flag carrier to the world. With bold horizontal stripes of purple, hot pink, and gold that swept the white fuselage and burst into an enormous stylized blossom on the tail, the plane would carry a new image of Thailand on the maiden voyage that would begin the following day.

No one had seen the plane until that morning. The paint job had been done fast and secretly in Zurich, and the -10 had flown in just the night before. As the group of officials moved toward the plane, there had been gasps, cheers, and applause. The excitement would be repeated in Teheran, Frankfurt, and Copenhagen, where parties would celebrate the design's triumphant debut.

The motif on the tail was the largest symbol yet painted by any airline on the rear engine and empennage of the DC-10 and it magnified the already high visibility of the mighty rear engine. It had been projected from small drawings up to super scale by computers that calculated precisely how it could hold its shape while curving over the sheathing of the rear engine.

The motif was part of a sophisticated "design system" that would be carried through every visual element of the airline—service trucks, ticket sales offices, cocktail napkins, stationery. The product of one of the world's leading design groups, Landor Associates, the system had been developed on Walter Landor's fabled converted ferry boat in San Francisco bay. To Landor, the objectives of packaging were essentially related, whether cigarettes, beer, gasoline, or airplanes. His challenge here had been to distill the essence of Thailand into forceful symbolism; to combine Thailand's exotic Asian flavor with implications of speed and competence; to find designs and colors that would say both East and West, for the airline was 30 percent owned by Scandinavian Airlines System, SAS. Landor's designers had played with every conceivable traditional Thai form, tending toward lotus blossoms, then discarding them when they learned that to use them might be a violation of religious codes. Scores of designs were explored and evaluated, slide presentations made to airline executives in Landor's screening room, as choices narrowed. The final decision was worried over, debated, made, and then further refined. It had been hard to bring enchantment to the efficient machine. But everyone agreed that the DC-10 "never looked better."

The new design system would transform an assembly line product into one of the Thai government's prime competitive tools in the aggressive fight for national prestige and the world's tourist dollars. It must have a positive impact on passengers, and help create a climate of confidence as the nation negotiated for landing rights and route swaps that would expand its access to the international tourist market. It must appeal to travel agents who, with the power to make or break resorts, airlines, and aircraft, had become a global tyranny. With tourism on the verge of becoming the largest foreign exchange source for Thailand, and the Chiang Mai resort in the mountains 500 miles north of Bangkok being heavily promoted, the DC-10 with the exotic tail must help.

And the design must be bold enough to overpower the gentle blue bird form on the tail of its Thai competitor, privately owned Air Siam. With an international fleet of only two leased wide-bodies, Air Siam had assigned its one DC-10 to the Honolulu-Los Angeles route, leased a billboard outside the L.A. International Airport, and was, as *Aviation Week* described it, "flaunting its wide-body fleet in advertising as part of the growing rivalry with 70%- government owned Thai International."

To compete, Thai International was acquiring *three* DC-10s. With their regal streaks of purple, gold, and pink, they would be appealing packages for a nation's spirit and powerful instruments for Thai ambitions. But even the most sophisticated of technological packages needed the traditional Buddhist blessing. With holy water, the priests sprinkled the plane, unaware, perhaps, that the big plane they blessed would bring the crowds that could overwhelm tradition.

Well-blessed, well-dressed, the plane flew off to Copenhagen.

Chuck Miller was still on medication for his heart, but the readings he was getting from his doctor were good. He was playing tennis as actively as ever and doing private consulting on systems safety for the aviation industry. And he had begun staging international seminars on air safety for the Flight Safety Foundation. He was lecturing in London on the anniversary of the crash and would soon be flying to Kuala Lumpur to lecture the airlines of Southeast Asia, a part of the world that hungered for information. He wished South America was as interested.

It was gratifying to play a significant role in the mission to raise global standards. But the scars of Miller's struggle within the NTSB would take a long time to heal. He had left the NTSB with grave self-doubts and had been immeasurably cheered when he had opened the year-end issue of *Aviation Week* and seen among the Laurels for 1974 one to *"Charles O. Miller, former chief of the National Transporation Safety Board's Bureau of Aviation Safety, who, at great personal sacrifice, exposed to Congress and thwarted the Nixon administration's efforts to subvert the board actions and policy, which he believed would adversely affect aviation safety."*

He was deeply moved and immensely grateful that the nation's most respected aviation publication had recognized his lonely battle. But White House influence was still intruding itself. And the ex-governor of Maine, John Reed—a pleasant and well-meaning New England potato farmer caught up in the world's most sophisticated technology, empowered to make recommendations affecting the safety of the millions who fly in American planes—was still chairman of the NTSB. Though Miller had always found him cooperative, Reed had become, in Miller's eyes, a symbol of a system of political appointments that had little place in the complex and specialized environment of wide-body and, one day, supersonic crash investigation. The GO team would soon be going to Concorde school, getting ready.

Miller would continue to monitor the NTSB informally from the outside. And to worry.

For Chef d'Escadron Jacques Lannier in Senlis the excitement was over. He was packing up, preparing to move on to Angers where he had been promoted to a district post. There, as Commandant Lannier, he hoped to make time in the evenings to complete his new book on police dogs. He had finished his work on July 27, nearly five months after the crash. He and his men had achieved adequate legal proof, either forensic or circumstantial, of 346 dead, and *jugements déclaratifs de décès* had been issued for them all. Dérobert at the Institut was having doubts—he thought there might have been more. But at least they could be *sure* of 346, the number that tallied with the airline list.

Lannier would leave the old stone gendarmerie and

la compagnie de Senlis in good order. Preparations had been made for the flow of families who would visit the forest on the first anniversary and for the Japanese service on March 11. Only minor procedural skirmishes were left. The British had violently opposed the choice of a French sculptor for the memorial, saying he was too expensive, and were proceeding with a British sculptor, using Cornish stone. The monument would be erected on the crash site at a location granted by the French government. The crash site in the forest was surrounded with high metal fence and padlocked. The blackened spikes of pine had been cut and cleared away. There was still a scattered carpet of residue: tattered swatches of gold-colored fabric that must have covered seats or floor, short sections of plastic tubing, jagged nubs of black metal, shoe soles, suspenders, sodden newspaper. But the half-mile swath was essentially neat and orderly, waiting the planting of new pines later in the spring.

In his office in the gendarmerie, thick books of files were stacked on a table, his record of the most remarkable assignment of his career. A big gray file was titled "Compagnie de Senlis, Brigade Recherches Senlis Procédure 1132 Infraction Homicides Involontaires." Another, "Dossier Photographique No. 2—Accident d'Aviation Procédure sur Commission Rogatoire, Procès-Verbal N. 65/R. Survenu le 3 mars 1974 a l'aeronef DC-10 immatricule TC-JAV de la compagnie aerienne Turkish Airlines." The crude assemblage of names begun on the day of the crash were now neat lists, full of information. He would leave them behind to his successor, with the envelopes of photographs.

He handed one to a visiting writer, a better way than words to describe what the crash had been to him and his gendarmes. In the shiny black and white of a press photo, a young fireman stood over the decapitated head of a woman, his hands dripping with blood and his face turned up as if pleading to God to let him escape the duty he must do.

Lannier obligingly took guests to the forest, unlocked

the padlocks, and strode over the rough, bleak ground again.

In the crash site, striding the barren swath, he was again the ebullient commandant, reliving it with the vivid recall of a soldier revisiting a battlefield: the lung hanging on a tree . . . the brains on the ground near his headquarters . . . the intact heart . . . the one who had cried out as he landed in the field at St. Pathus. . . .

At the Institut Médico-légal on the Seine in Paris, Professeur Leon Dérobert smoothed his hand over a thin red file, his final report on the Paris case. It was dated February 17, 1975, three weeks before the anniversary. It contained his report that approximately half the victims had been forensically identified. 188. Though only the Turks and Japanese had fully cooperated, he and his staff had achieved substantially more than the handful of identifications that had been predicted. It had been a triumph of skills and technical aids, but humanly unrewarding for a man who preferred to rehabilitate the limbs of the living. For him, there could be no triumph in a fatal plane crash, for he could not breathe life back into the "bits and pieces."

And there was the nagging question of the numbers aboard. 346 had been confirmed, and death certificates issued. But he believed there may have been between 356 and 360 people aboard the plane. If he was correct, who were they? Had they been missed?

A year ago, Stephen Mitchell had been saying goodbye to Prudence as she left for Spain. Now, he was standing on a stage in an auditorium in the City of London, introducing Jerry Sterns to a large group of solicitors and family members who had come from Leeds, Bristol, Manchester—all over England—to hear a progress report on the American litigation. To the solicitors, and especially to the families, the legal action was still an abstraction. They knew nothing of arguments over "paramount interest" and "domiciliary law," though the arguments had a very direct bearing on the outcome of their cases. The deaths were real. The money would be real. But to women like Nora Griffin, besieged by six children, trying to dry mittens and get the baby's formula made before the first returned from nursery school with questions and tears and needs, the lawsuit was as real as a lottery ticket.

On the stage, Mitchell could appreciate, as he did not in his day-to-day work, the profound change the crash had brought to his life. He had become a conduit between the American courts and this roomful of hope and expectation. His regular letters to the solicitors translated U.S. law and the status of the case into terms they could understand. He was in constant contact with Sterns by phone and Telex, discussing strategy. The cases were all processed through his office on the Thames. It was a position of leadership Prudence would have loved to have seen him play. "She always wanted her man to be a success." The terrible irony often occurred to him, as *Paris* thrust him more and more into a pivotal role in the most important aviation case in history: It was her death that had forced him to be what she had wanted him to be.

Several weeks before the anniversary, Sue Ellis had been preparing the postgame tea in the clubhouse of the Bury St. Edmunds Rugby Football Club. She worked to the usual background noises of men running, grunting, kicking rugby balls. But suddenly the noises stopped. She looked up and out toward the playing field. Both teams had lined up on the field and were standing at attention—the Bury boys and their opponents, the Racing Club of Paris. They had come over to play the first annual memorial game. She realized that they had stopped to observe a brief silence for Bryan and the men who had died with him. Even after a year, she was still surprised and touched by these unexpected gestures of feeling and respect.

As the day approached, Sue wondered if she would go to the concert being held in the cathedral in Bury St. Edmunds on the anniversary. The concert was a fund-raiser, not a memorial. She decided to spare herself the pain by going out to dinner with friends instead. But at home, she listened privately to the music they would play: Bruckner's Violin Concerto . . . Beethoven's Ninth Symphony.

She would go to the forest later, in May.

There, in a valley turning green under the irresistible forces of life and renewal, as all French battlefields had, she found some lily of the valley. She dug up a few roots and planted them in her garden in Ixworth. She didn't have much hope for them. But they took. And grew!

The lawyers would honor the anniversary by arguing the Warsaw Convention, an opportunity the judge seized with relish. Any decision he made here at the district level would not be binding, of course, but with Hall's prestige it would be swiftly printed in the Federal Supplement, grabbed and used as precedent; and if upheld at the appellate and Supreme Court levels, it would be binding on all future Warsaw cases. It was a chance to redress some of the inequities. As the club gathered in the courtroom, his eyes sparkled with the intellectual challenge. He leaned forward in his black robes, leaning on his arms, fingers interlocked tightly. "Warsaw has been boiling, case after case, and now, to my advantage, I have the most qualified lawyers in the U.S. before me, and they have briefed Warsaw." He clearly felt that he might never again have this opportunity, for during the next few days of argument, he would make more than his usual number of joking references to his own mortality. David Dann and Peter Martin had flown in from London for the occasion. The judge looked down on a full house of sober business suits, brought together on March 3, 1975, because a door had come out of a plane near Paris.

Warsaw was an appropriately funereal choice, for it was quickly clear that the lawyers had gathered to say the last rites over the withered old international treaty, a treaty the United States had never even ratified. Sterns drove in the first knife with his opening statement, "We come not to praise the Warsaw, but to bury it!"

Each lawyer passed by and made his ritual thrust. George Tompkins's was the unkindest cut of all. Although as attorney for the airline he claimed the Convention's Article 28 as a vehicle for escaping jurisdiction of American courts and believed that as long as the countries the U.S. flew to found it useful, the United States, in order to live within the international aviation community, must honor it, he personally didn't want it. He waved a worn green copy of the Warsaw Convention in his left hand, and said, *"Like the Convention itself, it's a little battered."* For him, and for Peter Martin, it was becoming more difficult to apply each year, as its limitations led lawyers to seek through litigation ever more ingenious ways to circumvent it.

Behind the formal proceedings in the courtroom, an agitated thrust toward settlement was going on in the halls and in the men's room. A month earlier, Kreindler had surprised the court with a proposal for a sharing arrangement between the defendants that he hoped might pave the way for settlements, for they could still not agree among themselves what share each should pay. He had proposed that the airline pay $10,825,000, and the three other defendants pay all amounts over and above that in the following proportions: McDonnell Douglas—80 percent; General Dynamics—15 percent; and the U.S. government—5 percent. There was grumbling consensus, based on the evidence that had appeared so far, that his numbers were fairly sound. Sterns had scathingly referred to it as Kreindler's "Metternich bit," for though he had grown very fond of Lee and never quibbled with his capacities, he was still aggravated by Kreindler's refusal to be a team player. High-powered aviation litigation, however, has never been a team sport. And since making his proposal, Kreindler had moved like a whirling dervish through the offices of the insurers and defense lawyers in New York. But nothing had come of it as March 3 drew near. And the lawyers flew in to Los Angeles for the first anniversary under growing pressures of awareness of the passage of time and lack of progress. There was a sense of urgency that the tragic symbolism of the first anniversary must be exploited to achieve a settlement breakthrough in a case that had become even more complex and rancorous with the filing, just a week before the anniversary, of F. Lee Bailey's one case as a class action, claiming *$670 million* in punitive damages. Still convinced he could be the architect of settlement, Kreindler stepped up his efforts to bring the defense factions together. During the hearings, he dashed in and out of the courtroom for quick, whispered meetings in the hall with one after another of the defense lawyers. But he had to admit to the judge that "of three defendants, the only compliance is with the airline." Tompkins had stood in court and made an offer of $10 million, a good-faith offer he and Martin had dreamed up over breakfast, one they hoped would break the deadlock. But Kreindler had discovered that the stubborn old conflict between McDonnell Douglas and General Dynamics—the vent door issue that had begun after the test blowout in 1970—was preventing agreement between those two. He told the court, "It is an outrage that survivors of 346 wait while the two defendants quibble."

By the end of the week, Kreindler had not succeeded. In spite of his vigorous efforts, in spite of the presence of David Dann and Peter Martin, the agreement between the defendants that must be a prelude to settlement had not been reached.

The vent door conflict had become a tar pit that had ensnared them all.

Chapter Twenty-Three

What Is
a Good Wife Worth?

SOMEHOW, IN SPITE of the impasse, settlement negotiations must eventually come. And in preparation, information on the dead was being gathered up in the offices of the plaintiff lawyers. Pictures, family and financial information. Personal testimonials and facsimiles of diplomas. The data that they would need to reconstruct each lost life in the intimate detail needed to negotiate for settlement or to go to trial. It was being built up in file folders, part of the process of conversion of a death, first, into a legal action and finally, into dollar value. It was what the litigation of crash cases was really all about. What *was* a human life worth?

Every plaintiff's lawyer in the case must face the task of putting a dollar value on death.

For Dr. Kai Nordlund and his colleagues, representing the group of twenty-two Turkish families, it was a most terrible task. At emotional meetings with the families in Turkey, Dr. Nordlund had the question thrown to him, passionately, by parents who still wept and grieved openly a year after the crash. "Is an Englishman or an American worth more than *my son?*"

The families had read stories in the foreign press, all translated into Turkish, telling them that if they took their cases to California, great fortunes would fall into their laps. Dr. Nordlund could not promise them that, and he tried to explain that although there could be some money awarded for loss of comfort—and even love—the size of awards would depend largely on lost income; that an American corporate executive leaving a widow and three children would be awarded vastly more than a twenty-year-old Turkish student. In that highly emotional, sorrow-charged atmosphere, families could only be impatient with facts of law that had nothing to do with real human value, law that seemed to discriminate against their dead children. Dr. Nordlund was powerless to answer the moral question of whether one human life *should* be worth more than another. He could only apply the law in the most favorable way possible for his clients. The Turkish cases would indeed be difficult.

In preparation for the task of assessing the value of the forty-eight Japanese they represented, Lee Kreindler's young colleague Marc Moller went at the Japanese cases with the same academic vigor that had made his senior partner's name a household word among aviation lawyers. He talked to a Far Eastern scholar at Columbia University; he searched the New York Public Library for books that might enlighten him; and with *The Chrysanthemum and the Sword,* anthropologist Ruth Benedict's classic work on Japanese culture, in his briefcase, he flew to Japan to try to learn what the young lives had been worth there, in human and financial terms. At Sophia University in Tokyo, he found an authority on finance and labor relations, Robert J. Ballon, and made Ballon's book *The Japanese Employee* his bedtime reading. Kreindler and Marshall Morgan, too, made trips to Japan. Bringing their research together, they discovered that for their clients Japanese law might be even more favorable than the liberal California law. In Japan, the value of life is measured by the loss of earnings to the decedent himself, and could be swelled by awards not only for pecuniary loss—loss of income—but also for *moral* damages that allowed payment for grief and anguish.

Though restrained on the surface, the grief of the

Japanese parents was overwhelming to the New Yorkers. The father of Takehiro Higuchi, who was on his honeymoon, had died thirteen days after the crash, immediately after his post-crash visit to Paris. How could you express loss this deep on a legal brief? Hideo Goto, who had lost his "beloved son" in the crash, had poured out his feelings to Kreindler about the discovery of his son's bloodied parka—the discovery that had convinced Goto that, for the seventy-seven seconds, his son had had clear, desperate knowledge of death. It might be an argument for grief damages. As they hunted for the most advantageous law, they were under pressure, for the Japanese were motivated by a quiet passion for moral redress that drove them to pursue the case with a systematic vigor that threatened to exhaust even Kreindler and Moller, whose own thoroughness was hard to match. The Japanese had already turned down an offer of $82,000 per case before signing with Kreindler, and Kreindler would have to produce awards substantially in excess of that sum to satisfy the Japanese and to justify their commitment to the searing emotional drain of a lawsuit.

Like Dr. Nordlund's, Moller's task was difficult. The Japanese were mostly young unmarried men, a traditionally low-value category called "nondependencies." They had died in the hiatus between college and the beginning of work. But they had employment contracts which spelled out their future income. Moller discovered that Japan's social system obligates children to care for their parents. "They take care of each other, and parents expect to get back what they put into the kids." And Japanese law *did* allow you to project *future* earnings—the money they *might* have earned—and claim these. Japanese law looked most favorable. And if applied by a California jury, it might produce awards big enough to convince the Japanese families that McDonnell Douglas's moral debt had been paid. But Kreindler could not simply argue the law of the domicile, for this might hurt his Kansas case, a state where there was a $50,000 limit on awards. In his brief on choice of law, Kreindler would argue for California law, except where the law of the decedent's domicile provided greater benefits. It covered both Japan and Kansas nicely. It was from just such expedience that *Kilberg* had been born, and that law evolves.

In San Francisco, information on English decedents handled by Jerry Sterns lined the walls of the tiny DC-10 room. Backhouse, Barrow, Wright, Sorkin became the daily companions of the young New Zealand lawyer, Jim Murray, who processed the material as it arrived. Murray had lost friends on the Pago Pago crash and would be forced by *Paris* to make the transition from personal to professional involvement in death.

From Stephen Mitchell's office he would receive the actuarial reports on pecuniary loss, the loss of financial support to a family. This loss of support would be used as the basis for putting dollar value on the economic losses suffered. This was the easiest area, for though it took painstaking calculations, there were tangible figures to work with. The actuary's quest was for *current value,* that capital sum which invested today would yield enough interest to keep a family going over a dead husband's expected working span. Even if awarded by California courts, it would be the English—or Turks, or Japanese, or Australian—standards of wages, inflation, interest, and taxation that would determine the dollar amounts. The income of a London street cleaner would not be replaced with the income of one from Los Angeles. But even in this relatively straightforward area, there could be wide fluctuation of value. Under California law, pecuniary loss was calculated liberally, taking inflation, promotions, and long life spans into account. By comparison, the United Kingdom was miserly, projecting—at the most!—a twenty-year working span for a young man. A widow of twenty-five might receive a sum that would sustain her for twenty years at the income level her husband had earned when he died, and if she did not marry again, she would be left unsupported when the capital ran out at forty-five.

With United Kingdom's runaway inflation, it might run out long before.

Loss of support was difficult enough to calculate, but it was the words that described the intangible loss that Sterns and his staff would agonize over. It was these words that had drawn the English to American courts, and in them lay the greatest dollar potential. Though not written into the California Wrongful Death Statute, a group of magic words had been recognized in cases, and upheld by appeal courts, as the law. *Care, Comfort. Protection. Society.* Usually lumped under the generic term *loss of society,* they were the words of sentiment that went beyond lost income to love and feeling, to the human relationships that life was really all about. But what were they worth? To a California jury? To the husband, child, or father who had lost them in the forest? Was a young Japanese executive worth more in these human terms than an Armenian seamstress? Was an accomplished diplomat worth more than his teen-aged son? What was a good wife worth? A mother? Or a grandfather? In this case, Sterns had a new lever for upgrading his claims. With timing that was beautifully fortuitous for the plaintiff lawyers, a *1974* Supreme Court decision, *Sea-Land Services, Inc.* v. *Gaudet,* extended the group of words to include two more: *love and affection.* They had arrived just in time for *Paris,* making American courts that much more appealing. The lawyers would all be citing *Sea-Land* v. *Gaudet* in their claims for damages.

But the breathtaking range of relationships encompassed in *love and affection* made it just that much more difficult to translate them into dollars. Human relationships could not be listed like assets in an annual report. Yet Sterns would have to come to the settlement table with numbers, numbers he could support under interrogation by the defense. Somehow, he must make each client stand out as a human being, as something more than a name on a brief. Each family must become real. It was easy for the defense to become familiar with the decedents in a small-plane crash, for there were

306

usually only one or two. But there was a danger in the mass-transport disasters that the individual got lost in the crowd. Sterns knew, too, that with potential settlements so high, the defense was going to balk at big figures; he guessed that they would resist anything over a million dollars on principle. Yet many, perhaps twenty, of his eighty-five cases could be seven-figure cases. For the levels of negotiation he intended to conduct, he intended "to build the right kind of foundation . . . to condition the defense, put them in the right frame of mind." He wanted the clout of each case impressed upon them and decided to give the defense "something they could get their hot little hands on." He made settlement brochures. Public relations pieces wrapped in shiny plastic covers, they are a delicate undertaking, for no matter how tastefully done, they served the deceased up as a sanitized, marketable product. Badly done, they could be maudlin, sordid. But 346 dead people were what the case was all about, a fact thrust to the fore by Judge Hall when he instructed that the name of the decedent be written on the first page of every brief and complaint. Sterns's job was to get as much money as he could, and he believed he could get more if he could "remind the defense they're dealing with people." He put a black-and-white photograph of the deceased on the cover. Inside, there would be family photographs and the story of lives lopped off mid-course, told, of course, in a good light. To make the stories as human and real as possible, Bernard Engler was sent out to interview thirty families, and here Engler came into his own. The administration of the cases had been largely lifted from his shoulders when the load became too heavy for his office in Manchester and had been moved to Mitchell's office, where young Jim Teff had been assigned to the cases full time. But in interviewing families, Engler's insatiable interest and warmth enabled him to draw human portraits that might have been done by a skilled journalist. He looked for the special qualities and conditions that do make each life unique, no matter how apparently ordinary. Both defense and plaintiff lawyers knew that an air crash was a slice of life, humanity in its old dressing gown. Families were not all loyal, loving, and vice-free. They often brought suit out of guilt and greed—*not* devotion. But a plaintiff lawyer had to put his client in the best possible light within the framework of truth. Dependence on every level—financial, emotional, physical—was stressed. Husbands did not drink, cheat, or gamble. Marriages were as durable as Gibraltar. Prospects were usually spiraling upward. The brochures would hold the same cleaned-up memory that most families held in their hearts. Most of it would be true. And supportable. It would have to be to justify the figures on the lower-right-hand corner of the last page, demands that would range from $200,000 to over $2 million—the starting point for negotiations.

Away from the politicking and attack mode in Los Angeles, Sterns and his staff would worry about and debate the bottom line over the year and more that it would take to gather all the material together. Sterns talked to other lawyers, checked current jury verdicts, and appraised his clients, trying to get a feel for the market value of human life. It was insanity, a never-never land, but the system required that lawyers played God. He traveled to England several times, meeting as many of the families as he could, getting a personal feel for the lost relationships. It brought him for the first time into direct contact with the crash. Pathetic, sad, broken people. Courage that made you want to cry. Such long marriages. Happy or not, they had lasted. Divorce had not yet cut across England as it had California, and he was touched by the clear affection and loyalty that had, abruptly, lost its focus. Like Lannier, Martin, and Miller, he had had to develop the defenses that would allow him to deal with death. It was impossible not to be moved by Nora Griffin, a widowed mother of five, wistful and pregnant at the time of the crash with the sixth child, whom her husband would never see. But he tried to view widows for their impact on a jury. A jury would empathize with Nora Griffin,

and the potential sympathy factor would help him negotiate her case. But a jury might resist Shirley Backhouse's chic, her crisp competence. Or Heather Brigstocke's. She had just taken over as high mistress of
London's best girls' school when her husband, a government official and classics scholar, had died, and she had
carried on in the demanding job, while raising four
children. Heather Brigstocke was tall, blond and, in a
sweeping plaid cape, a handsome and commanding
sight. To Sterns, she was Mrs. Miniver, with all the
classic strengths British women drew on. But would a
jury worry about her as they would about Nora Griffin?

And the family on the Isle of Wight. The three children, only eleven, twelve, and fifteen, had been born
with the same congenital deformation of hands and feet
as their dead father. The defect had been a shock to the
interviewer who had gone to the Isle of Wight to meet
the family. The father had triumphed over the disability,
becoming a chief draftsman and airplane designer, with
hands that withered into just two digits. Alive, his own
ability to overcome must have been an inspiration to
the three children struck by the same genetic defect.
But without him? The case would be a powerhouse in
a jury trial. But God, those poor kids! And the Polish
refugee family who had survived Hitler to make a new
life in England. The father had not survived the Paris
crash. These terrible ironies. Dreams ended.

It was an impossible task, but arbitrary value had to
be put on the words. What was the loss of comfort,
care, society, and protection worth? What did they
even mean? Sterns tried to create a formula, lumping
the words together and giving them a total annual
value: $10,000 a year in the death of a spouse, and
$2,250 a year in the death of a parent or of a child,
dropping to $500 a year after the majority of a child
who had lost a parent. But was the need of a parent
just one fifth as great when you turned eighteen or
twenty-one? And was the loss of the human benefits of
a wife or a husband really *four* times greater than that

of parents who had lost a sixteen-year-old son, or of an adolescent losing her mother? Phone calls coming in to the office from Fay and Tom Wright's parents in Berkeley were making it clear that the loss of even grown and married children could cause severe stress and even sap the will to live. The child/parent figure wasn't right. It was discussed and moved up to $7,500 a year. But Sterns was concerned, then, about double fatalities of parents. In terms of emotional devastation to the child, wasn't the loss of *both* parents far greater than the death of only one? They combed sociologists' reports on bereavement and decided that "One and one don't make two." Simply doubling the single loss—$7,500—did not compensate for the unique trauma of being orphaned. They compromised by multiplying $7,500 by three and a half in the case of orphans, rather than two, an arbitrary choice that was as logical as anything else. He and his staff kept checking current jury awards, keeping them always in the back of their minds as a test for numbers that seemed to be getting too grotesque, or too low. For a jury award was the final, legal test of value. But human beings could not be fitted into a formula. And special factors that could not be squeezed into the formula were tacked on at the end, like the Special Conditions that had tried to encompass the innovations in the DC-10 not covered by the FARs.

Each case had its unique circumstances. Would the money come through fast enough to keep the Armenian husband from being deported? The pressures for early settlement on his case were great.

How did you put a price on a sour love? And how would it feel to find that your wife had been with some-one else's husband when she died in the plane crash? Airlines kept passenger lists secret, and it is easy to fly off for an affair undetected. A crash was the brutal way some husbands and wives found out.

How did you measure the loss of your best friend? Especially if she was your daughter. As Murray pro-cessed the report, he marveled at the elegant sporting life a father, seventy-five, and daughter, forty-six when she died, had shared since the mother's death nearly twenty years before. It was a life that, with inflation and confiscatory taxes, was fading in England. Working with her father in his brokerage business since the late 1940s and one of the first "blue button" women members of the London Stock Exchange, licensed to trade on the floor, she had been his business peer. They had flown to meetings regularly in Brussels, Paris, Zurich, and for twenty-five years had lunched together daily at the Savoy Grill, a legendarily good and prestigious place to eat. They kept a box at Ascot and gave superb Christmas parties. The daughter had become better at horses, stocks, and poker than her father. The two were insatiable sports, skiing and tobogganing in Switzerland every winter, safariing in Africa, and salmon fishing twice a year in Scotland where the father maintained rights to a stretch of the river Tay. For trout, they went annually to Ireland. They shared a passion for speedboating on the Norfolk Broads, and for a life that, for most, had passed from England before World War I.

The trip on the DC-10 was the only one in twenty-five years they had not taken together. The father wished he had been with her.

It was the so-called nondependency cases that were the most difficult—and controversial. Where there had been no pecuniary loss, no loss of support, the case was based solely on the value of lost relationships, on *emotional* dependency. In England, a non-dependency case was worth a flat 750 pounds—roughly $1800. For a young, newly married couple who had died in the crash, Sterns would demand more than a million dollars. Two sets of parents had been left, their happy preoccupation with the young couple and their prospects of grandchildren stripped away.

And yet, there were people who were worth scarcely anything to anybody. Another nondependency case, a young baker's checker had no parents, no brothers or sisters—only an aunt and a scattering of relatives he rarely saw. He had lived alone, had no estate. He worked at a poorly paying job in a bakery. Yet, at a meeting in Wakefield, seventeen relatives with broad Yorkshire accents turned up to claim a share in his lawsuit. The case would probably be the lowest of all the cases being processed through the Sterns office. The demand would be $75,000, though word was out that defense would hold firm to a top offer of $10,000 for cases of his type where there were no close relatives. The settlement would be the only ripple that marked his passing. Without it, a human being might have come and gone without leaving a trace. With it, relatives who scarcely touched his life might find themselves richer by thousands of dollars—more than the young man might have earned in twenty or thirty years' work at the bakery. Though small, these were the cases defense and plaintiff's counsel fought over. They would be the source of angry stalemates as the case wore on, for they seemed to British solicitors like Peter Martin to be unwarranted windfalls available through no other kind of death. Was it right? The word *windfall* would become a banner of opposition in the settlement war ahead.

To plaintiffs, it was the *wrong*—the random, uninvited, violent death by plane crash—that must be recognized and paid for, no matter how apparently worthless, in human or financial terms, the dead were.

What was a good wife worth? It was always one of the most provocative questions, for the answers courts gave were an expression of changing attitudes toward the role of women. Courts in both America and England had been slow to put any value on a wife's functions as housekeeper and nanny. A decade ago, a $35,000 settlement was common. Now, the going rate for "mommies" in California settlements was $200,000 and up. Sterns had won $325,000 for the death of the mother of three teen-aged children in a malpractice suit in Fresno; $300,000 for a similar case in San Francisco. An award of $650,000 had been made almost coincident with the Paris case; $400,000 had been awarded in Southern California, reduced by the judge to $60,000, then reinstated by the Supreme Court of California four years later.

312

But a good wife had remained worthless under English law until very recently. An attempt was finally being made to equate her housework and nurturing with dollars, though still inadequately. An English insurance company would soon put an estimated value of a wife's services at 71 pounds a week.

It was not until after the Paris crash that common-law wives were recognized by the law. Stuart Speiser learned of this in London when he picked up his morning paper outside his hotel room. He was sure his friend had had it printed up as a joke, for it was inconceivable to him that a legal change that would so dramatically improve the prospects of his several common-law cases would fall into his lap so conveniently. Until very recently, too, English courts had treated widows as chattels in the marriage market, paying more to a young, homely widow with few prospects of remarriage than to a forty-year-old beauty who might marry again, or have a shorter period of widowhood. A system that penalized the bright, attractive, marriageable woman, it had been abolished by an act of Parliament just a few years before the Paris crash. It was no longer legal to take marriageability into account in assessing damages.

In California, even if a widow had married again by the time of trial, it did not compromise her right to recover. Though evidence of remarriage was not forbidden by statute, it was a matter of judicial policy that widows could be sworn in and identify themselves at the start of trial by their former married name, the name of the dead husband. The defense often cried, "Perjury!" and claimed that, with a new husband, a widow no longer needed the money. But the courts, in inviting a jury to look at a widow's status at the time of the death, had made a subtle decision. To make the new marriage an issue and to argue its value would be to give birth to a ten-headed monster. Both sides would have to call marriage counselors to debate the merits of the old and new marriages and husbands, the stresses under which the decision to remarry was made, the possible duration of the new marriage, and on and on.

Thelma Alden, watching and listening without visible emotion or expression while Judge Hall heard his cases, often speculated on just how sound marriages were, made by lonely, insecure widows trying to patch up their lives and find fathers for their children. Hearing them in court, she was grateful for a system that did not penalize them for the decision to remarry. In fact, juries were human, and a gorgeous woman, obviously pregnant by her new husband, would not help her case. Sterns always cautioned widows of the hazards they ran in remarriage before trial.

With dramatic improvements in the status of women all over the world, cases that asked "What is a good wife worth?" were being watched closely. Because this case would look at the worth of wives cross-culturally, it would be watched with special interest. Sterns's own experience made it clear that women were one of the growth areas of wrongful death litigation. Even the U.S. government had begun to recognize the economic value of a housewife; in 1972, the Social Security Administration had put an average annual value of housework at $4,705. For young wives with children, they gave a value of $6,500. With inflation, it had risen by the time of the Paris crash to over $7,000 a year. These figures did not try to deal with human value—just with the basic, measureable tasks like child care, cleaning, cooking, and so on—but were at least a beginning.

Sterns quickly saw that Gene Barrow would be an interesting test case. Loss of society should be strong, for with her death a family had lost its energy source. The Tudor home that glowed with the red and gold she loved had become "just a house." Harold Barrow still drove to his wholesale vegetable business in Eastbourne, but nothing mattered. He did the dishes by rote, and couldn't touch the garden. His face was the saddest Sterns had ever seen. For her three daughters, "losing her was losing the best friend you ever had." The eldest, Sally, had separated from her husband, for without Gene she had "needed somebody or something, and he couldn't provide it. Mother had been my support."

And Gene Barrow had had her own job, providing some 2,000 pounds a year to the family, with a promotion due in three years. She clearly played a large role in running the home, though the fact that she had a housekeeper four days a week would reduce that value. It began to look as if, even with England's lower wage levels, the case might be worth half a million dollars.

Reading the interrogatories and looking at the happy face, even Jim Murray, who had never met the Barrows, sensed that putting a dollar value on Gene Barrow was going to be like catching sunbeams in a jar.

Sterns and his staff kept working at the figures. For Gene Barrow, economic loss worked out to $212,405, using the actuary's calculations. Applying the formula for loss of society, noneconomic loss was $447,433.50. A total loss of $659,838.50. The defense would never buy it. As a compromise, Sterns would put $425,000 on the bottom line—a starting point.

What *was* a good wife worth?

Chapter Twenty-Four

Settlement!

"FUNDAMENTALLY LESS POSITIVE!" Applegate had said that electrical actuation was *"fundamentally less positive"* than hydraulic actuation of the cargo doors. The phrase from the infamous memo rang in their ears, as Sterns and Marshall Morgan dug through documents trying to find out *why*. And *why* had the decision been made to change to electrical from hydraulic closing of the doors, as originally planned? As they dug, the two lawyers began to sense that they might be on to the decision that, more than any other, had doomed the plane. They had found a basic and highly significant difference between the two systems. A hydraulically closed door, if closed but not properly locked, would back off and *ooze open* under pressure, bleeding off the pressurized air. The electrically actuated door did not. It relied on two actuators: one to close the door and one to drive the hooks over the spools, locking it. The vulnerability lay in the fact that a baggage handler did both operations—close and latch—by pressing one toggle switch. He held the switch down while the door closed, then, counting out the proper number of seconds, held it down a little longer while the hooks engaged over the spools. If he was impatient—if he held it down for *too few seconds*—or if the second actuator wasn't working properly, the hooks, unknown to the baggage handler, would not be fully engaged over the spools. And here was where the difference between the two actuating systems could become lethal. The electrical system was irreversible. As pressure differential built, the electrically closed door could not back off and bleed. If improperly locked, it held on until it blew. It appeared to Sterns and Morgan to have been the unreliability of the actuator that had led to most of the fixes—heavier gauge wiring, the vent door, peepholes, placards, a new indicating light on the operating panel beside the door—one compounding the other until *Paris*.

As General Dynamics' J. B. Hurt took the deposition chair, Sterns couldn't wait to get at him. And Morgan was waiting to follow up. For Hurt was not only the man who had squelched the Applegate memo. As project engineer on the DC-10, he had been involved in decisions on the doors. It was time to put pressure on General Dynamics, they felt, for the dispute between General Dynamics and McDonnell Douglas had invaded the lawsuit, with General Dynamics refusing to contribute a share of the pot acceptable to Douglas.

As he came into the deposition room, Sterns had a strange feeling that something had changed, that something was going to happen. Mid-morning, he was called from the room by a phone call from Fred Lack, General Dynamics counsel, who asked Sterns what he was planning. Sterns responded, "Fred, we've really got the goods on this actuator, and this morning we're going to hurt Hurt!" Lack asked him to take it easy on Hurt today, because a deal was in the wind. Ask him anything—where he went to high school, what his favorite color is—but cool it, because if he gets hurt, the deal may be off. Sterns returned to depositions and began to redirect his questions, exploring McDonnell Douglas's role in the actuator decisions.

The depositions ended at noon. The lawyers flew home. There were no depositions scheduled the following week, but they kept closely in touch, comparing rumors. Then, on the morning of May 27, ten days after the Hurt deposition, FitzSimons stood in court and in a terse, four-line statement announced that the defendants would "not contest liability." The defendants had reached a sharing agreement secretly among themselves and were ready to start settlement negotiations.

It was the climax of the case to date. The point of transition between the liability phase and settlements. But what did it mean? The defense would not *contest* liability. But they did not *concede* it. Normally, the defense accepted liability, then settlements got under way. Kreindler and Sterns were confused and suspicious. The inconclusive statement was wreathed in unacceptable conditions. Kreindler flatly refused the precondition that he waive punitive damages, since he regarded the claims as part of the strength of his case. There seemed too many loose ends. Sterns was concerned about how the volume of cases was to be processed. Which cases would be first . . . and last? And he was reluctant to see the momentum of discovery stopped. With Hurt, Sterns felt he had been at the brink of insights into the cause of the crash that, now, might never be disclosed. He still wanted a trial date. He, like Kreindler and Morgan, believed that the hovering threat of a jury trial on liability and punitive damages was still the best negotiating tool.

The judge, too, faced a critical decision. If it was a good-faith offer, the case was well on its way to completion. It would bring the contentious liability phase to an end—a phase that threatened to go on forever and to bury the court under a blizzard of paper and an unrelenting flood of third-party claims, cross claims, counter claims, causes of action, and defenses. In addition to the 205 filed complaints, there were 600 third-party complaints, cross claims, or counterclaims—a total of *over 800 pleadings*. Choosing the Backhouse case, No. 74-1993, as a random sample, his law clerk Delphine Ruman counted causes of action for negligence in design and construction, negligence in operation and maintenance, for strict product liability, break of warranty, willful misconduct, vicarious liability, breach of contract of carriage, and for fraud, oppression, and malice. In a liability trial, each would have to be individually tried and proved.

Settlements would put an end, too, to the interminable deposing of witnesses. Before him lay a list of 253 prospective witnesses, all but six requested by the defense. At two weeks each, it would take ten years to depose them all! But if he halted depositions, if he stayed discovery, and settlements were *not* reached, valuable time would have been lost, with the families more and more in need as the months went by. He weighed the risks.

The judge decided to trust in the good faith of the defense. Settlement negotiations would proceed. He put a stay on all discovery so that the adversaries could turn their full attention to preparing for settlement. Depositions ceased. The dispute between General Dynamics and McDonnell Douglas would no longer intrude, for it had been resolved with the secret sharing agreement. The hull suit had been settled and dispatched. The liability phase was apparently over. And lawyers slipped into their compensatory damages mode, with talk of "multipliers," "present value," and "pecuniary loss."

It was what they had all been after. Briefly, there was euphoria and a feeling that settlements were a mere formality. The families and the defendants shared a common relief, for it appeared that soon all could finally put the crash behind them.

Douglas wanted to shake free of the crash. With the closed-loop system, they had effectively "fixed" the door and were now building beefed-up floors and more venting into the new Japan Air Lines and SAS hulls, and in all subsequent new hulls, creating floors that could withstand a fuselage hole "three or four times" the new FAA requirement of 20 square feet—a vastly larger hole than the approximately one square foot that had been the industry standard when the DC-10 was designed. A strong reaction to the storms of criticism, it would substantially improve the plane's ability to withstand holes from any source, not just from doors com-

319

ing off. Under enormous pressure. Douglas had finally, voluntarily, recognized and dealt with the size effect. Brizendine had made the decision shortly after the crash, had the engineering worked out, and announced it publicly in August. It was a modification they would have preferred to delay until the next generation of jets, a safety modification so major that, in the inquisition atmosphere, it could seem to plaintiff lawyers to imply admission of a defect. Douglas would have complaints of cost from its customer airlines. But to their credit, they had done it anyway. On delivery on December 18, 1975, SAS's hull number 217 would have the strongest floors of any commercial passenger aircraft in the skies. And now, the FAA had issued a new AD requiring that every existing wide-body aircraft be retrofitted to conform to the new fuselage hole size of 20 square feet. The aviation industry had fought for a smaller hole size—12 square feet. Boeing and Lockheed had resisted an expensive retrofit forced on them by what they claimed was Douglas's problem. But, with the mandatory AD, both companies had come to Douglas for information on floors and vents. The industry was at last sharing its knowledge, dealing with the immutable facts that should have been faced ten years earlier. Though the Dutch would continue to argue that planes be designed to a 25 square-foot hole size, the new 20 square-foot criteria was a substantial step forward for air safety. It was, at least, larger than the area of the rear cargo door. By the end of 1977, the world's fleets of wide-body planes would finally be safeguarded against the size effect, and passengers would be able to fly without fear of another *Paris*.

The climate for selling planes was gloomy even without the drag of *Paris*. The effects of a general recession were being severely felt by the aviation industry, and though Douglas had received 27 firm orders and 13 conditional and on option since *Paris,* for accounting purposes a conservative goal of 400 planes had been set, though Douglas hoped to sell some 700 or 800 DC-10s through the 1980s. Several incidents had kept the press focus on the DC-10. There had been a near midair collision over the same airspace where the Windsor Incident had occurred, and *at altitude* where the fuselage structure was unlikely to withstand explosive decompression from a large hole. Sea gulls had been ingested into the engines of an Overseas National DC-10 during the takeoff roll at JFK Airport in New York, forcing a violent abort and causing a storm of criticism of the design of the CF6 General Electric engines used on the DC-10, the A-300 Airbus, and some 747s. The NTSB, concerned months before the accident that certification criteria for massive bird ingestion of large turbofan engines was not adequate, issued recommendations to the FAA that bigger and more birds be used in retests for compliance with bird ingestion criteria, that modifications be made to both the engines and the FARs, and that runway bird patrol sweeps be made before takeoff of CF6-engined jets. The FAA proposed an AD, trailing a month behind the engine's manufacturers, who had already instituted voluntary "fixes" on the engine structure. Dick Witkin brought his powerful pen to bear on the problem in *The New York Times,* and a new nightmare seemed about to begin.

And the ethics of the entire industry had been cast under a cloud by revelations in Congressional investigations of alleged payments by U.S. aircraft manufacturers to foreign customers to gain sales. With Lockheed taking the brunt of it, the scandal had threatened to bring down the Japanese government, and had thrown into high relief the even broader issue of corporate responsibility in selling any politically or technically volatile product, whether arms, nuclear power plants, or wide-body aircraft, to foreign nations. Did McDonnell Douglas, or any manufacturer, have an ethical obligation to limit sales to an airline or nation that appeared unready for a plane that could kill a small village of people in one crash? Any knowledgeable person knew there was a great range of quality and rigor of air traffic control, airports, management, flight crews, and regulatory authorities around the world.

Largely through American know-how, the situation was improving. Training programs were increasingly part of the requisite "package" you sold with every airplane. But, in the competitive international market, could—*should*—a manufacturer play God?

Through the gloom, Douglas was gradually emerging from its fortress, allowing glimpses of senior engineers in sports coats and short haircuts drinking tomato juice at lunch in the executive dining room, a symbol of sobriety that was reassuring even to plaintiff lawyers. For they, too, flew the planes these men built. Brizendine. Bates. Gross. Dubil. . . . Their skills were reflected in every longeron and rivet of the DC-10. As they began to articulate their postcrash feelings, the intense personal and professional distress of the experience came through. One sensed that though it was the insurers who would ultimately pay the dollars, it was Douglas engineers feeling the sting in the deposition chair who had paid any debt. Face to face, it was impossible to cast these men as conspiratorial villains. But as long as the litigation dragged on, with the threat of a trial on liability, the crash would haunt them.

With the prospect of settlement, the insurers, too, could get on about their business, which was to pay claims as quickly as possible and get on with the next risk.

But in London, Stephen Mitchell was nervous. Lawyers were acting as if the case was over, and not a cent had been paid! Anxiously, he watched the club drift away. Don Madole, finished with the nuts and bolts phase, was off to Puerto Rico with his partner Charles Krause and Madole's new wife, his firm's first female pilot/lawyer, to try the crash that had killed Roberto Clemente on a mercy flight to earthquake-stricken Nicaragua. Sterns was being tugged by *Pago Pago,* where he represented both the crew and Pan Am's hull suit. Marshall Morgan was defending a socialite accused of murdering her husband. Peter Martin was off to the Sudan and Norway on other crashes, and George Tompkins was flying to Honolulu on an anti-trust case involving Qantas Airways, for with the settlement agreement, Warsaw had become academic. Speiser was writing a new book on economics. And Kreindler was negotiating the *Bali* cases that had come to him through his connections with the Japanese in *Paris,* and preparing to take over the presidency of the International Academy of Trial Lawyers. In New York, FitzSimons was trying and winning a case against Speiser's firm, an F111B fighter case that, with General Dynamics as subcontractor, was an ironic twist on *Paris.*

But it wasn't over. And Mitchell had constantly to explain delays to the solicitors and families who had made him their liaison with the California courts. Some could not wait much longer. The momentum must not slow.

The judge appointed three negotiating teams of defense lawyers, confident that they could handle the job. Adding up the defense lawyers who worked for all the law firms involved in the case, he came up with a list of *493 lawyers,* enough, surely, to process the 205 filed cases speedily.

Negotiating began. Sterns's office produced the first of the elegant settlement brochures and hand-delivered them to Bob Packard's office, the lawyer he would work with. He made his first demands, and offers came back. They were discouraging. A fraction of what had been asked. In one of Bernard Engler's cases, a $1,200,000 demand had an offer of $200,000. A firm position had clearly been taken on the nondependencies—a flat $50,000, which Kreindler could never, never accept for his young Japanese. The experience of all the lawyers was the same. The defense were offering sums more in line with English standards than with California standards, *even though the judge had stated that California law would apply.* In a choice of law opinion that had the ring of a landmark decision, Judge Hall had gone beyond California's liberal "loss of society" provisions by adding the "love and affection" provisions of the Sea-Land case, creating the potential for even higher jury awards.

As lawyers on both sides compared notes, a pattern emerged. It became clear that the negotiating teams did not have the autonomy they had been assigned by the judge. They reported that all demands and offers were being run through the hands of one man: Jim Fitz-Simons.

At a settlement status hearing in the fall, Judge Hall was told that of all the filed cases, only three had been settled, and not one of these had yet been filed with the court of approval. The troubled courtroom would hear his voice break and see his head lower so that his bushy eyebrows hid his eyes, as he said, "I am disappointed. . . ." The three words would hold all his forebodings that his own time might run out before he could achieve his dream of a standard aviation law that would eliminate, once and for all, the forum shopping and confusion bred by that legal can of eels, choice of law . . . the human lottery that was Warsaw . . . the spectacle of lawyers so lost in the legal thickets that they lost sight of humanity. That time might run out before he could clean up *Paris*. It would be a terrible moment that would send a brief wave of guilt sweeping over the court. George Tompkins would be so moved by this great old man's expression of judicial despair that he would leap to his feet to try to reassure the judge that they *were* making progress, they *would* achieve settlements. . . .

Back in chambers, Judge Hall had Delphine add up some more numbers. There were 205 cases filed with the court, representing 337 decedents and 1,100 claimants. In his experience it took an average of two days to try death damages. If all these cases had to go on trial on damages it would take a total of 674 trial days. Conservatively, trials on damages alone would take over two and a half years. Logistically, humanely, it was an intolerable prospect. Why wouldn't they settle? All his other cases were moving along well. He speculated on whether the insurers were stalling to collect interest on the principal they would have to pay out, but this theory would be beaten back by Lloyd's chairman as "nothing short of absolute disgrace." In a November order the judge let the lawyers know that he was disturbed that "the final word on all settlements must come from one man, viz, one of ten attorneys who have appeared in court from time to time for McDonnell Douglas. . . . This court cannot in any justice whatsoever permit a procedure which holds up the finality of the rights of over 1,100 claimants for years . . . to be asserted or followed by *any one man.* . . . What seems to loom is the necessity for trial, not only of damages but also of liability."

Privately, he would smash his fist into the palm of his hand and with gentle eyes blazing, say, *"Halting depositions was the worst mistake I have ever made in my life!"*

Unless the plaintiffs could regain some leverage, they would be played like puppets. None of their ploys seemed to be working. Earlier, before the settlement agreement, the Speiser group had filed a thick motion for Summary Judgment—a documentation of all the key evidence produced so far in discovery. They hoped it would prove the defendants so incontrovertibly liable that the judge would be forced to declare it. But the judge had denied it from the bench. Mitchell flew from London to appraise the mess and flew to Los Angeles to hear Sterns argue aggressively, again, for a trial date. No date was set, though the judge declared that depositions would soon resume. Working with Kreindler over their next moves, Marc Moller commented that keeping pressure on the defense was all a matter of knowing what buttons to push. But no one seemed to know quite what the right buttons were.

Chapter Twenty-Five

The Kween Case

IN SEATTLE, two lawyers pushed the only button they could find. They had only one case, the Kween case—a double death in which a young London couple had been killed, leaving two young daughters and two sets of grandparents. By tradition, the two lawyers from the northwest should have been invisible. But from the start, they had shown a bullheaded tenacity in retaining control of their case. Richard Krutch, a successful trial lawyer, and his associate, Vernon Judkins, high-time pilot in the entire U.S. army when he retired and former pilot to General Westmoreland, had both learned in *Air Alaska* that having just one case need not be a deterrent to control. Nor need living in the wilderness. They now understood the system and had complete irreverence for the club. They had managed with Sterns's assistance to maneuver themselves onto the plaintiff's committee, in contrast to the lawyer representing the celebrated F. Lee Bailey who had been shoved off the committee and left hammering at the door with *his* one case. And they had allied themselves with Jerry Sterns, strengthening West Coast voting power. They were convinced that East Coast control was begining to crumble. They had sniffed it in *Air Alaska* and were seeing it confirmed in *Pago Pago,* running simultaneous with *Paris,* where three western lawyers had taken control of the plaintiff's committee.

But they hadn't got a cent, yet, from McDonnell Douglas for the Kween case. The original offer in England of $3,400 had been rejected out of hand. They had grabbed the airline's offer of $30,000 per seat and had received a check for $60,000 promptly. But they had received no response to the $700,000 demand they had sent off to FitzSimons. Optimistic when settlement negotiations had begun, they had received an offer of only $250,000. Though raised to $350,000 it was still far short of the $700,000 they felt sure the case was worth. The defense asked, "Would you take $500,000 . . . or $550,000?" They would not. Their demand was not an inflated negotiating figure. They were convinced after discussion with Sterns that it was fair value under California law. And they were going to get it.

They would proceed to trial on damages against McDonnell Douglas and General Dynamics. With an impudence that rocked the plaintiff's bar, the two men from Seattle had grabbed a languishing case by the tail and given it direction.

Krutch had believed from the beginning that there might only be one damages trial, and he wanted it to be Kween. It was the first damages case filed in Judge Hall's court. It would be the first case to be tried before a jury. It would be the test.

Krutch had had his opening and closing statements written for six weeks. Both he and Judkins realized how important their case had suddenly become. It would almost surely set a standard for *Paris* cases, and might well affect all future product liability awards. It would also have a profound impact on the several hundred English cases, for through the Kween grandparents, the controversial issue of dependency would be tested. They knew that what happened here could help or hurt Sterns's eighty cases. They asked him to join them in trying the case, knowing, too, that his overpowering effect on a jury could only help them in court.

Trial was set for January 20, 1976.

Sterns realized how important the defense considered the Kween case to be when FitzSimons arrived in Los Angeles to take charge of the defense himself, and

David Dann flew in from London to attend the entire trial. The three western lawyers found themselves facing the insurer's first string. The aviation insurance market was taking its stand, once and for all, to resolve what its vulnerabilities were to be for future product liability cases that could bring them to California courts. As battlefield, they had chosen the first trial of the largest piece of aviation litigation in history—a case in which damage demands in *excess of $760 million* had already been filed with the court. The results would be highly visible, and would have repercussions in every corner of the insurance world. For in risks so large there was no major aviation insurance group that had not acquired a portion of the risks as they had been laid off around the world. Though some might quietly dispute the strategy, all would be touched by the results.

It was to be as much a battle over principle as over money. The principles the plaintiffs had only guessed at now came into sharp focus. "The demands have been much too high." Jim FitzSimons put it bluntly in a BBC interview taped just before trial began. "They do not reflect what a jury would award were the cases to be actually tried. This is the nub of the problem." But beyond that, the more basic question was, "What law applies?" Could California impose its law on citizens of foreign countries? The law of the domicile had traditionally been applied. But most of the world now flew in American-built airplanes, and it was a question he and the insurers must have resolved. FitzSimons offered to the court an opinion prepared by an eminent Queen's Counsel in London that showed what damages might be awarded for the Kween case by the application of English law. The judge refused to allow it before the jury, for it argued the WRONG LAW. *California law, not British law, would apply on damages*. He had laid it down clearly in his opinion on choice of law.

It was an issue Peter Martin had raised at the influential air law symposium staged by the School of Law at Southern Methodist University of Dallas just nine months earlier. "We are now beginning to have to face the fact that there may be in the future more and more actions against the manufacturers of aircraft and their ancillary equipment and engines in the United States . . . by families of passengers killed in accidents to non-U.S. carriers . . . whether or not the litigants are U.S. citizens." Was it legally and morally right to have growing armies of foreigners flooding into California courts, as they had in *Paris,* abandoning their own laws, fattening the wallets of the plaintiff's bar, and going home with bonanzas that unsettled the existing scale of damages—and social values!—in their own countries?

In his speech, Martin had named the most passionate issue—*the non dependency case.* The Kween grandparents were claiming dependency. It was here, where there was no easily assessed financial loss, that "serious philosophical differences in the theory of damages occur." He and his colleagues would "go to the wall," he had said, before capitulating to massive damages that would be *"the largest windfall parents are ever likely to have in their lives—tax-free, and one that is only available in the very rare circumstances of a plane crash. Carriers and manufacturers can and must fight to prevent what they see as unjust enrichment as contrasted with fair compensation."*

David Dann had confirmed the stand in the same BBC interview on which FitzSimons appeared. "If we pay amounts which on the best advice we have available are outrageous, we are destroying the whole structure of law and insurance."

The defense was staging a holy war to save what remained of civilization from the cancer of American materialism. They marched into the Kween trial with the motto *PREVENT UNJUST ENRICHMENT* emblazoned on their banners. But though they were generally dismissed by the plaintiffs as hidebound reactionaries trying to hold back the clock, the social questions they asked were real and important. In aircraft, in settlements, was bigger always better?

Finally, there was the practical matter of finding out what premiums the insurers were going to have to charge manufacturers for product liability insurance. If "big money" were to be the norm, it could force insurance premiums—and air fares—up. The theory went that only by trying the Kween case, getting a jury verdict, and appealing it all the way would the London market have a true measure of what, before current California law, a life was worth. A few cynics suggested that an "outrageous" award might even be welcomed by the defense, for it might help speed the enactment of no-fault legislation for aviation, as well as for automobile crashes, a concept that had been very much in the air at Dallas when Peter Martin spoke.

There was one final reason suggested by lawyers on both sides as the real reason for the Kween trial, and for the stalemates that had led to it: the stubborn refusal of the one man in charge of the defense to see and understand the facts of life . . . the facts of *law*.

As trial approached, the insurers vented their frustration at being caught up in California courts on Jerry Sterns, whose "outrageous demands" confirmed him, in their eyes, as a typically "rapacious scoundrel." Sterns quietly believed a jury would prove him right. Coming out of Indian country into the world's largest piece of aviation litigation, he found himself, as the Kween trial began, standing virtually alone. He had started from a position of relative weakness and had suffered grave doubts as more famous men had made judgments very different from his own. But his early assessment of the case had, in time, generally proved right. He had seen California law as the only law the judge could apply. He had advised his clients against a class action he felt was doomed in this case. He had rejected the Summary Judgment motion as "an exercise in high profilism" and had resisted pressures to join in it. He had always wanted Turkish Airlines, with their jurisdictional uncertainties, out of the case so that maximum pressure could be brought to bear on McDonnell Douglas and General Dynamics—a goal finally achieved by the court's order for separate trials which would bring the two manufacturing defendants to trial on product liability. His early skepticism about the settlement agreement had been prophetic, for almost *nothing* had been achieved in nine months.

And ultimately it would be trial, the Kween trial, that would break the case that had become—as Peter Martin had seen a year earlier—a "microcosm of war." The trial, though, as Marc Moller saw it, "is no microcosm—this is *it!*"

Sterns ambled into court a living expression of the California legal system. He had been trained in it. He believed in it. And he applied it with deadly effectiveness. He thrived at the cutting edge of change and verged on poetry as he described the way in which each jury verdict became a fresh expression of values; each courtroom a dynamic laboratory for the evolution of law, a flexible instrument for social change; a citizen jury still the best measure of right and wrong.

For Sterns there was no confused complex of moral, economic, and global issues. There was just California law. And it must, he believed, be applied in a product liability suit of this kind. "California has the paramount interest in deterring negligent conduct or defective products, and in protecting the public from torts committed in this state. Manufacturers of defective products must be held to account by the laws and standards of the state in which they do business. They must accept the *consequences* with the *privileges.*" But it was not a one-way street. "If a victim comes from a country with a higher standard of damages, he, too, must accept California's standards—even if for him they are lower." It was Kreindler's dilemma with his Japanese clients. "Look, the system is fair, sound, logical . . . *AND IT IS THE LAW!*"

As the trial began, the judge could sense that it would never be finished in the originally scheduled four days, and would probably now run for eight. His doctor had ordered him home for six weeks' bed rest, but he had to see Kween through.

On January 20, a full courtroom watched as two tiny girls in white dresses walked into the legal carnage, followed by a single file of family members who had flown in from Seattle and London. It was a discomforting moment, for it was the first time that the very real fact of death had invaded the ritual and rhetoric. Melissa and Lauren Kween, age two and four, stood up on a bench to be introduced to the jury—five women and one man. They both said a shy hello and were led from the courtroom by grandparents, uncles, and aunts. They were orphans. Phyllis Kween, their mother, had been raised in Seattle, studied in Switzerland, had a university degree in teaching and languages, and had been a guide at the United Nations. Their father, only thirty when he died, was trying to build a chain of tobacconist stores in London, a venture into which he had brought his father, Cecil.

In the opinon prepared for the defense by the QC, the orphans would have faced a very ordinary and limited future indeed if their parents had lived. He felt that the children would be self-sustaining by age sixteen, and "there would certainly be no question . . . in this family, of the daughters enjoying a university career . . . I think that the most one could envisage, had the parents lived, would have been that the children might have taken a short secretarial course after leaving school, and before becoming wage earners."

Sterns could not believe that the daughters of an American woman with a degree in languages and an ambitious father would really have been raised as Eliza Doolittles. The opinion, he thought, was rooted in nineteenth-century British classism.

The QC had pointed out, too, that the children had benefited, in a material sense, from the death of their parents, falling heirs to their parents' house, car, and household belongings sooner than they might normally have expected to, and *the value of these would have to be deducted from any damages awarded.* It was English law. There was silverware . . . some jewelry, pictures, china, linen, and so on, to a value of £4,750, roughly $11,500, and half of that value was "clearly deductible."

The QC's analysis had not been allowed before the jury. But, as they began to present their evidence, it was clear that the defense was applying English standards. And that they would fight any attempts by Sterns to bring the human element—the loss of a mother's nurturing, the impact of being orphaned—before the jury.

As Sterns, with his Seattle colleagues, viewed his opponents, FitzSimons and Packard, and listened to their opening statements, he was delighted. A California courtroom was his habitat, and he was as confident here as a pilot in his cockpit. Finally, he was before a jury. He unwound from his chair at the plaintiff's table and moved to the lectern to make his opening statement. He spoke slowly, gently to the jury. "This is a case that arises out of the Paris air crash. This was an airplane crash in March of 1974, sometimes known as the DC-10 crash. And the two victims that we are concerned with here today were David and Phyllis Kween, K-W-E-E-N. Kween. They were both killed in that crash and this action is one that is called a wrongful death action. . . ."

He took the jury by the hand, through the lost lives. "David Kween started working at eighteen. He did well. He had plans, big plans . . . but these things were all in the future. I think things never looked better for the Kweens. They had just put together the shop deal and decided to take a holiday, and the holiday they took was . . . two weeks in Turkey . . . They boarded a plane together. They came down together. They died together."

Sterns and Krutch gave the jury a classic feast of apple pie and motherhood, providing moments when the courtroom would be so moved that even lawyers could not see clearly enough through tears to focus on the witness or jury.

In opening statements, both Sterns and Krutch had alluded to a Christmas tape that had been made just a few months before the crash by David, Phyllis, and the two girls for Phyllis's family in Seattle. On the stand, members of Phyllis's family had been mentioning the tape, too, and as eagerness to hear the tape grew the defense objected vigorously. Before making a ruling, the judge had taken the tape home to his apartment and listened to it, alone. The next morning he allowed it in as evidence. The court was, by now, so primed that you could almost hear the silent scream, "Let us hear the tape! Let us hear the tape!" The cassette was switched on. The voices of the two dead young people filled the courtroom, full of jokes and plans. "The shop is doing very well indeed. We're really completely up to expectations. Oh, I'm also looking at a second shop. At the moment it's just in the planning stage . . . If we do take over everything, David figures he'll have himself an empire. We still only have one shop, but we have lots of ideas . . . I love my bathrobe, and I love all the children's things. Lolly looks like the abominable snowman trying to walk in her snowsuit. She falls over like, you know, one of those clowns that is weighted on the bottom and keeps coming up . . . Did I tell you about Lissy the day she didn't have any pants on and she bent over, completely touching her toes, in the kitchen and singing goosey goosey gander? . . ."

The Japanese *au pair* girl was put on the stand and testified as to how she had told the little girls that their parents were dead. "I told them first—I told them that they were on a holiday; after all, they were just little children. But they started to ask me again and again, 'Where are mother and father? Why did they leave without saying good-bye?' " The parents had not wakened the girls from their naps when they left for Turkey. "So I told them that Melissa's parents, mommy and daddy, are not coming back anymore. You won't see them anymore, but they are watching you all the time and they love you a lot." It was perhaps the most heart-breaking moment in the trial.

Lissy, with dark curly hair and baby fat, was brought into the courtroom to count to twenty in English, French, and Spanish, clearly reaching the heart of the Latino grandfather on the jury. Krutch introduced

Phyllis's high school graduation picture and the wedding book.

With the introduction of each personal piece of evidence, Packard leaped to his feet to object. "Speculative and conjecture; remote!" "Cumulative, repetitive, and prejudicial to the defendants." But Hall reminded him, "Of course, one of the purposes of introducing evidence here *is* to prejudice you." It was the purpose of *either* side's introduction of evidence. He denied all objections. Sterns sensed that the jury didn't like the Kween story being interrupted by objections. He and Krutch devised a tactic by which they could get Packard to object *twice* to each picture. As the human story unfolded and objections continued to pepper the testimony, Sterns knew the jury was with them.

Midtrial, Mitchell called Sterns from England to say how sorry and concerned he was that "things aren't going well." It was the word going around the London market. The word passed back in daily reports from Los Angeles.

The trial went into its fourth week. During a break in FitzSimons's cross-examination of an American economist called to justify the plaintiff's claims, Sterns joined FitzSimons, David Dann, and one of McDonnell Douglas's senior counsel from St. Louis in the hall. They chatted amiably, but behind the pleasantries FitzSimons indicated that he was sure that the case would be reversed on appeal, no matter what the outcome. "Christ," thought Sterns, "that would mean a long appeal and retrial, and three more years!" Sterns despaired that his attempts to set up a settlement meeting on neutral ground would come to anything. Dann had indicated willingness, but still seemed ambivalent. And daily FitzSimons seemed more committed to carrying through this wasteful test. Sterns could see the costs and time stretching out before them. Going through this three hundred times. Insurers under pressure. Families waiting. It was so pointless. Sterns approached Dann, hoping to commit him to the long-discussed settlement meeting. He said to Dann, *"David, is this trip really necessary?"* He thought he perceived a look of willing-ness and good will on Dann's face. But Dann shrugged and returned to the courtroom to hear FitzSimons resume the attack.

McDonnell Douglas was now facing the plaintiffs alone, for midway through the trial Sterns had unex-pectedly dismissed General Dynamics from the trial. He was unhappy that lawyers for both General Dynam-ics and McDonnell Douglas were getting a crack at the witnesses, giving the defense "two bites at the apple." It was an opportunity he was sure had not been pro-vided by the wording of the secret sharing agreement. Judge Hall, on examining the document, agreed and summarily ordered the General Dynamics lawyer to "go hence," leaving the defense momentarily floundering, their plans for cross-examination in disarray.

The "8-day trial" moved into its fifth week. The time had come to present arguments and for each side to commit itself to a number. On a large sheet of white paper, Packard wrote a number for the defense. $300,000. The figure was based largely on a budget for the girls that had been presented in court by an ac-countant brought over from London by the defense. In cross-examination, Sterns had revealed that the budget allowed nothing for transportation, and only $7 a week per child for food, a number that had inspired a black juror, a mother herself, to remark after the trial. "They lost me with that one. You couldn't keep me in hog back for seven dollars a week." And how many party dresses could you buy on a weekly clothing allowance of $3, Sterns asked, as he drew out the admission that the accountant was unmarried and childless.

The plaintiffs wrote much larger numbers on their piece of white paper. Krutch started off by presenting the economic loss for support, education, and raising the children, asking for $600,000. Sterns followed by projecting the future earnings of David Kween. It was in establishing the strong potential earning power of the dead young man that the foundation for economic loss, and the real strength of their case, lay. There, and in loss of society. Sterns applied his best courtroom skills as he taught the jury, six "ordinary working class people," how to translate the effects of the loss of two lives into dollars. He totaled up all the elements: economic loss to the children, the future support of the grandparents, the loss of services, and the loss of society, and confidently stroked out his numbers. $2,100,000. Glancing swiftly at FitzSimons, Sterns saw an appalled look on his face. David Dann had already left.

Under growing pressure, as thousands of people waited for the results of the Kween trial, FitzSimons, Packard, Sterns, and Krutch used their full rhetorical powers as they explained and justified their numbers in closing argument.

Krutch had been rehearsing his closing statement for several weeks—to his wife, to Judkins. Every word had been polished to a flawless sheen. In one of the most effective closing statements a veteran member of the court staff claimed she had ever heard, Krutch placed the burden of surrogate parenthood on the jury's shoulders:

> David and Phyllis had the God-given right and the legal right to plan the children's future. They lost it when they died . . . They will have to trust and to believe in our whole legal system, based on the premise that six total strangers, thousands of miles away, can take and plan the lives that their children will live . . . and that is the awesome responsibility that you have . . . You will not be able to meet with the children each year like a trust department and say, "How did we do in our projections?" *You will only have one opportunity* . . . I do not think you will ever forget these children the rest of your lives. I think you will always wonder where they are, what they are doing. . . .

Packard's closing argument was everything Sterns had hoped for. It began as an apology to the jury.

> The point I am trying to get across to you ladies

337

and gentlemen of the jury is that if I have done anything, or if Mr. FitzSimons has done anything during the course of this trial, that matter should be put completely out of your minds. Because we are not the litigants here. . . . You, as jurors . . . should not consider any objections made by counsel. They have a legal right to make those objecttions. . . . So if anything we have done has offended you or prolonged the trial or we objected, you sitting there as six jurors have a duty to determine this case solely upon the evidence and the court's instructions. It would be totally unfair for you to feel that we did something unfair, so let's punish McDonnell Douglas for it.

FitzSimons, in his closing argument, tried to undermine the effect of Stern's apple pie and motherhood. He cautioned the jury that "in arriving at your verdict, you should not take into consideration any sentimental and emotional factors such as mental anguish, grief, and sorrow. . . ." He was still angry over admission of the tape. He had disapproved of the introduction of the wedding pictures. He knew the effect tiny orphans saying hello and counting in three languages would have on the jury. He had resented Sterns, who was a family man, too, getting up and telling the jury to "show those guys on the other side of the table what the value of a life is worth." FitzSimons said to the jury, "I know what the value of a life is worth as much as anybody else. You don't have to prove a point here. This isn't a battle. . . ."

In response, Sterns delivered an argument that made up in passion and spontaneity what it lacked in polish. He had listened carefully as FitzSimons and Packard, with their cautions and apologies, had shown him their vulnerabilities. Prepared speeches be damned. It was time to drive the knife home in the soft spot.

I think nothing could illustrate more what we are up against than the remarks of Mr. Packard this morning, where he spent most of his time, as far as I could see, apologizing for the way that he and his colleague have conducted this case. And I am frankly shocked, also!

Mr. FitzSimons indicated to you a number of things, including the fact that this is not a battle. *It most certainly is . . . and it has been a battle from the word go. Since that machine hit the ground in Paris almost two years ago. . . .*

FitzSimons left the courtroom and flew home to his family in Manhasset, New York, as the jury retired to deliberate. "Hell, I could tell how the trial was going."

Krutch flew back to Seattle.

After ten and a half hours of deliberation and five weeks of trial, the jury returned its verdict. The piece of paper was handed to Thelma Alden, then to the judge, and then back to Thelma, who read it to the filled courtroom. Packard, Sterns, and Judkins waited. "United States District Court Central District of California, A. Stuart Case, as Special Administrator . . . v. McDonnell Douglas Aircraft Company, a California Corporation. . . . We, the Jury in the above-entitled cause, find in the favor of the Plaintiff . . . and award compensatory damages in the amount of $875,053 for the death of David Herman Kween . . . and compensatory damages in the amount of $630,500 for the death of Phyllis Case Kween." They awarded total damages of $1,509,950.

The defense was stunned. The award was more than twice what the case could have settled for, fifteen times what the orphans might have received in England, *one hundred ninety times* the original offer made by the defense. The Kween grandparents were found to have had a dependency on their son, David, of 15 percent at the time of death and 10 percent in the future. The judge would decide how much the Kweens would receive.

Lloyd's had their answers. And lawyers had a fresh measure of what a good mother was worth.

As in the movies, reporters bolted from the courtroom to phone in the story.

A plaintiff lawyer in New York whistled when he heard the news and said, "There'll be blood on the walls of the boardroom at Lloyd's this morning." Word of the verdict flew around the world, ignoring time zones. Sterns delighted in waking Bernard Engler up at four in the morning to tell him. Stephen Mitchell and Engler were besieged by the British press and widely quoted. Every London daily gave the story blazing headlines. "THE MILLION-POUND ORPHANS." "ORPHANS SHAKE LLOYD'S." "VENGEANCE MONEY FOR MY LITTLE ONES." Casting it as one of Lloyd's great disasters, London's *Sunday Telegraph* said that "the Lutine Bell could be heard ringing all the way to Los Angeles."

And yet the insurers made no graceful concession speech. Lloyd's chief press officer in London termed the award "a money-grubbing exercise." It was being widely argued that the award was an "aberration" that would easily be overturned on appeal. Peter Martin stated that "the damages awarded are so far removed from reality in the context of what Mr. and Mrs. Kween might have earned in their lifetime that the figures make no sense. In particular, I am concerned about the award to the parents of the late David Kween which, by English standards, is wholly unjustifiable." FitzSimons was bitterly disappointed, for he hated to lose, but was out with his fists up within hours, philosophically unchanged. He still did not think it was right to apply California law. "Give a North Korean that one and a half million, and I suspect he'll buy North Korea! There comes a time when money doesn't make things better anymore. There are some things that money can't buy —the blink of your eye five minutes ago." And he felt that the jury had vindicated his stand on nondependency. They had said that the Kween parents would have been only 10 percent dependent in the future. "That makes me ninety percent right!"

There was rampant confusion over the effect of Kween. The plaintiffs had hoped that the shock of the high award would force the defense to productive negotiations. But FitzSimons felt that the award might even have taken the two sides farther apart. He reported that immediately after the Kween award, plaintiffs had started withdrawing their demands, preparing to amend and resubmit them with bigger numbers on the bottom line. Some of the plaintiff lawyers were worried that it would raise the hopes of their clients unrealistically. They couldn't all get $1½ million. The English papers had been translated in Turkey, and Dr. Kai Nordlund was preparing to fly to Istanbul to explain to the families there.

Arguments between the families flared in the press. Cecil Kween, David's father, had greeted the award as "a form of vengeance against the plane makers. If this is going to hurt them then it is wonderful."

Courtroom observers could understand why he might have said it. The slight, fifty-three-year-old shopkeeper had been grilled for two days as the defense had tried to prove that he had not been dependent on his son and had, in fact, been the "driving force" in the business. Kween had already watched his wife Betty deteriorate since the crash into a fragile, at times suicidal, emotional state. Under the barrage of detailed financial questions, he had become so unnerved that his shaking hands could not pick up a piece of paper.

Though crude, his statement may have been a release, too, for the smoldering frustrations still felt by a number of the families that the "guilty" had not yet felt the sting. Discovery's search for truth had faded out inconclusively. And even the French report, which would be the only official pronouncement of cause and responsibility, would, when finally circulated publicly in May, not place blame on any specific shoulders. The list of causal factors would not be greeted happily, though, in either Long Beach or Istanbul, for cargo door design, the uncompleted Service Bulletin, the misrigging and alien shim, the placement of cables below the floor, failure to look in the peephole, and failure to follow up with effective corrective measures after *Windsor* would

341

all be cited. But the French would make no criminal prosecutions, or name names.

Heather Brigstocke, a mother of four who had lost her husband, a senior shipping official in the government, answered him in *The Times*. She and her children wished only "to be allowed to mourn with dignity. Money would certainly be a help to me in bringing up the children and launching them on their careers. It would be even more help if it came soon. *But please let us have no talk of vengeance.* Let us not be greedy for damages, which can never be in any sense a compensation."

Everyone looked for signs. Stuart Speiser reported that as his firm had been about to go to trial on the first damages trial in the *Dulles* case in Alexandria, Virginia, the case had been settled, on the eve of trial, for $950,000—several hundred thousand more than expected. He was sure his clients had gained from the Kween verdict.

But the next week, Speiser's group settled the *Safran* case, the *Paris* case that was to have followed Kween, for a figure reportedly far lower than the demand. If that were true, it would give strength to the "aberration" theory, strip the Kween award of much of its power, and vindicate FitzSimons's strategy. Speiser, though, was content that the defense had settled on the eve of trial rather than face another "Kween," and that the numbers came very close to what a California jury might have awarded.

On March 8, 1976, the defense made the expected first moves toward an appeal. Appellate lawyers for McDonnell Douglas asked Judge Hall to grant a new trial for the Kween case. The specter of total paralysis of the case for, perhaps, three years was now before him. For if he denied the new trial, the defense would have to file their appeal within thirty days, setting the wheels in motion. With characteristic faith in the reasonableness of men, Hall took the matter under submission, hoping that this and other cases would be settled before he was forced to act.

It was a time of anguish. On April 5, the U.S. Supreme Court denied the class action. It was dead. Hall ordered depositions to resume. In mid-April, General Dynamics' Hurt took the chair again, and Marshall Morgan picked up questioning where Sterns had left off a year earlier. With hair clipped almost to a brush cut, his pipe and quiet precise words giving him a professorial air, Hurt did not seem, to one young lawyer sitting in on depositions, "like an ogre." But as his memory lapsed over details of a meeting held to discuss the Applegate memo, as he explained that his own memo in response to Applegate's had not been an expression of personal opinion but simply an attempt to show the other side of the coin, plaintiff lawyers could feel frustration building again over their inability to pin anyone down to personal responsibility for the failure to act on Applegate's terrifying prediction that a plane would be lost if the cargo door were not satisfactorily fixed. Applegate himself was scheduled to follow Hurt as the case lapsed back into the liability phase and flared up again into an angry war.

Condemning the "greed of many claimants and . . . the rapacity of some of their advisers," Peter Martin believed "the greed and rapacity are such that . . . a liability trial is becoming inevitable." Judge Hall set down October 12, 1976, for what Speiser had forecast would be "the most monstrous piece of civil litigation ever to be brought to the courts." In preparation for it, the club flew to London in late May to take testimony from Mahmoudi, who Sterns had managed to wrench free from his inaccessibility in Paris. They all watched —FitzSimons, Packard, Des Barry, Sterns, Morgan, Robinson—as the much-maligned "illiterate baggage handler" entered the room. In a beautifully fitted three-piece suit. With strong Arabic face, a handsome head of thick black hair, he was a tall, charming, articulate young man who may not have read English but spoke three other languages. He had been promoted by both his union and his employer Samor since the crash, and had just filed his own suit for defamation against

343

McDonnell Douglas. Des Barry scribbled a note to Marshall Morgan, asking, "Where did you get a witness like that?" Morgan sent a note back, "Central Casting in Hollywood." It would be quite a trial.

But in Los Angeles, there were positive signs of change. Judge Hall, the innovative old master, had been quietly setting up a system he prayed would work. He had been ordered to bed, but before he left for Palm Desert he had called nine judges out of retirement, named them as "special masters," and assigned them to three non-binding evaluation panels. Within weeks of the Kween award he would have the first panel ready to start reviewing and evaluating the cases, using California jury awards as their standard. Plaintiff lawyers were afraid that retired judges from southern California would be far too conservative to produce acceptable figures. But as the antagonists gathered before the judges for the first of the unique "settlement conferences," plaintiff lawyers sniffed a realigning of the defense forces. There was no talk of English damages. That choice of law issue would be kept in storage for appeals. And settlements were occurring. As Jim Butler and Des Barry took the first batch of cases through the panel a handful of settlements were reported, achieving as much in a week as had been achieved in the previous two years. By the time the first round of cases had been completed in mid-May, the Speiser-Butler group had settled sixty-three cases. Sterns had settled seventeen. And though Kreindler was probably going to have to go to trial on the Japanese cases, he was optimistic about his American cases—for one, a judge had suggested a figure of $1,500,000! By the end of May, the cases of 110 of the filed 337 decedents had been settled. By intruding impartial third parties, the judge might at last have found a way for both sides to save face, and get the cases cleaned out. It looked as if he might have found the way to "keep 'em movin'."

In London, Stephen Mitchell followed the post-Kween drama with hope. He was the only lawyer who carried a thread of intense personal concern through the case. If it had not been for the death of a beautiful red-head in the forest, he would still be in the Lloyd's camp. Forced to cross the line, he had seen the shocking unwillingness of English judges to deal with the needs of families struck by an air crash. But his had never been a moral crusade. Though he had shepherded over eighty British cases across the sea, he was still heartsick that "the personal loss can only be compensated in terms of money," still saddened by what they had all felt compelled to do. He hoped that the Kween verdict could speed peace and finality. For the crash would never be fully behind him until the litigation was over.

Mitchell watched the calm movement of river traffic along the Thames. Something had been achieved. There had been a breakthrough in public awareness of the insurer's role in liability cases, a healthy bit of education. But the profound questions of moral values had still not been resolved. He knew that somewhere lay the balance between British and American values, settlement sums that would have the effect of "avoiding thalidomide, without discouraging the discovery of penicillin," as *The Economist* had put it after the Kween verdict; a balance between abandoning technology's victims and encouraging everyone who stubs his toe to run for a lawyer. Mitchell spoke out. "Lloyd's have an honourable reputation to live up to and I feel that they must see the sense, now that we have the first feel of California juries' views, that it would be better to get around a table and see what kind of money we can agree upon. The American lawyers acting for our clients are quite prepared, with myself, to get together tomorrow—preferably somewhere away from the heat of the action. . . ."

Bermuda perhaps, which though still comfortably British was, symbolically, closer to the United States than to England. Though he and Sterns had been able to forge their close friendship under fire, neutral ground might be needed to soften the defense and attack modes that had become conditioned reflexes. When he and Sterns had flown to hear Peter Martin speak in Dallas, the academic setting away from the battlefield had somehow helped them bridge the distances. In *Paris,* Martin was their adversary. But there, he had dropped his shield and poured out with unaccustomed passion the frustrations he felt as he dealt with crashes around the world. The dismal record of 1974 had cast its gloom as he had spoken. There had been 1,657 transport crash deaths worldwide, up from 1,569 the previous year. Yet it was still just a few hundred more than were drowned annually around Britain's coasts, and a small fraction of the nearly 60,000 killed annually on America's and U.K.'s roads. Martin knew that statistically, a businessman could fly ten trips a year—12,000 miles a year—for 38,000 years without the risk of death. The grandmother flying only one 2,500-mile trip a year to visit her married daughter could fly it for *12½ million years* before the odds would catch up with her. The lawyers who came to Los Angeles to attack the industry lived in planes and flew without fear. Fatal accident rates had been declining steadily for the past ten years, were still declining. Yet some airlines *were* better than others. Accidents *did* occur, leading to the widening flood of litigation that so concerned Martin, raising "nightmare anxieties about the wickedness of big business, and the inefficiency of governments." Damaging public confidence in flying. Compromising air safety, in his view. Yet he had recognized that American litigation served a needed function. The U.S. tort and criminal law systems did sometimes "serve as a deterrent to unsafe behaviour . . ." Warsaw's inadequacy had made litigation inevitable "if injustice and hardship are to be avoided." Martin had pleaded then—as Mitchell did now—for the humane middle road. *"Accidents are about death and destruction, not litigation, and ought to be looked at in this way by those with the power to influence change for the better. Just for once, could not the divided parts of our profession combine to produce a major change in the law instead of feeding on the inadequacy of the existing system?"*

It had seemed possible in Dallas. It must be possible now, for the second anniversary was almost here.

Chapter Twenty-Six

"La Grande Catastrophe"

ON MARCH 3, 1976, families went again to the forest and this time saw the gray stone monument that had been raised by the International Association in memory of those who had died in *La Grande Catastrophe*. A rough-hewn megalith of Cornish stone pointing to the sky, its primitive dignity denied high technology and answered human needs. This massive tomb at the grave of 346 would be a permanent focus for the memories, grief, and love that would continue to flow out over the years ahead; a reminder. Like a cenotaph, it would evoke feelings larger than individual loss and help make sense from the confusion of fears and commitments and hopes that invest an aircrash with such special significance, that make it the symbolic catastrophe of our age.

The air crash has become what the shipwreck historically was—a sacrifice offered up to an unforgiving element that must be plied in the interests of progress. Clustering at airport terminals, waiting for news, has replaced the gathering of black-shawled women on a cold bluff above the sea. But it lacks the stoic resignation. When men went to sea, they made a compact with fate. But complying with fate is not our way. We insulate ourselves from risk, try to avoid and defer death. When a crash does occur, we avert our eyes. For, as Professor Dérobert knew, "neither the sun nor death can be looked at directly." We don't develop the rituals and releases, the laws and procedures we need, but respond in a piecemeal, ad hoc manner, hoping it will go away. We grab at "fixes" rather than at preventive systems. Even the enormity of *Paris* had not shaken the world to deep change. It had simply blown the old problems up to jumbo proportions.

But *Paris,* by its very size, had forced all those thousands caught up in it—the families, lawyers, insurers, governments, manufacturers—to see that change must come. Technical energies had been marvelously concentrated into building, selling, insuring, and filling the skies with jumbo jets. But, crashed, one had caught the world unprepared. Three hundred and forty-six deaths had finally forced engineers to confront the size effect and to overcome its lethal implications. But the horror of Ermenonville and its aftermath had shown them all that in driving technology on to higher, faster, bigger planes, society had at last "outtraveled its own soul." Now, the soul must rush to catch up.

Glossary

AD Airworthiness Directive. Mandatory modification ordered by the FAA

ATLAS and KSSU European Airline Consortium

BEA British European Airways

CALPA Canadian Airline Pilots Association

DC Douglas Commercial

DOT Department of Transport

FAA Federal Aviation Administration

FAR Federal Air Regulation

FCO Foreign Commonwealth Office (in Britain)

FMEA Failure Mode and Effect Analyses. Engineering analysis of design for potential failure modes.

"G" Gravity

IATA International Air Transportation Association

ICAO International Civil Aviation Organization

IFALPA International Federation of Airline Pilots Associations

MDL Judicial Panel on Multidistrict Litigation

NASA National Aeronautics and Space Administration

NATO North Atlantic Treaty Organization

NTSB National Transportation Safety Board

RAF Royal Air Force

RLD Netherlands' Department of Civil Aviation

SAC Strategic Air Command

SB Service Bulletin. The most commonly used way for manufacturers to recommend or suggest voluntary changes in the aircraft

THY Turk Hava Yollari (Turkish Airlines)

Technical Consultant:
T. Michael Harris, B.App.Sc., M.Sc.

Received his degree in engineering physics from the University of British Columbia; Master of Science degree in aeronautical engineering from the Cranfield Institute of Technology (England). Has been a military fighter and transport pilot; accident investigator for NATO forces; engineer/ test pilot and head of flying qualities and simulation section of Cornell Aeronautical Laboratory; crew integration officer on X-20 space program; currently a program manager for Flight Systems, Inc., a flight test, research and development firm in Newport Beach, California.

THE AUTHENTICITY of the technical and flying-related segments of this book must accrue to Michael Harris. He has not only been a rigorous taskmaster in "getting it right," but also has proven to be an imaginative philosopher of flight. With broad aviation experience that frees him from "tunnel vision," he has given the book a perspective I could not possibly have provided. And he has put a level of energy and dedication into the project that far, far transcends his role as professional consultant.

Though he relinquished his engineer's vocabulary with good grace where compromises had to be struck for the sake of clarity, he will never quite forgive me for comparing pressurized air to "rampaging elephants."

Acknowledgments

SIMPLY THANKING a long list of people cannot begin to express the experience we have all shared, all of us who for whatever reasons—have been touched by Ermenonville. The hundreds of interviews, phone calls, letters, and wires that form the basis of this book have been charged with a special sense of commitment. We have managed to communicate through the sensitivities, conflicts, and fears that quickly built up around this most terrible and historic crash. I have dealt with sorrow and suspicion, and am overwhelmingly grateful for the bounty of trust and candor that has flowed back from people on all sides, from all factions. This book has really been written by the participants. Believing this project to be important, families have reopened wounds to give their stories; world-ranking aviation specialists have gone beyond their roles in the book to tutor me in aviation law, in aerodynamics and flying, in system safety, in crash investigation, in psychology, in corporate and government processes, giving me the rare privilege of working with the best. Some whose names scarcely, or never, appear have given selfless hours and days, and can, I hope, feel my gratitude, My only promise has been that I would attempt to give a fair and balanced view. I have tried to do that.

Though I regret that I cannot, in this space, thank everyone who helped, there are several people I do wish to single out for their special contributions. Bin

Cheng, Professor of Air and Space Law at the University of London's University College, gave generously of his knowledge of international law. Max Hope, Consul General for New Zealand in San Francisco and former air attaché for his government in Washington, D.C., brought a special wisdom and held me to a high standard of integrity. Two distinguished aviation specialists, physiologist Dr. William R. Pierson, chairman, and aviation psychologist Chaytor Mason, associate professor, of the Human Factors Department of the University of Southern California's Safety Center, helped me "fly down" Flight 981. In addition to IFALPA's recently retired executive secretary Captain C. C. Jackson and the numerous captains who came from their cockpits to talk to me, two pilots educated me to the unique concerns of the human element in the loop and to the realities of international commercial aviation; Captain Charles Simpson of Air Canada, who has served as president of the Canadian Air Line Pilots' Association, and as principal vice-president of IFALPA; and Captain L. Blomberg of KLM, active in IFALPA and the Safety Committee of the Dutch Airline Pilots' Association—a pilot whose long global experience was of enormous value. Delphine Ruman's grasp of complex aviation litigation has not been adequately credited in the text of the book, nor has her enthusiastic help. Air safety consultant Frank McDermott gave me useful insights into governmental regulatory agencies; Dale Ruhmel gave vital insights into the engineering challenge of designing airplanes and the high level of integrity and competence that characterizes aerospace engineers. W. R. (Bob) Laidlaw, experimental test pilot and aeronautical engineer, read the manuscript and drew on his wide experience in aeronautics and aviation to make valuable comments.

Among the press, I am grateful to producer David Graham of the BBC for sharing his extensive research, and to Hugh O. Field, assistant editor of *Flight International* magazine, for sharing his surpassing knowledge of the industry.

Among the many aviation organizations that have provided me with information—IATA, ICAO, the FAA, the Aviation Consumer Action Project, *et al.*—personnel of the NTSB have been particularly cooperative.

The book might never have been written or published if three extraordinary people had not believed in it. Ernest Scott gave me early encouragement and exhibited a generosity of spirit I will always thank him for. My agent, Helen Brann, worked with an energy, intelligence, and enthusiasm for the book that buoyed me through the critical periods. My editor at Morrow, Carol Hill, applied a sensitive and creative eye to a big and unwieldy piece of work and patiently helped me weed and prune. I am deeply grateful for her sustained belief in the book.

I will never be able adequately to thank my friends for spurring me on during the lonely months of writing. Janet Peterson in Paris and Libby Plum in London proved to be superb researchers. Pell Fender prepared an excellent cultural analysis of all the nations significantly involved in the crash. Cheryl Yee carried the heavy secretarial load. Much of the book was written in Jonathan Rice's quiet library in San Francisco. I wrote, too, in the homes of the Sarasys across the Golden Gate Bridge and the Hurleys in Manhattan, and am grateful for these gifts of peace and space.

And finally, my family. This book has truly been a family affair. My brother, Michael, was technical consultant. My mother, Christie Harris, author of fourteen books, lent her deep concern for cultures and human dignity and her sharp literary eye to help shape the book. For many weeks, she put aside her own important work to help me in capacities ranging from typist to writing collaborator. Above all, my husband, Donald—an ex-military pilot—and my two amazing children, Woolsey and Christie, created and sustained a climate of encouragement that allowed me to undertake and complete this massive project. I feel blessed to have such a gifted, supportive, and loving family.

Synopsis

PART I: THE HUMAN EXPERIENCE

1. The 77 Seconds
   *The boarding of the flight at Orly; the last
   nine minutes before the world's worst
   crash; impact in the forest.*

2. Did They Feel Anything?
   *A reconstruction of the passengers' and
   crew's responses and behavior during the
   crisis.*

3. Was It a Door?
   *American safety professionals speculate,
   and the GO team flies to Paris to investigate.*

4. The Windsor Incident
   *The chilling dress rehearsal for the Paris
   crash, in which a DC-10 survives explosive
   decompression.*

5. "Could You Check the Lists, Please?"
   . . . the Ones Who Waited
   *England, and the world, respond to news
   of the crash. A young solicitor loses his
   fiancée; an ancient British town loses its*

355

rugby team; the American School in London loses nine children.

6   They Must Do Their Best

THE SITE

The burden and the chaos of the disaster fall on France and on the gendarmerie of Senlis. An ebullient French captain heads the hunt for life, removal of remains and debris, and early attempts to identify.

IDENTIFY!

A "mad scientist" on the Seine begins the appalling task of forensic identification of the shattered flesh.

7   Waiting . . . Waiting
Frustration builds as British families wait for confirmation of death, funeral plans. Press takes up crusade, families travel to Senlis to identify.

8   The Litigation
Tensions find expression in leaders and release in American lawsuits. Press flays plane's manufacturer.

9   The French
Drawing on tradition and experience, the French cast law and order over an uninvited crash. The official investigation is launched.

PART II: WHAT HAPPENED?

10   The Size Effect
The Dutch worry over the potential decompression hazards of wide-body jets and try to caution the aviation world.

fornia. Search for a lawyer takes English solicitor on odyssey across America to San Francisco.

17 "Extremely Improbable"
San Francisco lawyer learns FAA/corporate facts of life in Wichita with small planes and Pankow case. Televised Senate hearings show him that Paris case has same problems, writ large.

18 The Gentlemen's Agreement
Senate hearings ask: Might Paris have been prevented if FAA had ordered mandatory rather than voluntary fixes on cargo door after the Windsor Incident?

19 The Great Birthday Card Debate
Lawyers set up housekeeping in Los Angeles and vie for control of case. Judge Hall assigned. Conflicts bared in fight over birthday card for Judge's eightieth birthday.

20 The Birth of the Plane
Through discovery, lawyers learn the story of the DC-10 and see step-by-step decisions that led to Paris. The Applegate memo emerges.

21 In Court
In a classic courtroom hearing, lawyers try to break logjam. New York lawyer makes headlines and gets Japanese cases.

22 The First Anniversary
The aftermath, a year later. An intimate look at the adjustment of families and the activities of principal participants.

Half a Million Hardcovers in Print

Over Ten Months on
The New York Times
Bestseller List

Charles Berlitz

The Bermuda Triangle

THE
NATIONWIDE
#1
BESTSELLER!

The Bermuda Triangle book
that will continue to astound the world
long after the others have "disappeared!"

COMPLETE WITH PHOTOS, MAPS, CHARTS, AND DRAWINGS

BT 12-75